DIGITAL MARKETING

...A Guide To Marketing In Today's Digital World

by

Tim Griffiths

DISCLAIMER

The information herein is offered for informational purposes solely, and is universal as so. The presentation of the information is without contract or any type of guarantee assurance.

The trademarks that are used are without any consent, and the publication of the trademark is without permission or backing by the trademark owner. All trademarks and brands within this book are for clarifying purposes only and are the owned by the owners themselves, not affiliated with this document.

Tim Griffiths

DIGITAL MARKETTING

TABLE OF CONTENTS

INTRODUCTION

Thank you for downloading **"DIGITAL MARKETING: A Guide to Marketing in Today's Digital World."**

In the ongoing age of the Internet, digital branding is the obvious choice for businesses. In contrast to traditional branding, its digital counterpart revolves around what consumers see, hear, feel and consider about a business online. Digital marketers keep themselves engaged in creating consistently appealing and positive images, as well as messages to promote any brand.

To put it in simpler words, online or digital marketing is all about advertising and promoting businesses, along with their brands, through different digital media channels.

The channels, usually, include websites, radio, TV, mobile handsets and various social media platforms in one hand, while on the other covers traditionally non-digital media like billboards and transit signs. Any marketing media, which is delivered electronically, is accepted as digital, electronic or Internet marketing.

A good number of blogs and websites would say that digital marketing or online marketing is a type of marketing and sales approach that involves the use of accessible and authoritative online channels and websites such as Facebook, Twitter, YouTube, LinkedIn, etc. in promoting a product or service; such an approach increases traffic and popularity to their website and ultimately to their business.

— Revolution of Digital Marketing

We define Digital Marketing as a branch of marketing that makes use of integrated digital technologies to disseminate communication that is targeted and measurable with the end goal of acquiring and building relationships with new and existing customers.

This type of marketing campaign should be integrated in such a way that multiple avenues are utilized harmoniously to work towards one goal - to reach and communicate to a "targeted" online market. With the opportunity to engage and build a strong relationship with the consumers as the most important benefit of running a digital marketing campaign, businesses now can interact and connect with consumers real-time.

This fantastic guide talks about digital marketing and strategies to promote your business online and reach your audience.

Let's Begin!

CHAPTER 1: UNDERSTANDING DIGITAL MARKETING

On a simpler note, digital marketing is nothing but the marketing of any product or service done via internet. It is a kind of "new-age" marketing technique which is different from the conventional or traditional systems of marketing. It is different from traditional marketing because digital marketing offers the advantage of monitoring the entire aspects related to your marketing strategy. And of course, this monitoring can be accomplished on a real-time basis.

WHAT IS DIGITAL MARKETING?

Today nearly 80% of all the media that we consume come through digital channels. Massive internet usage and digital media have given rise to a new marketing concept called Digital Marketing. It is a broad area and considered to be the future of business development.

Digital Marketing is the most commonly used term for online marketing, and it has several advantages over traditional offline marketing. With the help internet and mobile devices customer, these days have access to information from anywhere in the world. Marketers these days use digital tactics to attract and convert audiences online.

This new age marketing method helps to gain a good reputation which is essential for a business to survive. It is the best way to reach out to your targeted audience.

With the help of digital marketing, one can reach many customers at a minimal marketing budget. Unlike traditional methods, you can measure the success of digital marketing campaigns with the help of analytical tools. Every year more and more marketers put aside traditional marketing and focus on this approach. Successful marketing campaigns can be accomplished by integrating conventional methods with digital marketing techniques.

HOW IS DIGITAL MARKETING DIFFERENT FROM TRADITIONAL MARKETING?

Digital Marketing is cost effective in terms of better reach and results.

Internet Marketing lets you target a specific audience based upon demographics, interest and devices.

Internet Marketing gives us factual data that can be statistically analysed. For instance, if hoarding is marketing your product, you have no clue how many people saw the hoarding, read the content and became customers because of that hoarding.

However, in digital marketing, say we run a campaign marketing the same product, we can analyse the data produced by different marketing platforms that can show us how many people saw the product, how many became consumers and which consumers came via which of the used platforms. It allows us to find glitches in our campaign and work on it to make it even more action driven.

CHAPTER 2: METHODS OF DIGITAL MARKETING

There is no question that we live in the digital world and from this perspective; it is significant that your business has a magnificent presence in the digital space. Internet marketing or digital marketing is the marketing future across the world with full of advantages as compared to traditional marketing. Here are some standard methods of digital marketing for every business:

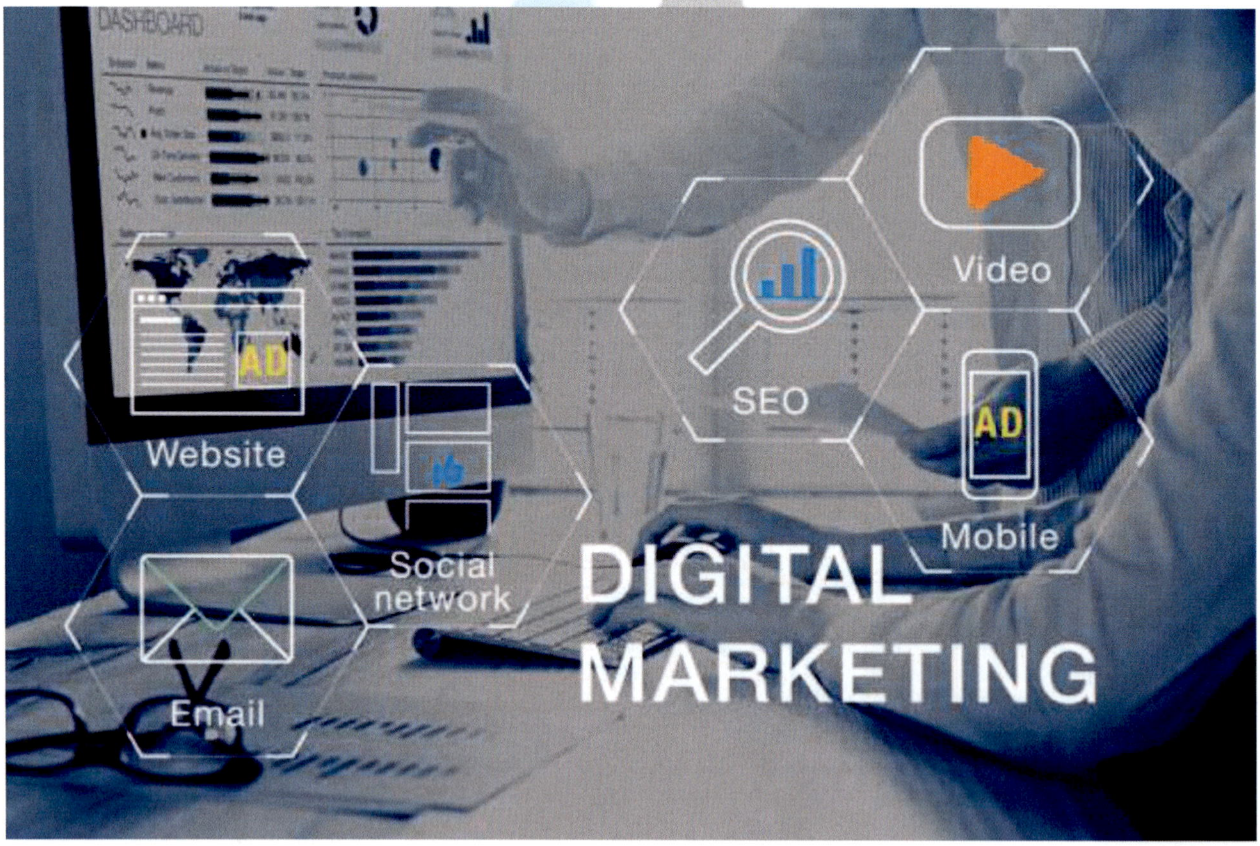

— **Search Engine Optimization**

It is an organic way of optimizing your online content to improve the ranking of your website on the search engine.

There are a lot of factors involved in the ranking of a website such as a title, keywords, relevance etc. SEO helps to ensure that your site is accessible and improve the chances of being found by the search engine. It is classified into two types on the page and off page optimization.

On page, optimization is achieved through the careful distribution of keywords and the quality of content on your site. Off-page optimization involves factors that are beyond the control of your website.

The primary goal of link building is to get other websites links to yours to improve SEO.

— **Search Engine Marketing**

When someone searches for information or a keyword, SEM makes sure that your site appears at the top of search engine results. It uses a variety of techniques which helps the search engine to deliver your site to the web searchers.

One must clearly understand SEO before using SEM. It is one of the most efficient ways to spread your business across in this competitive world. Some of the components of SEM are ad auction, bid and quality score. Your maximum bid for a keyword with an excellent quality score determines your ad position.

— **Pay Per Click**

The fastest way to reach your target audience can be achieved through P P C campaigns. You pay each time when someone clicks on your ad. For example, if you spend 1 dollar per click and when 1000 people click your ad, it will cost you 1000 dollars. Based on the CTR (click through rate) the performance of your ad campaign is determined. It generates faster results by targeting the right people at the right time and in the right place. Since it costs money, it is suitable for businesses that sell product/services.

— **Social Media Marketing**

The process of marketing through various social media platforms such as Facebook, Twitter, and Instagram is known as Social Media Marketing. The primary objective of SMM is to produce content on social media that help an organization to increase brand awareness and customer reach. In social media companies can share content to achieve marketing goals.

Also, Linkedin, YouTube, Google+, Ushi, Xing etc. These are web-based systems that allow you to connect and share information such as ideas, links, photos, videos with like-minded people.

They can also generate income for your business and so can be routed to market for your business. They can be great ways to connect with people who you may not be able to get to by any other means. Twitter can be a great source of publicly available real-time information and has reported major global events ahead of the world's press.

Social media marketing is not a mere marketing add-on. Neither is it a blogging experiment whose purpose remains forever unclear. It is not a justification for conversations, engagement, and whatever buzzwords generally find their way into a discussion about social media. More than anything, a social media program is neither simple nor easy. It is not what most people think.

A fully deployed social media program is a completely integrated communications mechanism that amplifies the impact of every function within an organization by leveraging the power of human networks via social networking platforms. It is a complement to all other forms of neither tactical communications nor a replacement for any of them.

An SMP can provide organizations with detailed, virtually instant feedback from customers and valuable market intelligence. Used with specialized monitoring, measurement and analysis tools, it can amplify not only activities but the acquisition and analysis of useful data, from consumer insights to the calculation of ROI.

An SMP also brings into heavily compartmentalized companies the potential for enhanced collaboration, increased departmental efficiency, cost reductions, and of course growth of the business.

Forget about blogs, Facebook, Twitter, Instagram and all the social media channels and platforms for a moment, and focus instead on what matters to your organization: Is lead generation an area of your business that could use some help?

You can create an SMP that will help you acquire new leads. Are you losing customers to competitors? You can develop an SMP whose focus will be to help you enhance your customer retention activities.

An SMP can plug into every type of business function you need it to and help you make it work better, smarter, and faster.

A fully developed SMM program can, for example, protect a brand in times of crisis; alert an organization's decision makers to new trends in consumer interests and sentiment, influence hundreds of thousands of consumers discover a company, organization, or product at a fraction of the cost of other forms of "traditional" media.

Because mobile devices such as cellular telephones increasingly incorporate social media capabilities that go beyond simple texting, voice, and email digital social networks now live on mobile devices, not just personal computers. It matters because portability means both increased use and lower barriers to adoption. Because of this, the acceleration in global social media use is rewriting the way humans communicate, share ideas, recommend products, and connect. Not being a part of this means not being a part of the world.

Just as the telephone, email, and mobility could not be held at bay by companies reluctant to accept change, social media cannot be ignored either. The company that chooses to resist this latest step in the inexorable evolution of business will find itself having to work increasingly hard to stay afloat.

Conversely, the company that chooses to adapt and implements a business-focused SMP will have the opportunity to gain an advantage over its competition at minimal cost and improve its position in the market.

— Email Marketing

It is one of the commonly used ways of online marketing.

Email marketing enhances business communication, cost-effective and Eco-friendly. By this method, a message could be sent to a group of people by the use of electronic mail.

It is an efficient way to stay connected with your audience while promoting your business and also one of the easiest ways to reach your target audience.

Also, emailing is one of the easiest and inexpensive ways to advertise your business and products or services as compared to all other digital marketing strategies.

Below are some of the reasons how email marketing can help in the growth of your business:

- — Email has a wider reach
- — Email delivers your communication
- — Email drives conversions
- — Email results in higher ROI(Return on Investment)
- — It is an open platform and will remain there forever

All the above reasons show that email marketing is the most effective marketing channel that can help you to connect with the audience and drive sales and revenue for your business.

— Display Advertising

It is a form of conveying a message with elements like images, logos, graphics, audio or video to communicate to the target audience. Also known as banner ads, it gives a unique opportunity to re-target the ideal audience. You can also display ads to people based on their search behaviour. Generally, display ads are seen alongside search engines such as Yahoo, Bing and Google.

— Content Marketing

This type of marketing is done by creating and sharing free content to attract new prospects and retain existing customers. Informative content is divided in the form of articles, videos, infographics etc. It helps in building strong relationships with your audience by providing them with relevant, high-quality contents.

Your business goal should be aligned with a content strategy to gain critical success.

— Lead Nurturing

It is where a prospect gives you their email address in exchange for something free. It is usually an eBook (in pdf format), video, the course of emails on how to do something.

— **Viral Marketing**

The sending out of a message which is so compelling that people forward it on to other people unknown to you. A great way to send out a message if you get it right.

— **Video**

An increasingly popular method of sharing ideas, passing on information and selling on the web.

Great for selling more complex products or services. YouTube is the most popular at present but, the video is becoming embedded into more digital media.

— **Music/Podcasts**

Spotify is becoming the most popular legal file sharing system as it gives you access to a broad range of music. Podcasts are voice recordings about a particular subject. They can be downloaded for listening to on a computer or MP3 players at a later date. Great for relaxation or for learning about a new subject while travelling.

— **Chat/Instant Messaging/Skype**

Chat and Instant Messaging are systems for conversations using a keyboard which are done in real time. I.e. one person types something and the other responds. Both need to be present and online for this to work. Users of Facebook, Bebo etc. use this, especially the younger generation. Skype is an internet based video and phone system that allows Skype users to call each other for free or at low cost and is becoming increasingly popular for business use and will grow now that the video version is available on Facebook.

— **Smartphone or Mobile Apps**

Smartphone or mobile apps (or software applications which is where the term is derived from) are small pieces of computer software that runs on your phone that allow you to do things that you would typically do on a computer. The need to work anywhere, anytime means that these will become increasingly popular with business systems starting to appear on them.

Great for anybody who works away from the office including executives, technical and salespeople. Also, watch for a growing number of consumers using their mobiles for online purchases as they fill their time waiting for something.

— **Cloud-based storage/File Sharing**

The Cloud is for most purposes another name for the Internet. So Cloud-based storage is the ability to store information on the internet including backups and sending large files to customers and suppliers.

DropBox and Yousendit are examples of systems for sharing large files between unrelated users. There is a wide range of suppliers of remote backup systems now with most corporates including them in their backup strategies. Personal File sharing is also available for two or more computers to be linked together to share information including music and videos.

Personal File Sharing is generally not a business tool for larger corporates.

— Cloud-based systems

These are systems that allow you to work anywhere. Google has Google Docs, Microsoft has Office 365. A lot of third-party software providers are moving their systems onto the Cloud so that customers can access them from anywhere and don't have to worry about their own IT infrastructure. Companies are moving their IT infrastructure on to the Cloud to reduce costs as all the support is managed by a third party.

— Extranets/Web-based Systems

Companies are now looking to give customers, and suppliers access to their information (through Extranets) and their systems (through Web-based systems).

It allows customers and suppliers to access to information relevant to them and enables them to do any processing on a DIY basis saving you both time and money such as the entering and progressing of orders and checking stock levels.

— Remote Access

The ability to work anywhere means that you sometimes need access to your computer at home or work. Remote access through web sites such as Teamview and LogMeIn is a great way to get at critical documents away from the computer.

Some of these systems allow you to do online demonstrations of your product and service. It saves you and your customer time and money.

— **Online Games/Gaming**

More gaming companies are moving their operations on to the web so that their services can be accessed anywhere anytime. Also, notice that more consumer applications have games technology or ideas built into them to make it more fun to buy.

The term is called gamification. It could be a challenge for parents as the line becomes blurred between buying something and playing a game.

— **Push digital marketing**

Just as the name suggests, push marketing projected to push the advertising information directed toward the target clientele.

Often, marketers will initiate push marketing through email, RSS, or SMS, indeed targeting the receiver or clientele with a personalized message. It means it is also influential in that it is easy to track, monitor, and measure the relative efficacy of the marketing.

The benefits of Digital push marketing is that it targets "warm prospects" or people who are already on your list. It targets your niche. Additionally, you can personalize the message. For example, in an email, you can have it address each person individually, "Dear ______." Lastly, it is straightforward to track the effectiveness of this type of campaign.

The disadvantage of push marketing is that it reaches a smaller audience and usually takes more time, money and effort to put together.

— **Pull digital marketing**

The pull method of marketing is aimed at garnering customers to come to you. The marketing for this means will be communicated to compel the individual to make a call to action or visit your business. The most visible or pervasive example is a web page, website, or any other Internet-based medium.

While this means of digital advertising is not as easy to personalize or track, it is still active and powerful nonetheless. The benefit and disadvantage of the pull strategy go hand-in-hand. More steps are involved here, for the potential customer. But, if they are taken, there is a higher percentage chance that the potential customer will buy or opt-in.

An example of successful pull marketing is SEO (search engine optimization) and having your article or website ranked on the first page of a Google search.

CHAPTER 3: IMPORTANCE OF DIGITAL MARKETING

The world is rapidly getting to be noticeably computerized. Individuals are expanding electronic substance speedier consistently. Organizations and the world when all is said and done are beginning to perceive the significance of going advanced.

DIGITAL MARKETTING

And it is fundamental that showcasing offices adjust rapidly to the new conditions and effectively contract experts in the field of digital marketing.

The new strategies are quicker, more down to earth and adaptable than the old conventional ones.

The New Media age has arrived, and it's the ideal opportunity for individuals who have not yet adjusted to open themselves up to this strategy for cooperation and comprehend the different advantages of digital marketing by Digital Marketing Company.

1. More Cost Effective

It is more financially savvy than conventional advertising. It is particularly imperative for independent companies as they don't have numerous assets or a considerable measure of capital. New media can give you a less expensive and more powerful promoting channel.

2. Use Content to Connect with Customers

Utilizing electronic content either supported or free enables you to associate with customers substantially more adequately than boards, post office based email or PR battles. The quality of your online awareness now straightforwardly connected to the accomplishment of your business.

3. Cater to the Mobile Consumer

Innovation has developed so much that ingenious contraptions are never again viewed as minor other options to PCs or tablets. 91% of grown-ups in the only US generally include their cell phones inside achieving separation and routinely utilize them to peruse the web.

The biggest gathering of purchasers is utilizing their cell phones every day, so it's fundamental that you utilize an advertising arrangement that objectives these gadgets appropriately.

4. Realize Higher ROI and Revenue

By expanding your digital outreach, you can build your income. The more information that you can separate from your effort crusades, the better your expectations and along these lines ROI will be.

5. Track Your Customer's Journey

Utilizing analytics like Google analytics, you will have the capacity to screen all your client's activities, inclinations and show signs of improvement understanding into their conduct. Investigation enables you to assemble the persona of your client with the goal that you can offer them the ideal experience.

6. Increased Conversions

On the off chance that you have an online business and you are promoting items and administrations on the web, you can without much of a stretch measure your prosperity by approaching movement that gets changed over into endorsers, leads or deals and along these lines you can compute and enhance your transformation rates.

7. Encourage Social Media Engagement

On the off chance that you need your organization to develop, you can procure new customers utilizing different web-based social networking channels. Ensure continually to concentrate on your customers in light of their ages, interests and country. Along these lines, you will have the capacity to support engagement through digital marketing better.

8. Get More Likes

A few people disparage the significance of online networking as a significant aspect of their advanced advertising effort. The more "Facebook likes" or "tweets" you get, the more your organization can develop and manufacture trust and validity with your clients. It can likewise convey activity to your site on the off chance that you utilize these channels to advise your adherents about rebates, new items, blog entries and friends news, and so on.

9. Get Ahead of Your Competitors

Most business has officially surrendered conventional publicizing techniques and concentrates instead on Google AdWords, SEO or Social Media. With such a substantial number of contenders out there, it is to a significant degree challenging to promote your private venture and extend past the pack.

In any case, you can use Google Alerts to hint at change thought of where your adversaries stand. You can screen their publicizing methods or things so you can learn things that could improve your own business.

10. Earn People's Trust

Digital marketing showcasing develops from social confirmation, web-based social networking signs and genuine tributes from customers who have beforehand utilized, joined, obtained or benefited by an administration or item promoted by your business. Most customers would believe an administration or an issue when individuals they know give positive input or data about a specific brand.

It is vital to comprehend the significance of actualizing advanced advertising in your business procedure. The utilization of new media in the 21st century is not only an intelligent venture choice it's fundamental; it's a standout amongst the most effective advertising channels with many advantages that can help develop and extend your business.

CHAPTER 4: CHANGING YOUR DIGITAL MARKETING STRATEGY

Digital Marketing is continually evolving, and this may seem unsettling at times. Strategies that were working in the past might not be useful in the present.

Do you know why many businesses fail to get ahead of their competitors? It's merely because they are not willing to adapt to the ever-changing world of digital media.

But, the great thing about a digital marketing strategy is that you can change them on the fly in response to real-time results and analytics data.

While this may seem tricky as if you change things too quickly, you may not be able to find if your strategy worked for long-term.

But if you wait for a long time, you are likely to waste your two valuable resources: time and money.

With that said, how do you know when its the right time to change your Digital Marketing strategy? To help you keep up with the fast-paced industry, this will help you to identify when to change your digital marketing strategy.

Below are the 5 signs to help you decide when to quit your existing strategy.

1. Focusing on low-value metrics

If you're concentrating on low-value metrics like impressions and clicks, you may be missing out because impressions and clicks only let you know about your marketing visibility. And not the real accuracy of your strategies.

2. Only focusing on your brand not on audience needs

Every marketer wants to spread their brand name, but you should not overdo by pasting your brand name all over everything.

Make your content educational that focus on your audience problems and needs. It would help you in targeting buyers in the initial stages of the buyer's journey.

3. Over usage of keywords

Although it's required to place keywords in your content, Google's priority always lies in providing reach user experience and relevancy of content. Google has nothing to do with how many times your site shows the keyword like "Digital Marketing Strategy."

4. Don't rely on your instinct

Your prior experience is positively precious. But your decision-making process should not be only based on what worked in the past. It's a horrible idea as what worked tomorrow may be completely irrelevant today. Therefore guiding your marketing strategy through objective data will only get you better results.

5. Not integrated

Whether it's about a veteran digital marketer, sitting in IT or a startup company, it's too familiar for digital marketing strategies to be finished in silos. It is a more natural way, but of course, it's not useful. It's true that the digital approach works best when it's integrated with traditional channels. Now you know that if you need to change your digital marketing strategy or not, here is a complete guide to help you build a new, powerful marketing strategy to achieve your online goals.

What are the essential steps for creating an effective digital marketing strategy?

When creating a marketing strategy for your business, always keep your audience first. Set goals, plan your strategy, implement it, and finally measure your success:

— Research on your target market and competitors

— Know your audience because if you don't like them, how can you help them

— Integrate different marketing strategies and use only the correct tools

— If you don't have the required skills set, don't hesitate to purchase special services
— Identify your online value proposition and apply it across all digital marketing channels
— Last but not least, prepare yourself

But before you do something ask yourself a few questions. Asking yourself the right questions and having their answers in place will certainly help you make the right decisions.

Here are some Q's & A's below to help you out.

Which digital channels are most effective for you and why?

With so many digital channels around, it gets difficult to choose the best one. So you can identify it with these simple basics:

— Identify the avenue where most of your potential customers like to hang out
— Analyse your target audience behaviour
— Build awareness with Twitter
— Attend industry events and conferences
— Social media and newsletters to reach out to your potential customers
— SEO or combination of SEO and PPC to help you attract more visitors

How to evaluate your digital marketing activities?

Unfortunately, some companies don't know how to answer this question correctly.

- If you're also one of them, don't feel embarrassed! Just hop on and find out how can you determine the right metrics and evaluate your current digital marketing activities.
- Identify your target KPI (Key Performance Indicator) to help you understand what's working
- Monitor your website traffic and sales to know the necessary statistics about your customers
- Track and measure your metrics through Google Analytics
- Survey your site visitors to find if they're satisfied with your solutions
- Track ROI, conversions, market share, and sales

How to make your business stand out from the crowd?

In today's competitive digital market it's challenging to make your business stand out from your competitors. But an effective strategy can help you stay ahead of them.

Let's see how.

- Effectively communicate and educate your customers
- Stay honest and transparent to build customer's loyalty
- Talk less, listen more
- Be authoritative and helpful in what you do

— Know your competitors and learn from them

— Be creative, open-minded, and try new technologies

— Speak in your audience language

— Use proof points and testimonials to show you're the best

ESSENTIALS OF DIGITAL MARKETING

The marketing of any product or service on a digital medium is called digital marketing. The medium can be computers, mobile phones, tablets or even iPods. There is a reason why such marketing overpowered traditional advertising. On televisions and billboards, advertising is a one-way street. Customers don't have a platform to communicate with manufacturers and companies themselves. This gap in communication is eliminated by the internet.

Online platforms selling products like Amazon and Flipkart rank products based on consumer ratings and allow customers to give in-depth reviews about the product in question. It creates a direct line of communication between consumers and manufacturers as the latter can grasp what the former truly needs.

HOW WOULD A FRESHER BENEFIT FROM DIGITAL MARKETING?

In the digital world, online marketing is essential for running a successful business. Marketers these days are adopting from traditional to the digital approach.

CHAPTER 5: TOP 10 DON'TS OF DIGITAL MARKETING

Digital marketing is the method of marketing in which we use various electronic devices such as computers, smartphones, tablets, etc. It also entails the usage of software programs, apps and technological platforms such as email, websites, social media, etc. The world of digital marketing is a vast one in which we can easily get lost.

Because of all the advances and changes in technology, it can be hard to keep up on all the latest trends and methods encompassed by digital marketing. Digital marketing strategies include visual marketing, mobile marketing, and online marketing techniques of various kinds so it can all get very confusing and overwhelming.

We not only need to know what to do in the digital marketing world; we have to know what not to do. Below is a list of ten of the don'ts to help you trek through the massive digital marketing universe hopefully.

1. Closing Your Eyes on Mobile Marketing - The number of people who spend more time on the web with mobile devices is growing at an astounding rate. If you own online business, you can no longer resist mobile devices as part of your digital marketing arsenal. The first step would be to make your website mobile device friendly.

Many site builder programs such as WordPress have plugins and automatic features to do that for you. You can also add a line of code to your site that will format your site to the device being used.

Be sure to try your website on your mobile devices to find out exactly how people see it. Go through the mobile shopping experience yourself, so you have a full understanding of what you need to do.

2. Too Much Social Media - Social media is so much a part of the internet these days it is impossible to expect to build a presence on all of the social sites.

You need to pick 2 or 3 of the top sites and start building your brand and setting up your social presence. The most used social sites as of now are Facebook, Twitter, LinkedIn and Pinterest. You can get most of your social traffic from Facebook and Pinterest. Next in line is Google+, Tumblr and Instagram. If you can understand your target market, you can become a part of the social sites in which they would most likely participate.

3. Information Overload - The digital marketing world is so vast we can quickly become lost in the information. We need to narrow our focus and learn only what we need to learn to build our business successfully. Find a few good sources for this information and stick with them to learn the ins and outs.

4. Not Having a User-Friendly Website - Many of us are tempted to create the most prominent, brightest, flashiest website possible, but this is a big mistake. You want your site design to be simple, easy to navigate and very user-friendly. Add only what is needed to inform your customers.

You do want to add some extra content to provide information to your visitors but make sure it directly pertains to what your site is about. Do not clutter up your site with many ads, irrelevant information or extra steps to get to your call to action. Fancy features and flashy extras will confuse your customer and possibly drive them to another site.

5. Not Keeping Up with SEO Changes - SEO is very pertinent to your website, but the rules and regulations are always changing. Find a good source of SEO information and follow it regularly to keep up with the changes so you can make any necessary revisions to your business website.

6. Not Utilizing Visual Marketing - By using visual marketing, you could increase your conversion rate by as much as 86%. It is a phenomenal statistic.

Place a video on your landing and homepage. Strategically place quality graphics in your blog posts and content. Use visuals as much as possible in your social media marketing.

Create and use your infographics for your blog and social media. There are free tools for making infographics. Use a compelling photo or graphic in your articles. It could mean the difference between your item being read or rejected. Look over articles with photos. Does the picture pull you into the material and make you want to read it or does it leave you flat? Take note of the type of image used and what emotion or action it brings out in you. Placing a well-made video on your homepage or landing page will make a substantial difference as well.

People will get the message much quicker than by reading and could be the deciding factor as to whether they stay or go. Be entertaining in the video but be sure to deliver your message.

Your image and voice will also help your potential customer bond with you. You also want to get started in a reasonably new visual marketing technique called meme marketing. It combines humour and real-life situations with amusing and heartwarming images.

7. Not Testing and Tracking - Take advantage of Google's free tools to study your stats and track your visitors. Google Analytics can help you tweak your site to its performance peak. Test ads, web pages, article resource boxes, etc. Find out what brings the best results and most response and stick with it.

8. Not Establishing the Relationship - Doing business with people digitally is much different than being able to talk with them face to face. It is harder for people to trust a webpage than an actual person so be sure to do all you can to build that relationship of trust and respect. Answer all email inquiries quickly and appropriately. Be reliable, if you say you are going to do something, be sure to do it. Be consistent if you are sending out a weekly newsletter do not get lax and start missing weeks.

Update your blog and product information regularly. Do not let your site go stale. Be consistent in your social media. Respond to all questions and comments promptly. Let people know you are available for them and can be trusted.

9. Focusing too Much on Traffic and Not Enough on Conversions - Traffic is the lifeblood of an online business, but you also need to focus on quality and targeted traffic.

Getting 1000 visitors to your site doesn't do much good if they are not interested in what you offer. Participate in groups and forums where people who are interested in your services might be. If you offer B2B products and services, join groups and conferences of home business owners. We all want more traffic, but we need to aim for the traffic to whom we can sell.

10. Charging Blindly Into the Marketing Abyss - Starting an online business and charging headfirst into the digital marketing world is not a good idea. You need to do some planning ahead and research what you are getting into. Know who your customers will be and where to find them. Make sure you are offering a sellable product or service. Be somewhat prepared for your dive into the digital marketing world.

These mistakes are widespread but need to be addressed. If you are attempting to build an online business, you need to be informed and constantly be adapting and learning.

CHAPTER 6: DIGITAL MARKETING IN HEALTHCARE

For any organisation to create an active digital brand presence using these devices, the first step is to create a digital strategy.

A digital strategy answers the fundamental questions of who an organisation will engage and how. Implementing a digital strategy puts a public face on an organisation, thereby increasing outreach capabilities and raising an organisation's public profile.

THE BUSINESS CASE FOR DIGITAL

As statistics reveal, performing well in digital is critical to healthcare organisations:

- — More than 72% of people use the Internet to find health information and services. (Pew, 2012)
- — Half of online health information research is on behalf of someone else. (Pew, 2012)
- — One in five internet users has consulted online reviews and rankings of health care service providers and treatments. (Pew, 2012)
- — Caregivers are more likely than other internet users to take part in a wide range of health-related activities online. (Pew, 2012)
- — 42% of people living with a disability have looked online for health information. (Pew, 2012)

Digital is not a short-term trend. It is the way the world is moving because no other medium compares in its ability to reach and engage such a wide variety of audiences. Overall, digital budgets continue to trend upwards. According to David Moth of Econsultancy, 71% will increase their digital marketing budgets. Robust growth in digital spending will continue, with spending topping out at $4.51 billion ($4.55 billion) in 2016 (eMarketer, 2012).

Despite the continued growth, today many organisations still have not caught up to this reality, and therefore are misallocating their marketing dollars.

Organisations that properly allocate their marketing dollars and implement coherent digital strategies early will enjoy more significant long term benefits. Starting as early as possible is essential.

As more and more organisations join the digital sphere, space can become crowded, thus requiring a more significant investment of time and resources to have the same impact. Also, investing in digital early provides the time necessary to build institutional knowledge and develop habits that are consistent with industry best practice.

Increasing consumer reliance on the Internet for information means that health care organisations can significantly increase their revenue and brand by engaging audiences online. Whether a client is looking for directions, helpful hints or researching services, an organisation may establish itself as an early leader.

Joining the digital revolution is a process that takes time, dedication and most importantly, a thoughtful and well-executed plan. While the importance of a solid digital plan is well known, it is not a race. It is never too late for an organisation to realise the benefits of early implementation.

THE BENEFITS OF EMBRACING DIGITAL

The benefits of embracing digital are clear-especially for healthcare organisations:

Increased sales: As consumers increasingly turn to digital channels to seek out information regarding essential decisions, smart marketers are converting that interest into handraisers and sales. Well-managed digital marketing methods have a better probability of turning a casual browser into a client.

Stronger community relationships: Digital provides an efficient means to reach out to and cultivate an audience of residents, staff, patients and their families, leading to a greater sense of community.

Quantifiability: Unlike traditional advertising vehicles, marketing your organisation can track, optimise, and improve every interaction through digital. This approach results in the best possible customer interactions and higher conversion rates.

Improved brand perception: When asked, 94% of prospective patients said the reputation of the facility is vital in hospital selection (Google, 2013). Brands can pay attention to what people are saying about their organisation online.

While it is impossible to stop negative comments completely, organisations can respond appropriately and mitigate their effects with actual content. By engaging they make it personal and have the opportunity to improve brand perception.

Reduce operating costs: When compared to more traditional forms of outreach, digital messaging tends to be more cost-effective and can help to reduce pressure on conventional patient acquisition vehicles.

TRENDS TO LEVERAGE A SMALL BUSINESS OPPORTUNITY

This section focuses on how small businesses can leverage digital marketing to achieve greater success and enhance their market opportunities.

Digital marketing should be a tool that every serious small business should utilise. Digital marketing goes by many names such as e-commerce marketing, online marketing, and internet marketing. Digital marketing can be defined as "*the marketing of products or services using digital channels to reach consumers.*" The key objective is to promote brands the usage of the internet.

Digital marketing extends beyond internet marketing to include channels that do not require the use of the internet. Some digital marketing channels include websites, social media platforms, email marketing, search engine optimisation (SEO), blogging, podcasts, and online advertising to name a few. Beyond technology gimmicks, businesses should know their customers and their core competencies. Digital marketing is not a silver bullet. Digital marketing is a tool for the savvy business professional.

Catherine Juan, Donnie Greiling, and Catherine Buerkle, authors of Internet Marketing: Start to Finish, suggest that effective digital marketing requires plenty of careful planning. They add, "*The heart of getting real traction out of your internet marketing program is to tie marketing and sales data together, with metrics. Track what you're doing, track the impact, and track the resulting sales.*"

Looking at the landscape of technology and internet innovation, small businesses should think strategically about the following five digital marketing trends:

- **Artificial Intelligence** - Some people develop elaborate doom-day scenarios of machines to control the world. However, artificial intelligence (AI) is becoming a way of life in marketing. AI can be defined as 'the theory and development of computer systems able to perform tasks that normally require human intelligence.'

Voice Activation technology like Amazon's Echo is bringing AI into public attention. By 2020, customers will manage 85% of their purchases without interacting with a person.

- **Internet Searching** - Buyers are more knowledgeable than ever with access to the internet. 81% of shoppers conduct online research before making big purchases. Thus, exploring how to utilise search engine optimisation and getting your business at the top of searches is an invaluable step.

- **Mobile Communications** - Most Americans have grown accustomed to instant gratification and easy access to technology. Mobile and tablet e-commerce will reach $293B by 2018. Smartphone and tablets are part of this wave of innovation. Mobile will account for 72% of the U.S. digital ad spend by 2019. Marketers recognise that mobile marketing is an untapped business tool.

- **Social Media** - Social media platforms, like Facebook, allows buyers to connect virtually. 65% of business-to-business companies have acquired customers through LinkedIn ads. Marketers realise this value.

- **Web Content** - Good content will attract customers. Customers are more likely to purchase from sellers with useful, relevant videos/photos on their website. 52% of marketing professionals globally name the video as the type of content with the best ROI.

Faced with the tenants of competition, small businesses need to utilise digital marketing.

Some small businesses may be hesitant to explore digital marketing due to their lack of trust and understanding of the internet. Philip Kotler and Kevin Keller, authors of Marketing Management, note "Top firms are comfortable using technology to improve the way they do business with their business-to-business customers."

CHAPTER 7: TRADITIONAL MARKETING VS DIGITAL MARKETING

Traditionally, the term "*market*" refers to the place where buyers & sellers meet for the exchange of goods & services. The market is the universal term, known to all, but depending upon the number of products handled, there are wholesale market & retail markets.

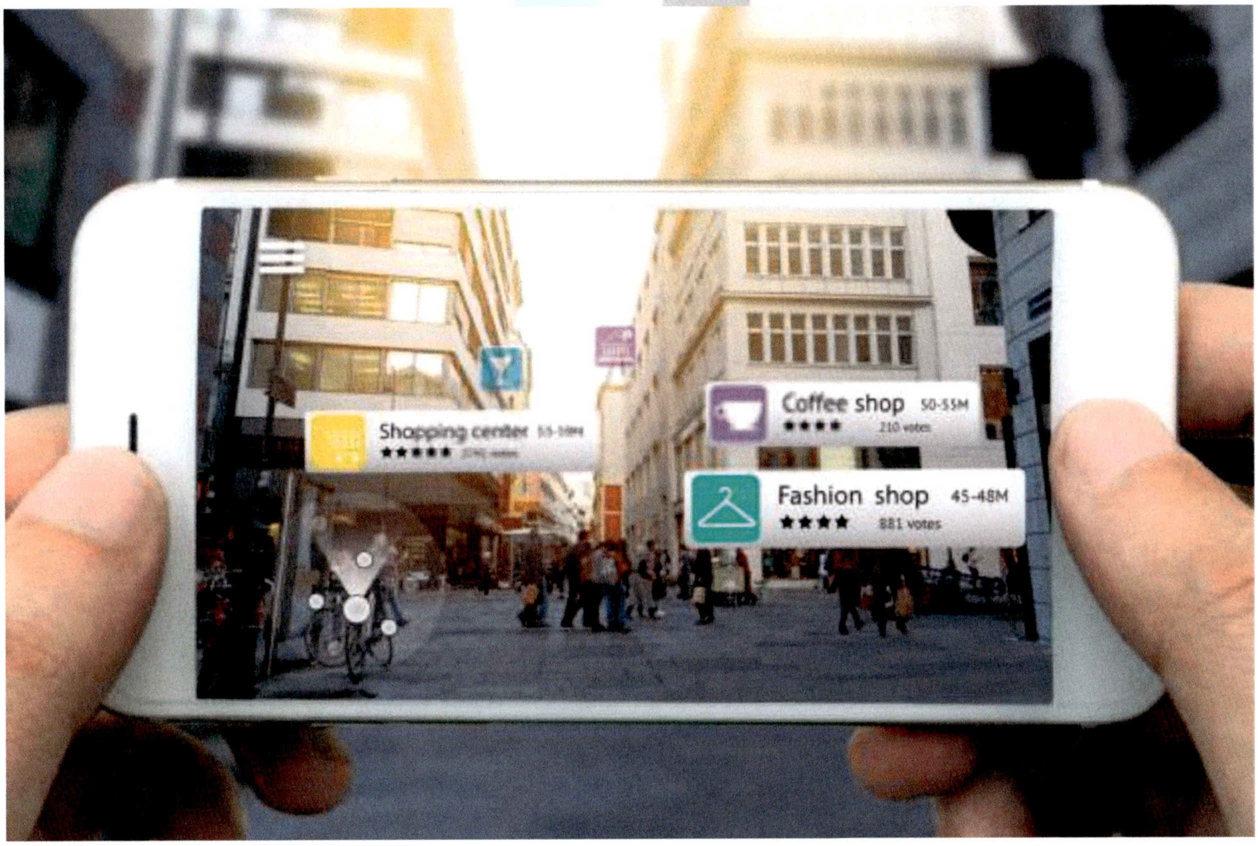

In the modern concept sense, the term "market" has a broader meaning. It refers to the sets/collection of actual or potential buyers of products & services. There are various categories of marketing, but there are two main segments, first being the traditional marketing & second, being digital marketing. In this section, we will discuss these methods in details.

TRADITIONAL MARKETING

Traditional marketing refers to any promotions, advertising or publicity, which are generally used by the companies/ business entities for a more extended period, & that has a proven success rate.

In old times, marketing was defined as the flow of goods & services from producers to consumers. It is a product-oriented definition of marketing. The producer concentrates only on the products that what they can produce / manufacture, & need of consumers are not taken into consideration.

Methods of traditional techniques include print advertisement, such as newsletters, billboards, newspapers ads. Other forms are television, commercials, radio -broadcasting advertising about the product or service of any company.

NEED OF DIGITAL MARKETING

Since the technology is advancing in nowadays, that demands the change in everything. Digital marketing is a part of the computerisation. Talking for about 20 years back, there was no computers, no mobile phones & of course, no internet connection. But as the technology grows, after some time mobiles phones & computers are introduced into the life of human being. After some more time, internet facilities got added, which bring about the digital revolution.

Examples of digital marketing include websites, social media networks, emails are standard.

Digital marketing is similar to the traditional one but by using digital devices & information technology. It is faster, reliable & easy to find medium & therefore accepted worldwide.

DIGITAL MARKETING

Digital marketing is a broad term that refers the marketing through the online medium like search engines, websites, social media networks & emails. Digital marketing is sometimes also called online or internet marketing.

Digital (latest) marketing technique includes the SEO (search engine optimisation), SEM (Search engine marketing), content marketing, and campaign marketing, e-commerce marketing & social media marketing.

There is various reason for the growth of digital marketing.

1) Digital marketing techniques are more cost-effective than traditional concept.

2) Digital process faster than the old one, thereby result oriented.

3) Any individual/company track his/ her performance.

4) All method being reliable generates better revenues.

5) Digital media facilitate interaction with the targeted audience.

However, various factors affect the process of a firm's ability to develop & maintain successful transaction & relationships with the target customers.

There is generally two types of environment inside any organisation. One is stable, not changing with time & changes are very frequent. Second, being the dynamic field that keeps on the move according to the demand.

IMPACT ON CONSUMER PERCEPTION

Consumer perception is the most crucial factor for all business entities since it helps in developing their brand awareness and understanding. Thus, both for online and offline marketing it is essential for management to understand consumer perception more effectively and efficiently.

There are some of the reasons behind the maintenance of consumer perception of the business and industries:

1. Creating brand awareness
2. Building brand loyalty
3. Enhancing consumer loyalty
4. Developing a brand image
5. Competitive advantage

Before purchasing or experiencing products and services, customers tend to develop a particular perception. Perception usually varies from customer to customer, product as well as service quality. Hence, from a business or marketing point of view, it is essential for them to track down the customer behaviour pattern and their perception and therefore need to address the same effectively and efficiently.

During purchasing a product or services, customers always tend to gather knowledge about the same over the internet. Thus, based on the online presence and rating, mainly from Google, customers landing into conclusion for buying decision process.

Therefore, developing perception before buying is essential for the business to track down. Customers also develop after purchasing behaviour, and it depends on the user experience. Based on the user experience, perception varies, and it is essential to address accordingly.

Organisations, to have a competitive advantage ahead of their competitors, need to develop and maintain its brand awareness and image. Based on the market presence and performance, customers used to create their perception that guides them to undertake purchasing decisions.

It is essential for the management to address all the consumer complaints and issues to have customer faith and resolve all the related problems.

Digital marketing is a platform that accelerates the marketing activities to a different level that provides the organisation ample enough opportunity. Thus, a digital marketing platform operates under using digital technologies, and the primary and the most effective medium is the internet. This, therefore, helps the organisations to attach with a million customers within a short period.

Some of the various platforms, organisations do undertake while implementing the digital marketing process are search engine optimisation, search engine marketing, social media optimisation and email marketing.

Some of the digital marketing platforms like Google Ad words, Google Webmaster tools, Google Analytics, Facebook, Twitter, LinkedIn, which help to track customers, perform customer engagement and thus interact with them effectively and efficiently. Therefore, it also stated as the online marketing platform that allows to connect with the clients and the audiences and thus helps in active customer engagement.

Now the main title of the chapter used to focus on digital marketing and its impact or the effect over consumer perception. Due to digital presence, it is easy for the organisation to connect with the customers more efficiently and effectively.

From the customer end, they face problems, and often they share various recommendations and reviews. It is essential for the organisation to respond to those queries and the digital marketing platform provides mobility in such a process.

These digital marketing platforms thus make the communication more effective and result oriented and thus helps in managing the customer perception more effectively. Facebook, Twitter and other social media sites help to target the broader community, and therefore it becomes easy to connect with the audiences more effectively.

Combining all the digital marketing activities and developing customer perception, helps the organisation to create consumer awareness. Developing useful customer perception helps in redefining brand awareness and brand image.

While conducting a digital marketing process, it is essential to maintain the proper pace and quality. It will ensure adequate customer attraction, which helps in developing better customer perception of various products and services.

The social media platform has helped in attracting or tapping the targeted customers more efficiently and thus ensuring customer engagement, which helps in developing perception. Therefore, from the above discussion, it is evident that digital marketing does create a substantial impact over consumer perception thus enhance the brand image as well as awareness.

Lastly, it is essential to conclude that not only business professionals but students also need to have proper grip and awareness over the field of digital marketing since it also provides prospect in their career.

CHAPTER 8: FUTURE OF DIGITAL MARKETING

Traditional marketing has been challenged by digital marketing in today's world of smartphones and laptops. People are available more online than on television sets or outside hanging out with friends. The culture has become such that people like to shop online, talk online, and eat online. In a nutshell, the internet of things has made everything mobile-driven.

With internet connectivity reaching out to every household, people are becoming tech-friendly and hence spends most of their time booking things online and saving the rest for the things they love. Putting up hoarding on the main road and playing the ads during the prime time is not going to help that much in today's world than placing ads on social media sites and YouTube or applications.

The application of digital media marketing is making the companies surge with demand and supplies of products to the customers at a higher speed. Therefore, applying smart techniques with the help of various tools of digital marketing would benefit the companies to take advantage of the increasing demand in the customer segment and earn a profit.

— **Digitisation**

Everything is becoming digitised and would be fully automated in the days to come. If people are using things that are connected to the internet, then advertisement agencies and digital marketers should also come up with ways where there is the maximum possibility of traffic coming. With everything becoming digital, the application of search engine optimisation, social media marketing, AdWords is going to help the marketers to bag new opportunities and lure customers to purchasing their product.

— **Network**

With more and more network tower coming up and new satellites being set up in the universe to make communication effective, time is going to come when the network would be stronger than ever before. It is going to make things easy, quick and transparent. Network availability and access are going to prove it instrumental in creating digital marketing the only way to reach customers.

— Increased Demand

The coming years are going to see the customers getting prosperous than ever before. With more purchasing power, people would want to purchase more products and services. It is going to facilitate things in the companies by making them available online to the customers and working with high speed to get the product delivered to them without any hassle. It is going to be another essential tool that would lure customers, and the fight would be about this aspect within the competitors.

Things are changing fast in the world. MNC's are becoming aware of future trends and analysis is done to see whether traditional marketing is necessary to be carried out or not. Traditional marketing would continue to serve the foundation of digital marketing, but the evolving nature of the marketing field as a whole is never going to stop. It is so because marketing keeps the customer needs at the centre. The more active the customer, the more complex would be the marketing.

WONDERS OF SOCIAL MEDIA MARKETING TO A BRAND

The universe of digital marketing is wide and varied, but the one factor that is dominating it is social media. Through online platforms, companies can reach a global pool of customers that are in billions. Any corporation that is not utilising; this source is not only skipping on a fantastic growth window but a cash cow of profitability.

Be it poor PPC services or sharing content on social media, when a company utilises any platform, they spread awareness of their service or product. Furthermore, they indicate to search engines that the brand is reliable, valid and consistent. Let's take a look at how else social media affects an establishment, positively.

— **Get the customer engaged**

Marketing is about winning the attention of a person and then conveying your message. Social media is the easiest and ideal way of interacting with customers. It is the one path that allows for two-way communication at lightning speed. Catering to the wishes or interest of the patron is fast-paced with online platforms. When more consumers are engaging with your brand, there is a more significant probability of conversion.

— **Get more customers aware**

Facebook, Twitter or Instagram are not just avenues to converse with current customers. They are pathways to reaching an added audience in real time. Unlike most other marketing stratagems, social media is a hassle-free way to enhance the visibility of a brand. Just a few hours every seven days has shown, in more than 90% of companies, a greater awareness of product or service in customers.

The gist is to create all social media profiles, use them regularly and begin networking to generate a broad audience

— **Make customers more loyal**

Without a shadow of a doubt, the one benefit social media has for customers are the ease with which they can find brands. The convenience of connecting heightens user experience and benefits the company. How? A patron becomes loyal to a brand when they receive satisfaction.

When a customer can communicate with the corporation within minutes of facing an issue or wanting to know more about a product through social presence, it ups satisfaction. This, in turn, leads to brand loyalty.

— **Gain an understanding of the marketplace**

The reason social media is considered the MVP of digital marketing is not that it gives brands the freedom to introduce their products to a broader audience but because it offers comprehension of the marketplace. When a company can talk with their patrons through online avenues directly, they get to know precisely what is needed.

Over and above, a brand can observe the online activities of the consumer and get to know their opinions and interests. It would not be possible without pages and handles on social media.

Think of social media as a research tool which can be employed to know the demographics when the brand following becomes large.

— **Be more economical**

Advertising, in the traditional sense, is not an inexpensive strategy. But promoting through social media marketing is hugely cost-effective.

— Creating an account on any platform is free.

— Developing a brand through your handle costs zilch.

— Even paid advertising is dirt cheap on social media.

To top the cake with a cherry, a company can invest the smallest amount and get a high rate of return. Significantly raising conversion rates is not hard with social media adverts; you need a little capital and the right time.

— **Gain a brand voice**

Through an online platform, a brand can create a voice that speaks directly to patrons and generates a healthy brand image. When a customer receives a tailored reply to their query on social, instead of a cookie cutter reply, they appreciate it more. It shows that the company values the consumer enough to take the effort to write a personal response. A brand voice, therefore, allows for effective communication, networking and healthier satisfaction in clients.

— **Become an authority**

Every time a small or big business posts original content on social media or each time, they resolve a question posed by a customer, they establish authority. As more and more original posts go up and resolutions occur, in the eyes of the patron, the brand becomes an expert on the subject or topic.

Just like satisfaction and loyalty affect the bottom line of an organisation, authority touches it too. Why? Because it leaves an optimistic picture in the mind of the consumer. It makes them more probable of buying a product and talking about it to other potential customers.

— **A Succinct Layout**

No marketing guru or entrepreneur can deny that media is a magic wand. It creates miracles for budding and established businesses. When you post consistently, the benefits the trade accrues are:

— Better SEO

— Increased traffic

— Improved brand loyalty

— Healthier customer satisfaction

Remember, chances are the competing businesses are already exploiting social marketing to reach probable patrons.

CHAPTER 9: EFFECTIVE LEAD GENERATION THROUGH DIGITAL MARKETING

Lead generation is a critical component of many different businesses. Take an insurance agency, for example, whether you're providing car, life, home, life, health or business insurance, you need to understand how to get more customers and utilise your sales funnel consistently.

A lead is a person who has shown interest in your company's product or service in some way.

You want them to buy something from you, but you need to spend some time building up the benefits and wooing them to entice them to choose you over your competitors.

A lead generation funnel centres around a large number of names being poured into the funnel. Over time, you identify which are viable targets, then hopefully turn those targets into prospects and finally convert to buyers as they move down the funnel to purchase.

Direct marketing goes way back in the world of insurance sales, but the internet has made it much easier for insurance companies to get new targets and automatically follow up with potential clients.

If you're using online marketing strategies, it doesn't matter if it's the middle of the night and your business is closed - your insurance agency can get new clients anytime, anywhere.

There are 3 steps to this process:

1. Generation

It is the first part of the journey, where you generate the initial spark of consumer interest or enquiry into your products or services.

Ideas to start trying to convert targets to paying customers to include:

- Asking people to sign up for your email newsletter
- Encouraging people to fill out an online form for a free consultation
- Using an exit intent popup on select webpages

If you're doing SEO, SEM, social media marketing and content marketing well, you should have a large number of visitors to your website and social media accounts, where you can initially engage new clients.

Make sure you ask people if they'd like to sign up for your newsletter before you start sending your finely-crafted marketing materials to their inbox!

2. Qualification

Not every prospect you capture is going to become a sale. You need to have an active process of filtering through all your leads to find the best ones. Otherwise, you'll waste time on audiences that will never convert.

For example, a prospect who lands on your site visits your "Pricing" page and enters their information into a form to download your free report is more valuable than a person who lands on your site, reads a blog article, then leaves.

Here's an example of lead generation through digital marketing from everyone's favourite gecko.

3. Nurturing

It is the step where you're focusing your efforts on providing relevant information at each stage of the buyer's journey. Some examples are providing targeted marketing content and email personalisation.

Studies show that compared to traditional marketing, content marketing and email marketing generate 50 percent more leads. It's important to create original, quality content if you want to attract customers - especially because a lot of insurance information is confusing to the average person.

Content marketing helps you get discovered on social media and in search engines.

Then, you can help drive new referrals organically. Appeal to potential clients' needs and pain points with solution-based content, and you'll get their attention. Through continuous nurturing with valuable content, people will start to think of you as a trusted source and authority.

The Importance of A/B Testing

You'll never know quite how successful any campaign is without testing it! A/B testing is a popular way of determining what works and what doesn't.

You should be testing the effectiveness of one element at a time to determine what is responsible for an increase (or decrease) in traffic or conversions. The more time you spend testing, the better results you'll see.

Some things you can A/B test include:

— Adding or decreasing text or white space on your website

— Changing a call to action in your email or on your site

— Changing a headline or block of text on your sales landing page

Finding new clients is hard work. So is working hard to stay ahead of your competitors. Will it be easy? No. But if you put in the time and energy, you'll see your insurance marketing strategies pay off!

How to Target Your Ideal Clients With Digital Newsletters

Regardless of the size of your business, they're an efficient way to reach current and potential clients and to easily measure the results of your efforts. Not sure if sending newsletters is something you should do? Here are 5 reasons to consistently send newsletters that will generate leads.Before you send out newsletters for digital marketing purposes, you need to make sure you're targeting the right people with the right messages.

Here are 5 ways to get started:

1. Identify the objectives of your company newsletter.

The first question you need to ask is: Who are your ideal clients? You need to understand that first and foremost. Ask yourself questions such as:

— What pain points do my customers have?

— Why do they want what I'm offering?

— What are their interests?

If you don't have customer data to study, start by putting yourself in their shoes. Think like a customer receiving your newsletter - what would you like to see? What would make you open your newsletter?

2. Have a newsletter content plan in place.

Coming up with a content calendar is a must if you want to ensure you're sending the most relevant emails at the right times.

How else will you remember how many times you've promoted a particular product or shared an article on a topic?

Beyond keeping your email newsletter content organised, a content calendar is great for remembering holidays whether you're targeting customers on Thanksgiving or National Donut Day. You can also create monthly or seasonal themes.

3. Think outside the digital newsletter template.

Today's email marketing services offer hundreds of template options you can use when creating your company newsletter.

However, digital newsletter templates can make your readers feel like they're getting a cookie-cutter email rather than a customised message.

Consider hiring a professional marketing company to design a personalised email newsletter template that will make your brand and messaging stand out.

4. Track, refine, repeat.

All of the first email marketing services have some form of tracking in place so you can measure your email campaign metrics.

It is an essential part of the targeting process, as it gives you valuable insight into what your customers love and what they don't.

For example, if your clickthrough rate on your "Weekly News" section is dismal, you can test replacing that content with something else.

If an article you included was opened, shared and liked by a lot of people, look for related content to include in a future company newsletter.

5. Segment your newsletter audience.

Sending different emails to different lists is key to customer engagement. The more you can narrow down your audience's interests and buying habits the better.

Sending customers who have just bought your product an email promoting that same product isn't a good use of your time or theirs. How about showing them an accessory to the product they've bought, or a thank you email with a promo code?

CHAPTER 10: RUNNING A SUCCESSFUL BUSINESS IN THE DIGITAL AGE

The fact is that if you are going to have a successful business, you are going to have to do it in the digital age, which we all should have embraced fully at this point. It is a reality, and once you get comfortable with digital marketing as well as other digital tools, you will probably enjoy it.

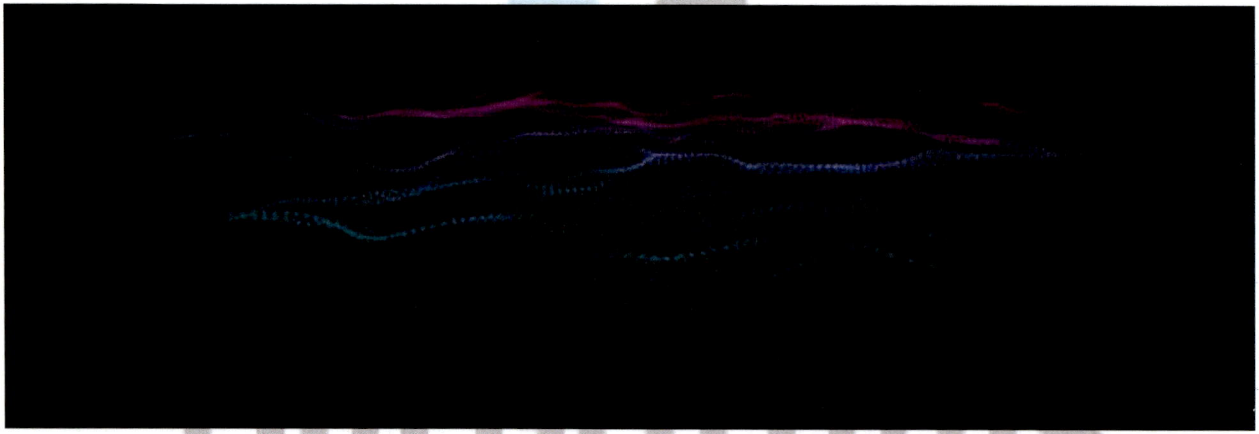

— **How the digital age has affected the way that businesses are run**

If you are at the point where you are starting a business, you will probably have an easier time of it and become successful more quickly than you would have before technology was functioning at such a high level.

Having a solid knowledge base that you can apply to sell your brand and your products and services will make all of the difference to your success in business, and without it, you will not get very far in your industry. Part of that knowledge is having a good understanding of the marketing angle of your business. Marketing is critical to all businesses, and it is necessary for you to either be able to market your brand or to get someone else to do it for you. All that matters is that it is done successfully.

— **Everyone loves an entrepreneur**

Nowadays, entrepreneurs and entrepreneurship are well respected for everything that they are trying to do (and, hopefully, succeeding at). That attitude has been evolving over the last several years and entrepreneurs are taken just as seriously as all other business people.

If a person who is starting a new business has a feeling that his or her efforts will probably not pay off, provided that the person has a unique angle to what he or she is trying to do, there is a reasonable likelihood that the person will succeed (at least for a while).

So, the conclusion to draw here is that not only should the entrepreneur take the endeavour seriously but other people will also take that person and his or her efforts seriously. To go one step further, those other people will probably also be willing to recommend the entrepreneur and his or her offerings to other people.

— **The qualities of an active entrepreneur**

An effective entrepreneur is one who has a lot of positive energy, holds the attention of the target audience member effectively, is genuine, and is clear and concise at the same time. As a person who is reaching out to others to explain the heart of the business, it is vital to be able to do that with as few words as possible.

Of course, your passion for what you are doing must be evident at the same time. You want to entice the other person with your ideas and your words, and you want to get them to want to buy what you are selling.

— **You are selling yourself as much as you are selling your products and services**

The reality is that if you are selling a product and function as a relatively new business owner, you also have a responsibility to sell yourself. Nobody will want to buy anything that you are selling if you can't convince them that you are worth buying from.

That means that you must possess certain qualities: sincerity, trustworthiness, credibility, and you must be a subject matter expert in your niche and industry. Of course, some of the other attributes that you should also possess are passion and ambition. All of those qualities put together make up a successful business person and one who will become even more successful over time.

— **Follow certain rules for success**

As an entrepreneur, you are bound to learn a great deal as time goes on. First of all, you will need to have an attitude of receptiveness, and you will want to embrace the idea that you will learn a great deal of valuable information that you will be able to leverage in your business.

Of course, your learning process will not always be easy. It will probably be more painful more often than it will be easy. However, it is essential for you to keep in mind that you will perhaps learn the most from the unpleasant (or trying) experiences. The learning experiences will enable you to adjust what you have been doing (and what may not have been working) to achieve more favourable results (results that you can use to improve your business practices and business approach).

The fact is that if you can identify what you have been doing incorrectly, you will be able to fix those things so that you can achieve positive results for your business. You should never consider that whatever isn't working is a failure on your part.

You need to look at it as a learning experience. It is crucial for you to remember that you will walk away richer (in many different ways) than you were before.

AVOID CERTAIN PITFALLS

Although you probably do many more things right than wrong, there are inevitable common mistakes that you (and many other people) may be inclined to make. You never want to be:

— **Unprepared**

Being unprepared is completely avoidable under most circumstances. When it comes to your products and services, you should understand (and be able to recite) every aspect of it (or them) in your sleep. No matter what question is brought up, you need to make sure that you have an intelligent, insightful answer every time. If you care about what you are selling (as well as being passionate about your products and services), it will come through in the way that you answer the question(s).

— **Unenthusiastic**

Enthusiasm goes hand-in-hand with passion. If you have amazing, creative ideas but you can't express your interest in those ideas, nobody else will buy into what you are saying and in what you are trying to do. It is a simple concept. It is also where the concept of selling comes into it. You need to sell yourself to the other person before you can sell anything else.

— **Arrogant**

Before you can get anywhere at all in business, you need to believe in yourself and in your power to make your dreams come true. Additionally, you need to like yourself as well. If you do that, others will feel the same way about you.

— **Speak more than listen**

Of course, undoubtedly, you will need to be able to communicate clearly in as effective a manner as possible. However, you also need to listen effectively. The chances are excellent that the other person has a lot of valuable information to impart to you to help you make a raging success of your business.

Running a successful business in the digital age comes with its own set of challenges, although, in many ways, you probably have an easier time achieving your business' goals now than you would have before. Nowadays, you have a lot of tools at your fingertips that can make a positive difference to your business.

If you are passionate, persistent, and enthusiastic, you are bound to succeed. As an entrepreneur, you need to be willing to take calculated risks as well. That doesn't mean that you should be reckless. You need to balance the potential danger with the approach and what you have now and what you stand to gain. At that point, you will be able to make an intelligent, informed decision.

CHAPTER 11: CHATBOT MARKETING WITH ARTIFICIAL INTELLIGENCE

ChatBot Digital Marketing which makes use of Artificial Intelligence technologies can be used as a critical component in any company's marketing strategy in terms of guiding customers through a marketing sales funnel.

The marketing funnel that would be programmed into the AI ChatBot would be defined concerning the products and services being offered into the market place from the company in question. Implementation of the particular social media digital marketing strategy may well be devised by a full-service digital marketing agency.

When it comes to active digital marketing strategy development and subsequent execution that requires marketing research, strategy formulation, content planning, linking strategy and the publication of the content in question, in addition to the above, careful posting on relevant content portals and blogs in necessary to expand the digital marketing footprint of the company as well as developing the equity of the brand.

The point being made is that publishing content on its own is not enough; there has to be a key focus on that of promoting the company and that of building the business's brand.

If the company chooses to take care of the content marketing in house as opposed to making use of a digital marketing agency then all of the necessary software and keyword analysis tools will need to be purchased and subscribed to in order to be able to determine the correct direction that needs to be taken for maximum social media marketing effectiveness.

So bearing in mind that the content itself is not the main issue per se, we can turn our attention to the strategic use of how companies are using chatbots for marketing the content will be created and published strategically on portals, blogs, websites and via social media channels then in turn users make their way to the company website where they interact with the artificial intelligence chatbots in order to implement the business' digital marketing strategies.

From the various social media marketing channels that may be used to publish related company content; along with the [say] the company blog and other authority blogs. Remembering that there will be associated links within each piece of content in turn, users are directed to the company website which will lead to the strategic AI chatbot with all of the associated calls to action coming into play.

The activation of the AI ChatBot and interaction with the customer and associated data that will be collected will, in turn, provide valuable marketing intelligence for the company in question. It could be in the form of questions asked by the ChatBot which carefully guides prospects through a defined marketing or customer support process.

AI INTEGRATIONS THAT ARE REFINING MOBILE APPS PERFORMANCE

From intelligent chatbots to speech recognition, mobile apps are now evolving to be the smartest of business tools. Artificial Intelligence or only AI is one of the computer science fields that help machines or technology tools to act like a person. People these days rely heavily on mobile apps to get their problems solved or some needs fulfilled.

While this pushed many businesses to build an app for promoting their brand further and reach out to more markets, now the influence of AI will help them respond to the pressing needs of customers in a more personalised way.

Apps made with the notion of AI can deliver them functions like speech recognition, predictive analysis and critical thinking. It will resultantly cause more engagement of customers and enhanced user satisfaction.

App developers all around the world are looking ahead to ways they can captivate AI in apps. However, here are some already prominent tools of AI, famous for taking the performance of apps to the next level.

— **Chatbots**

Chatbots are intriguing AI tools that are reducing the gaps between businesses and their customers.

Most branded services providers or companies are incorporating it in their prevalent apps to revolutionise the way customers interact with them. They no longer have to wait for sales or customer service agents to reply to their queries or issues via email.

Chatbots have then reported to boost up query response, increasing more conversions for the businesses.

— **Image and speech recognition**

AI has even transformed the way people search for information. They are now able to look for anything with images, i.e. QR (Quick Response) codes and also with their voice.

They can get more than just general information with QR code scanning, like products' release date, upcoming service offers, and so forth. In other words, with image and speech recognition features, apps are standardising the search experience in apps, enhancing both user experience and conversions.

— **Voice control**

The digital voice assistants are too result of AI and are helping mobile users to initiate a lot of tasks which they cannot, physically. There are many instances when people are unable to reach for a device, like while driving a car when voice assistants can provide them with accessibility to do specific tasks. They are the most intuitive way for users to interact with apps that cultivates a close connection between them.

— **Face Detection**

Among all the significant AI developments, face detection has been the most rewarding one that recognises a face to give access to users in an app. This feature got more purpose in the security-based apps as verifying the users with their faces will safeguard all confidential data from outside intrusions.

Expert app developers are now hence thinking to bring face detection as a prudent feature for apps that require online payments. The app will allow payments by scanning the user's face but not credit card details, protecting the confidential card information from leakages.

AI is currently becoming the most radical progression in the apps and businesses are increasingly showing interest in its utilisation to make their marketing more customer-centric. While the potential of apps will expand beyond just face recognition and digital assistants, it is worth seeing how they will be amplifying user engagement.

CHAPTER 12: TIPS FOR BLOGGERS TO LEVERAGE DIGITAL MARKETING

Digital Marketing is not a new concept now. Still, a lot of companies and experts lack a real understanding of the subject. There are still many dark areas to explore for many. Every blogger also needs it.

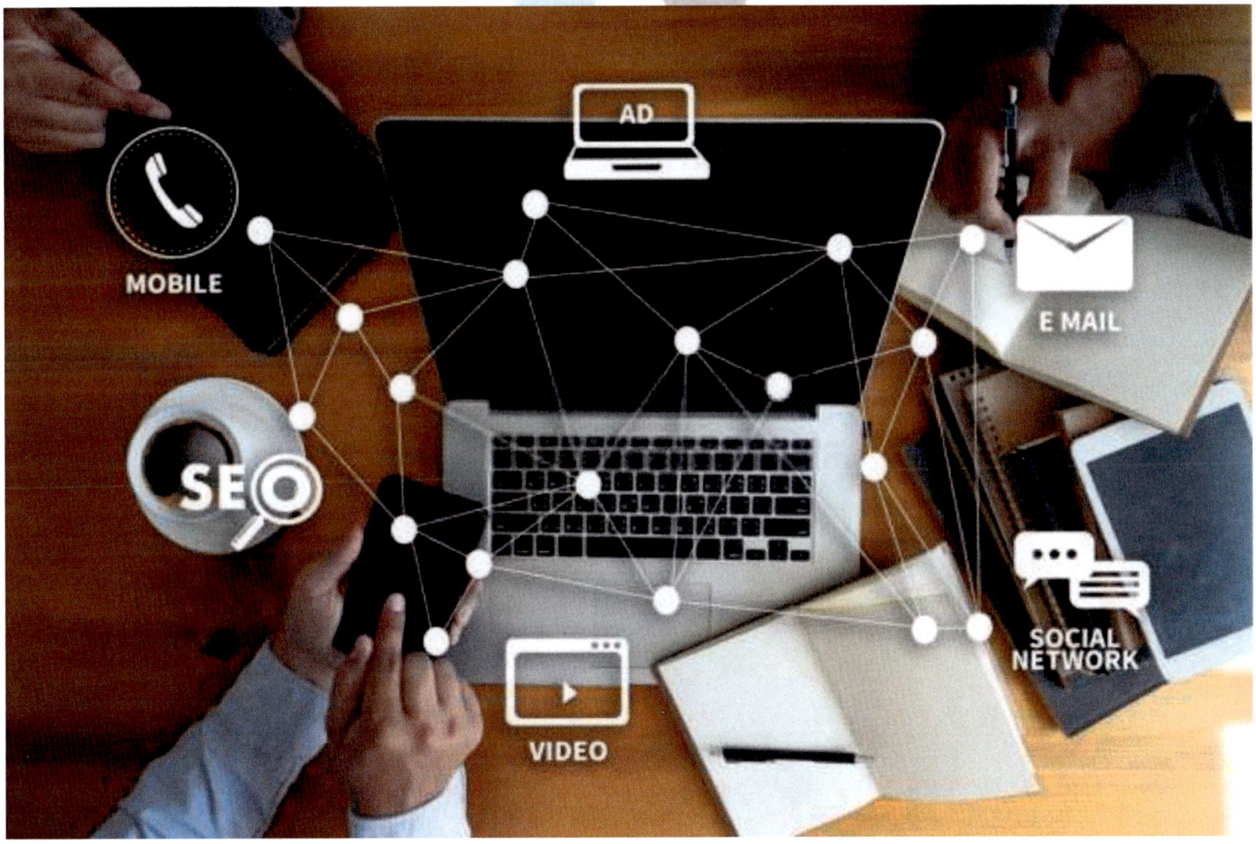

So, here are some tips for bloggers to leverage digital marketing. It is easy if you apply common sense and go for it with a proper strategy. It doesn't require you to pay to somebody else for it. If you acquire some basic understanding, you can do it yourself.

So, let us try to take a deep dive into the subject to understand it better. The Internet has been a revolution in everybody's life. Technology gets a new meaning with it. Similarly, marketing has become more comfortable and faster. Definitely, for businesses and entrepreneurs, it might become essential to hire an agency or an expert.

The reason for that is businesses can't afford to lose their sales because of the lack of their knowledge in the field. That is why they can even think of outsourcing their marketing to an agency. But bloggers can't do that. Contrarily, they also need to market their posts appropriately. So, here are a few tips for bloggers to leverage digital marketing.

1. Manage Your Online Presence

Every blogger needs to know how your readers perceive your blog and posts. If you look at the blogging arena, it is no less than an ocean. Every day new bloggers are born at an exponential rate.

So, imagine why someone would like to spend the time to read your 300/500/700/1500 words post. While your blog is your home ground, but you also need to play on various social media platforms that are not your home ground.

How do you make your presence on various social media platforms? What is the frequency? How do you ensure every new post you write that is worth mentioning through different platforms reaches your followers well in time. Mind it that it is not only your followers that would get to know about your new post. Some people keep a track on new posts based on keywords or hashtags.

If you are a blogger, do go through these tips for bloggers to leverage digital marketing. Understanding your niche is quite essential. For instance, if you review products, do you post reviews on other review sites? Do you visit related forums and participate in topics of your interest? How is your post performing in Google Search? What more can you do to improve its rank?

2. Your Time Is Your Marketing Budget

Now, since you are not spending money on outsourcing an expert, you have to invest something substantial at your end. That is your time. You need to spend the time to research thoroughly and understand well the crux of the matter. Otherwise, the benefit of these tips for bloggers to leverage digital marketing will not be that fruitful. At times, you might feel that you are in a tunnel with no end and light visible. But the situation will not remain the same for long. You will become an expert swimmer only if you practice daily. Merely standing at the pool will not bring that expertise. Similarly, you need to have that urge to dive deeper to draw out more.

3. Your Blog Post Sharing Is As Good As Your Marketing Campaign

When you share your new post on social media platforms, does it fetch some interest? Do you get organic reshares, likes, and comments? If not, there is something wrong with your marketing strategy. Either your post has juicy content, or you have not been able to present it well on social media.

Learn about the concept of relevant hashtags, keywords, and context to attract more people. Use some tools to find out which social media brings more traffic to your blog. What is the reason that another platform is not fetching that much response? Try to post in some engaging manner. It has to be a perfect mix of the right post with the right pitch.

4. Gain Knowledge Of Marketing Trends

It's being covered in the point above.

5. Test Your Posts

Keep an eye on your posts. Some posts will always do better than others. There was something in those that could attract more visitors.

Similarly, if comments are not something happening regularly on your posts, some posts inviting comments means there is a reason behind it. Try to analyse. Spend time on these posts to understand what was better that is lacking in other posts.

6. Make Marketing Your Top Priority

Remember that your blog and posts are yours. If you are not convinced, you will never be able to convince anybody else.

Spend time daily on this exercise. Take these tips for bloggers to leverage digital marketing as starting points. Once you are on the right track, you will find your ways to excel further.

IDEAS TO GIVE A ROBUST DIGITAL BOOST TO YOUR BRAND IMAGE

Every brand wants to stand out. Each ecommerce business expects extraordinary growth and development.

In this scenario of demands and expectations, and with the high competition in the market, it is too challenging for the new businesses to outrival the opponents.

Growing a wildly profitable business is a hard thing to do. It is a game of numbers. You need more new customers, well-retained old consumers, and less cancelled orders.

More leads generation than cancelling sales? You'll grow.

If not, you will go off the track, and the competition will gulp the significant market share in front of you.

At the same time, you cannot employ every new idea to spread and maintain the tone of your brand voice.

It can be challenging to get the public's attention, especially if you are a new brand competing against the well-established large corporations. However, you can scale up your brand image with right business promotion strategies.

— Develop a Consumer-Centric, Strategic Plan

A strategic tech plan is a must-have to capture the pulse of the target audience. It should be tactical, insights-driven, fast, well-connected and adaptable. Fill the gaps in brand image development through following ideas.

— Tap into Audience Emotions

Empathy can do wonders for your brand image development. As humans, people love to relate. So, you need to create an emotional charge and connectivity between your brand and the audience. As you successfully tap into the power of audience emotions, say with the help of storytelling or visual representations, etc., you can drive them to take action and convert into customers.

Stay emotionally connected with your potential consumers. As they empathise with your version of a story, they will be more humanised and persuaded to be part of your business journey. Don't miss out the trend of telling your stories to the audience and asking for their feedback.

Win their trust by asking them to share their accounts with you. Look for the common ground and leverage them with the sense of belonging to you. Eventually, it will strengthen your brand image.

INTEGRATED MARKETING (ORGANIC + PAID)

So, you have a product. Did you show it to the world? Not yet? What are you waiting for? do you want somebody else to accidentally perceive the idea and display before the same target audience as yours. Imagine the loss your business and brand value will face.

It's essential to market your brand, products, and services in front of the right audience without delay to capture their attention with full power. Marketers often talk about different tactics for brand promotion.

Some are free (organic) to low-cost such as social media marketing, and for a few, you need to pay more, e.g., search engine marketing, and PPC ads, etc.

For robust brand awareness, you should go for an integrated marketing plan. It means to publicise your brand message clearly and consistently through social media, paid digital ads and PR. It is the best way to make your brand capture more exposure.

— Offer Free Webinars and Podcasts

Want to get more people to see your brand? Offer them free webinars and podcasts regarding industry trends and how your brand is making a difference. For this, you need to learn about customer behaviour. Develop the audience personas and predict what interests them the most.

As you understand the audience personas and their preferences, you can quickly create webinars and podcasts to capture their attention. It will also help you with search engine marketing processes because of the rising trend of voice searches. People feel more comfortable with listening and watching things of their interests instead of reading a pages-long text.

— Personalised Business Solutions

Now, if you are running a B2B business, then opt for custom solutions both for your employees and clients. For example, you have more than one team in the organisation, and you want them all to work in collaboration than custom software such as time management, workload management or project management, etc., will speed up the working process. Secure communication is another plus.

Personalised business solutions will give your company a crucial edge in the competition.

— **Custom mobile apps development**

Fuel your brand image worth with customised applications. You can bring organic traffic to your business site, and if you offer the consumers custom services, they will come back again.

For example, if you are a restaurant owner them, online ordering app will help you build your brand in a much better way compared to your competitor without any such POS system.

Now, possibilities are high that all your opponents have their mobile apps. It's a downside. But, you can survive like a warrior by differentiating yourself as a distinctive vendor offering the same service but of high-gen calibre.

Learn about the consumers' pain points and offer them a seamless user experience while using your mobile app with integrated features and functions that well-assorted, easy-to-use and different than others.

— **Harness the Power of Video Productions**

Visual content plays an integral role in boosting your brand worth. Quality video productions help to maintain the brand's consistency. The majority of people tend to watch short videos rather than reading the same message in digital ads.

Brands with humorous touch can make the best out of their video content. Experiment freely in this regard. People remember creative motion content.

Several brands across different industries considerably realise the power of storytelling through videos and the opportunities it provides to reinforce brand image. It helps to engage new consumers and win back the churned customers to increase revenues.

CHAPTER 13: SEO FACTS THAT ALL DIGITAL MARKETERS SHOULD KNOW

Search Engine Optimization is a very crucial part of digital marketing. Here are some Search Engine Facts which a digital marketer must know. These SEO Facts 2019 can help them to plan for different marketing strategy.

1. Most of the users click on top 5 search results: According to the latest researches, 75% of the users click on the first 5 search results shown by the search engine. To be more precise, 32% of users click on the first result compared to 18% of users going for the second result. This stat very clearly shows that the higher your website will rank the more visits it will get.

2. Users don't usually scroll past page 1: Only a mere 20% of the users are persistent enough to navigate to page 2 of search results. So if your website is on page 2, then you must work on your digital marketing and SEO strategies.

3. Mobile Friendly Keywords are the need of the hour: Around 50% of users start their searches on a mobile device. When people use their phone for a search, they tend to use different keywords. Also, when it comes to looking for local business, 88%of the searches are initiated on a mobile device.

4. Mobile SEO and Local Business: As mentioned before, users tend to search for a local business on their smartphones. The number of smartphone users is increasing year after year; hence, it is essential to plan your keywords according to the rise in mobile searches.

5. Websites with more pages are likely to attract more traffic: The number of pages on a website plays a direct role in determining the amounts of traffic it generates. It merely reflects the importance of relevant keywords.

6. Around half of the search queries are 4 words or longer: It is a clear fact that short keywords will help you to show up higher in the search results. But at the same time, it is tough to ranks those keywords as short keywords are very competitive. So, instead of going for short competitive keywords, you should use longer ones effectively.

7. Organic Search still trumps over Social Media Traffic: Although social media traffic is increasing day by day, organic searches are always the way to go. Organic searches account for 41% of the total search which is 3 times the social media traffic. Hence, moving ultimately to social media platforms to generate traffic is not wise.

8. Quality Content: Google adores fatty and definite substance which gives per users esteem and answers questions. Whenever you're attempting to get a site on the first page of Google, ensure you incorporate a lot of substance.

VIDEO TRENDS IN 2019

As marketers find more innovative ways to attract audiences, video continues to be an essential part of the strategic conversation. Building a relationship with your customers and stakeholders, narrating your brand story or highlighting your USP in a crowded market place - videos can do wonders for your enterprise!

Did you know over 50% of marketing professionals worldwide name video as the type of content with the best ROI? And this number is increasing thanks to the effectiveness of videos and its ability to grab eyeballs. With increasing internet bandwidths, affordable video technologies at hand and secure distribution platforms, 2019 promise to be a fun-filled year for videos!

Let's look at some Video Trends that are sure to catch up in the coming months:

— **The age of Live Videos**

Live videos are here to stay thanks to better internet connectivity, increased mobile phone penetration and easy to use tools and apps. Live videos can help enterprises reach up to close and personal with their target audience. Live videos can make an event genuinely global without additional distribution costs. Live videos can also help you monetise. Statistics show that about 45% of live video audiences are ready to pay for live, exclusive, on-demand videos if it suitably interests them.

— **Stream, Host, Analyse and Stream more**

It's not so much about picking the cheapest or the most popular live video streaming platform, but the one that possesses the most attributes that will benefit your business.

The most effective and convenient platforms will be all-inclusive, allowing you to broadcast, host, embed, monetise, search and analyse video content, while granting you total control over your content. With video streaming apps and online platforms competing to grab your attention - you are in for an exciting time ahead!

— **Virtual reality may soon become the reality**

Virtual Reality is still an unexplored territory. It's more fun than business! With an affordable headset that provides you 360-degree access into a virtual 3d world - the year ahead promises to be exciting for marketers brave enough to use these technologies to build immersive and interactive customer interfaces. We pin our hope on great marketing strategies in 2019 designed around VR.

— **Holograms for Marketing? Yes, it's happening**

We were fascinated by holograms when the technology came into usage. Artists readily picked it up as an alternative medium to the canvas. But it's yet to be fully utilised as an effective communication medium mainly due to the daunting technology at play here.

Holographic videos, however, provide immense scope for multi-location telepresence through realistic 3D images of speakers and products. Will 2019 provide us with communication strategies woven around holographic images and videos? Let's keep our fingers crossed!

— **Video mapping is changing the customer experience**

An excellent tool for experiential marketing - the craze for video mapping promises an upward trend in the coming years. The technology is affordable and provides scope for enterprises to reach a broader target audience quite inexpensively. Using available flat surfaces like buildings or monuments, 3D projections can get the right message across quite impressively. It's larger than life projections make sure people don't miss out on your messaging.

— **Next level of personalisation with videos**

A great way to break open the inboxes and make a real impact is to customise videos for your target audience. With Facebook leading the way, personalised videos are something your audience might expect you to deliver as well. From recorded messages for your customers to explainer videos with specific services and even simpler 'birthday wishes' - make sure your communication strategies are not aimed at a faceless crowd! Thanks to machine learning, personalisation and embedded searching are quite stapled for your videos now.

— **Users/customer are becoming content publishers**

The onus of creating videos is quickly shifting from producers to users. Videos are more comfortable than ever to develop thanks to rapidly progressing mobile technologies. Hence brands are turning to their audiences to share their products and services instead of crafting their communication.

With attention-spans dropping drastically user-generated content is a great way to keep audiences involved in marketing campaigns. The focus is on building experiences and connections. From passive receiver of your messages, make your audience the active creators of value for your brand.

— Video is on its way to ruling digital marketing

More consumers and clients are interacting with videos today than ever before. Video marketing is a powerful strategy to promote, brand and grow your business online.

Videos help build engagement, impact results like click-through, shares, lead generation, and sales. 55% of online traffic watches videos every day.

CHAPTER 14: DIGITAL MARKETING B2B

How you allocate your time as a salesperson is critical. In particular, maintaining a healthy pipeline requires that you balance your efforts between:

— Focusing on closing the possible deals for this quarter.

— Nurturing those prospects with potential for next quarter.

— Generating fresh leads to go in at the top of the sales funnel.

To get the balance right can be a challenge. Key to the efficient use of your time is a system for prequalifying prospects and opportunities on which you are going to focus. But, too often, pre-qualification is applied bluntly.

Applying the popular BANT (budget, authority, timing and need) criteria too rigorously to an inbound enquiry or cold-call could exclude the bulk of the marketplace, including many companies that do not have a budget for your solution now, but still, represent potential customers.

As well as selling to those who are already actively searching for a solution in the marketplace, every sale organisation must generate, and foster and nurture, demand for its solutions.

That means sales and marketing must work together, with marketing substituting for pre-qualification at the lead generation stage. While some leads are classified as sales or sales meeting-ready, others not ready for the next step are not left to waste but are nurtured.

Later in the sales cycle, pre-qualification becomes more critical, as the time and resources you must commit to an opportunity increases. Progressive pre-qualification that is, asking the right questions - ensures that you can adapt your sales approach continually (if you are talking to the wrong people, or addressing the wrong requirements) to ensure you have the maximum chances of success.

Pre-qualification, like all aspects of selling, is not something that is done to, but rather is done with, a prospect. It must be a two-way process - that means asking the customer what stage he/she is at and what they want to do next if anything. It is important to remember that you have to earn the right to ask progressively more direct and searching questions.

Your approach should reflect the stage of the buying cycle (if, indeed, there is one) that you are both at, as shown in the table below, ideally incorporating as many buyer-focused questions as possible.

The decision to engage in the buying process, in itself, is a significant commitment of resources by the buyer. For this reason, it is generally made in stages, with the sponsor in the buying organisation first being required to present a justification for a buying decision and a business case being prepared.

- Only a limited number of projects can be evaluated at any one time. It means that, although a project is of interest, the timing may not be right. As a vendor, you must show buyers how your project can impact on their immediate business priorities.

- Given the cost and time required, organisations will want to 'kill off' poor projects as early as possible. You may have to do most (or all) of the initial running for a project to gain traction.

- Organisations are standardising their approach to buying decisions, including steps to be followed, templates for documents, etc. It makes the process more repeatable and consistent, thereby saving time for them. You need to know and support the approach required.

- Involving another supplier in operation costs time and money, so don't expect to be able to squeeze in late when you hear that a project is under consideration, even if your solution is ideal.

- Buyers want to limit the time/cost of the buying process, which means being informed about time spent with sellers. When you want access to all the stakeholders, you need to be conscious of the fact that this represents an additional draw on their time and adds to the cost of the decision.

- Buyers want to get something back for the time spent with vendors. They may need to meet with three vendors because their internal process requires three vendor quotes but, if each vendor requires 20 to 40 hours (including briefings, presentations, proposals, ongoing communication, etc.), it's understandable that the buyer wants some immediate payback.

- Once a vendor has been selected, it makes sense for the buyer to want to develop and deepen that relationship, as opposed to going through the entire process again.

When customers defect to another supplier, they face real switching costs related to the process of evaluating, educating and learning to trust another vendor.

DIGITAL MARKETING MISTAKES YOU COMMIT

There is a need to look at the what-should-NOT-be-done side of things as well. It is essential so that you do not fool yourselves into thinking that you are on the right path and keep wasting money without getting an ROI.

When you know that you don't know something, you can find out.

However, when you don't see that you don't know, such a situation is risky. Here, is a list from my side to make you aware of some undetectable errors you might commit in your digital marketing pursuit.

1. Promoting Rather than Problem Solving

Beating your drum is something that doesn't go well with the internet-savvy people looking out for any product/services. They are bombarded with promotional information continuously, and you don't want to do the same thing and get lost in the crowd.

Don't boast about how excellent your product/services are, tell them how it can help solve their problems. They have come to your site or your ad, looking out for a solution, provides them with that, and you will hit the bulls-eye.

While it is okay to display your achievements, stage even that to appear more for 'you-the-customer' rather than the 'I-me-myself' attitude. How? Show client testimonials! And let your audience think if you can solve the problem for your existing clients, then you can search for them as well. Be customer-centric, portray your product/services as solutions and see the magic.

2. Relying Heavily on anyone Marketing Channel

Making this mistake would not only throw your digital marketing budget out of balance but can reverse slingshot your revenue. You may have implemented many strategies throughout your experience, out of which say one or two may have worked the best.

And it's the digital marketing mantra that one should maximise efforts on what works best; relying too much on this mantra could be dangerous. What if this channel suddenly becomes ineffective? What if the organic traffic that you were so proud of drops overnight thanks to the unannounced updates search engines come up with.

Such a repercussion would cause severe damage to your bottom line revenue. Therefore, resist the temptation to pour all the efforts into one channel and create a robust, well-rounded multi-channel based marketing strategy.

3. Ignoring some Marketing Channels

This point is similar to the point above, yet different in the way that it proposes using every channel whenever the time is right for your business. It is understandable that a few channels like pay-per-click might instantly thrust you into the limelight, but you should not ignore the other seemingly slower channels.

While it is essential to leverage the high-ROI-producing channels at the beginning, at a later stage venturing out into the others should be the aim of your marketing strategy. Invest your outstanding efforts in SEO, no matter how time-consuming. 6 months down the line, when the search engines would start paying you back with relevant traffic, you will thank yourself you did it.

Go social; get your name out there. But, select the social channels carefully. LinkedIn and Twitter work best for B2Bs and the famed Facebook is the go-to channel for B2Cs. As you progress, throw in email marketing into the marketing mix, you will be surprised with its potential.

4. Not Assigning Numbers to Campaign Goals

"Isn't this basic", you may think! Well... we usually deep-dive into the advanced stuff and forget the basics most of the times. So, set measurable goals for your campaigns! Say, you want to increase the number of leads generated for a B2B company, set a goal of +20% in a given month, then work towards it.

Don't just say, and I want to increase the leads - that's just wishful thinking! If you define your goals in terms of numbers is when you'll be able to scale your efforts.

Otherwise, you'll keep stepping in all directions without moving an inch ahead. Also, remember, you are investing money in your efforts; the person who is carrying out the campaigns doesn't come free. Moreover, if you are investing money in paid marketing, not setting measurable goals is a sure-shot recipe for disaster.

5. Poor Data Interpretation

If you have ever seen the analytics dashboard, you'll see how it shows different traffic channels like organic, direct, paid, referral etc. Now, direct traffic interprets into people manually typing in your website's URL and coming in.

However, you need to make sure that the direct traffic numbers don't consist of your internal employees. Ignoring this would result in data dilution and wrong interpretation of data.

Besides, choosing the wrong metric to define your data could be disastrous. For example, if you have a high 'pages per visit' or 'average visit duration', you may feel that your customer is spending more time on the site, whereas the reality would be your visitors are not finding what they are looking out for.

CHAPTER 15: CHOOSING THE RIGHT METRICS

Measuring your results can genuinely bridge the gap between struggling and making returns on your investment. There are numerous ways to gain insights into your digital marketing efforts, but it's essential to choose only those relevant to your overall strategy.

Let's discuss the essential metrics and how they can help you succeed. There are three categories, Traffic, Conversion and Revenue.

TRAFFIC

1) Site Traffic - This metric will provide insight as to whether your digital marketing techniques are valid or not. Remember to focus on unique visitors your site receives rather than website hits and page views.

2) Source of Traffic - How did your visitors land on your site? Maybe the keywords you used brought them there, and maybe it was a search query or even referrals. This metric will let you know what channels you should be focusing on.

3) Click Through Rate-The CTR of any digital marketing plan is the number of viewers who clicked on the ad/offer. A great way to increase CTR is to combine it with compelling content and an active Call to Action.

4) Mobile Traffic - This needed to be on the list considering the growing mobile internet traffic in the digital marketing playing field. As more and more people gain access to the internet via their smartphones, new opportunities arise for bigger and better revenue sources.

This metric provides insight on how to structure and plan your marketing strategy and achieve beneficial engagement with viewers.

CONVERSION

1) Conversion Rate - Conversion is the primary goal of your strategy. You need to convert traffic into sales/leads. Monitoring your conversion rate can help steer your plan in the right direction.

2) Bounce Rate - If your site is irrelevant to the viewer, they will skip or 'bounce' off the page. Some insight into this will help you approach the right target audience/ potential leads.

3) Rate of Return - Your site's popularity is not only defined by your traffic but also the rate of return by viewers. Knowing your rate of return can help improve your site to convert traffic into leads and to solidify the engagement.

Cost Per Conversion - Also known as cost per lead or cost per referral. This metric determines your overall profit margins.

A higher CPC may turn negative if the costs are so high that they reduce your net income. There are even digital marketing training programs that include this as a course, thus making it art that needs to be paid attention to.

REVENUE

1) Return on Investment - Insights on your ROI will determine which parts of your site are truly driving sales and bringing in revenue, and which parts require more effort on improvement. Your ROI is the ultimate measure of your success as it proves your marketing campaign to be either profitable or not.

2) Cost Per Acquisition -CPA is all about revenue and is accounted for only once a visitor becomes a paying customer. This metric will determine how much you spend, to get a customer to spend on you. Tracking your CPA will decide whether the strategies you've employed to gain leads is working or not.

Effectively spending your digital marketing funds and measuring metrics will ensure that you are doing the best for your company in this spectrum. The parameters will provide a pretty accurate picture of how you are doing and where you need to place more efforts, thus enabling you to adjust to the rhythm and convert traffic into leads.

GOOGLE TOOLS FOR ENHANCING DIGITAL MARKETING

Pretty much all the major businesses, regardless of industry or status, use Google to fulfil some requirement.

Be it Google Drive, Google Docs or ever familiar Gmail, and it seems as if everyone depends on at least one of Google's Services to support their daily life work routine. That being said, there are a few hidden gems in Google's Toolbox which at times do not get exposure and consequently remain underutilised.

Although it is true that Google has many apps, however, there are some which can have a severe positive impact on digital marketing initiatives for businesses and those seem to be on the low a bit.

Moreover, Google's products generally have "freemium" models, which offer an invaluable opportunity to improvise with a variety of unique techniques and dive in on what suits the niche brand most.

Everyone is testing out the latest and most effective tools from the world's most gigantic Internet powerhouse. So it is advised to give a few of these seemingly under-recognised tools or products a try for better results.

GOOGLE TRENDS

If you are looking to boost up your SEO strategy, Google Trends is a tool that should not be neglected. It allows you to see how frequently a Keyword is searched so you can get a measure of its popularity. Google Trends instantly creates a graph of the search volume categorised by language, country, region etc. revealing how the key phrase has evolved over a specific period. It also predicts how these phrases will trend shortly, thus helping you in making more precise and prepared decisions.

Most importantly, Google Trends makes it relatively very easy to stay up-to-date with a particular product's or service's marketing language so that one can jump into interactive conversations about topics which are relevant to his/her niche.

THINK WITH GOOGLE

Think With Google is more like a creative brain-faith we can depend on when searching for inspiration and improvisations for our digital marketing strategies. The resource contains valuable insights on industry trends, analytical research and statistics, tips on marketing techniques and different outlets to give us new ways to venture for further success.

When devising your online SEO marketing strategy, especially if you have an Ecommerce Website and you are investing on a quarterly and yearly plan basis, do not skip out Think With Google. This tool also helps when a marketer is suffering from a writer's block too.

GO-MO

According to experts' reports, almost 66 percent of people say that a mobile-responsive website makes them more likely to buy a product, use a service or engage in reading in the case of blogs.

So it is essential to tap into the mobile revolution, or one's business may soon be left behind due to lack of innovation.

Go-Mo uses Artificial Intelligence and helps in making this transition to the digital world, a very comfortable experience. It is free for the first year.

It instantly generates a mobile friendly version of one's website. So you are no longer restricting you are targeted on the go customers with a website that is almost impossible to navigate through.

GOOGLE ANALYTICS

Studies show that Google Analytics is an overlooked tool among small and medium scale business enterprises. Without Google Analytics, executing website marketing strategies is like walking blindly in the dark.

Website analytics reveal critical data and results on how existing and potential customers interact with marketers online. When evaluated efficiently, the analytics insights offer plenty of opportunities for customer engagement enhancement and higher conversions as well.

So it is a must use tool for digital marketers who want to evolve and succeed gradually.

Lastly, as the horizons of technological advancements are widening day-by-day, one can expect a tech giant like Google to introduce more such practical and helpful tools for improving the digital marketing platform. However, it is not only the responsibility of technology leaders but of users too to take the platform to a more evolved, matured and practical level.

CHAPTER 16: ESTABLISHING YOUR DIGITAL IDENTITY

Nearly half the world has internet access, which provides a gateway for small businesses to now enter a global market. It is more important than ever before that businesses not only have a digital identity, but one that is present and relevant. In many cases, digital identity will impact the success and longevity of a business.

Here are five tips to consider when establishing your digital identity or enhancing your presence via social media platforms.

1. Research Platforms

Research the platform(s) you are considering, and the primary audience engaged with the platform. User demographics can be easily found for notable platforms. Due diligence in understanding the nuances of each platform is integral to your success.

Do not merely learn about the demographics, and you should also learn about the prevailing trends and behaviours of the users. How often do users log in daily versus monthly or weekly?

How long does the average user stay logged in during a single sign in? When using the platform, what features of the platform are used most? Are users more drawn to posts, updates, videos, or graphics? The answers to those questions and others will assist in determining when a platform is appropriate for your business or personal brand, as well as how you can use the platform to its full potential.

Once a platform is chosen, exploring analytics options to track who and how people are engaging with you or your business is highly recommended. Many platforms will provide a range of analytics for free to all users, and have options to enhance the type and amount of information tracked. Free analytics, provided by the platform is robust in the information submitted to users.

2. Know Your Purpose

While the platform may be a current trendy option, that cannot be the sole purpose for a business to utilise the application. Some businesses will use specific platforms to be strictly informational and serve as one-way communication to their consumers, like utility companies.

In most scenarios, it is in the best interest not to, but some businesses may choose to link their social media accounts so that the same post will appear on multiple platforms.

It sounds good in theory, but as you learned in step one, different platforms have varying demographics and behaviours. The deliverable needs to be presented in a way that resonates with users and aligns with the trends or ethics of the platform in use. The appearance of being present and at the moment is integral to the establishment of your digital identity. Often, viewers can see if a post was made from another platform and will choose to disengage with the content presented.

Expansion of the consumer base is another common purpose for establishing a digital identity. The demographics of a specific platform are typically easily accessible and can be used to target a new consumer audience.

Businesses will also consider ways to enhance public relations through their digital identity. Professional sports teams and organisations may select to highlight their engagement with community and fans domestically and globally.

3. Voice and Content

Once you have chosen the platform(s) of choice, consider your content and voice. The beauty of social media is that it allows people to be tangible and engage with others.

Consider how you want to interact with your viewers and potential consumers. What type of content should you share and how often? Social media generally is most effective as moments are happening or shortly after. Limited posts or interaction with others usually will lead to a downtrend in followers and engagement.

Social media marketing campaigns and hashtags serve a dual purpose. Both are great ways to drive content that can be shared, and attract new users to your digital presence. The other way it should be used is to conduct market research within the norms or social activity of the platform.

Voice is critical because it represents your digital personality. Explore your timeline or news feed to explore users that have a pleasant voice. Consider being informative, diverse in content, and providing a selective amount of individuality. Voice and content should give the illusion that user interaction is with a person instead of an office or corporation.

4. Brand Alignment

Purpose, voice, content, and platform(s) of choice should align with your overall brand. Your brand is a holistic development strategy for the success of your business over an extended period.

Digital identity is just one of the many components that comprise a brand. Colours, content, voice, shapes, sounds, logos, typography, and a host of other elements are all things that should be considered when establishing your brand and digital identity. Brand recognition is key! Think about significant brands or fast food companies. Regardless of how and where their content is delivered, the viewer or user at some point recognises the brand, whether it be by sounds, logos, colours, or other features.

5. Be Creative

Innovation is almost a necessity for the success of your business and its relevance. As technology continues to advance, so will your business' digital presence. Be mindful of the integral components, mentioned in steps one through four, which comprise your digital framework: platform(s), purpose, voice, content, and overall brand.

Be open and willing to explore new platforms, and options within them, for the betterment of your business. Regular evaluation of your digital identity is essential to ensure that it is consistent and relevant to current standards. Explore practical ways to engage with your viewers and consumers that your competitors have not. Being an entrepreneur requires taking a certain amount of risk, and so will establishing a robust digital identity.

CREATIVE TIPS FOR CLICKABLE VIDEO ADS

Video advertising is one of the most effective ways to reach and engage your target audience.

— Video Production For Mobile

As predicted by digital marketing experts, mobile usage surpassed desktop usage to access the internet in 2018 and businesses are taking notice. The shift indicates that more consumers are using their mobile devices to do their research about products and services. Therefore, it makes sense for businesses to want to engage their customers on mobile devices and a powerful way to do this is with engaging and effective video content.

The shift to mobile has come with a shift to video content. Mobile users have been shown to prefer digital video over all other types of content. Thus, it's reasonable to invest in video ads for increased engagement with your customers.

— Video Production Tips For Clickable Ads

Many businesses that attempt to produce their video ads before approaching a professional corporate video production company find out the hard way that there is more to video marketing than meets the eye. They find that they are not getting the return on their investment as expected. Many end up making losses because their videos lack strategy, clear messaging and excellent production quality. The following are some video production tips for effective video marketing for mobile:

1. Ensure your logos are large and clear

Everything designed to be viewed on mobile should be large and bright. It is because mobile devices have smaller screens than desktops and laptops. Large and bright logos will increase viewer familiarity with your brand and improve the chances of people recommending your brand to their networks. Small logos are likely to be lost on smaller screens. Packaging and branding your videos is vital.

2. A Call to Action is a must

A call to action (CTA) gives the viewer a clear path to take if they buy your sales pitch. It can be a simple statement, such as 'click now to buy your goods' or "for more information - website address". Not including a call to action is likely to result in dead-end users who don't take any action even if they are interested.

3. Mention the brand

It's important to mention the brand in the ad to build brand familiarity. This mention may be verbal or visual. It also doesn't matter when in the ad you specify the brand.

4. Use different ad tones

There are different tones you can use in video marketing. These include rich, dramatic and informational tones. These can be adjusted and interchanged to suit the situation and the audience. It is essential to be aware of your customers' expectations and preferences to use the most appropriate tone.

5. Align your ads for different screen sizes

Ads will not appear the same on different screen sizes. It is therefore essential to align the ads to suit the screen size. Test the ads on different screen sizes to align for the most excellent efficiency.

6. Don't make a long video

The traditional length for an ad is 15 to 30 seconds. It is the ideal length to pass information to your audience. Your audience is likely to lose concentration with a video that is too long.

7. Limit your ads to 15 seconds

15 seconds appears to be the optimal length for video ads. It is adequate for passing information. Ensure your ads are engaging, exciting and concise. A 15-second ad can lead to a more extended version when using social media platforms like Facebook and Instagram.

8. Use auto-start

Not everyone likes ads that auto play. However, they are an effective way of getting through to your target audience. You are likely to get through to your audience with a relevant interactive and visual ad if you make it engaging and concise.

CHAPTER 17: NETWORKING IN A DIGITAL WORLD

A dedicated support system is crucial for personal and professional success. Networking has and will play a vital part in your business. Face-to-face networking and handshaking is still a fantastic way to do business, but with the Internet at our fingertips and available everywhere, there's a new way to connect and communicate with people.

Networking is the process of searching for contacts. Not just to be a collector of people, but to get involved, get connected and to help build each other up. It may still be about handshaking, passing out business cards, giving your elevator speech, and wearing name tags, but we should view networking as establishing and maintaining authentic relationships.

So, why do we network?

- — Engage with people who will have a positive impact on us and our business.
- — Swap ideas and stories with others.
- — Find clients and partners.
- — Find a job or recruit potential employees.
- — Gain feedback and insights.
- — Get inspired!
- — Present yourself as an SME (Subject Matter Expert)
- — Generate and build leads.
- — Establish meaningful relationships, personally and professionally.

LinkedIn is a global social networking site for people in professional occupations. In a sense, it is a bit like Facebook you create your profile for others to see, but it is used for professional purposes. Members build a profile of their job history, interests and experience an online Resume if you will and 'connect' with former colleagues and people in their line of work.

Like most social media websites, your journey on LinkedIn begins with creating a personal profile. Many LinkedIn profiles are abbreviated resumes due to LinkedIn's professional tone, but with the new concept of Social Selling, we need to think of your profile as a brand. Employers look for inside information on candidates such as professional interests.

10 ways to build you and your brand on LinkedIn:

1. Update your profile is the first step in marketing you and your business.

a. From the top toolbar, click Me.

b. Click View Profile.

c. From here, you can take the time to edit your profile by adding education, experience, volunteer experience, and so much more. Click the pencil next to a section to edit, or click the more button (three dots) to access more features.

d. Make sure to save all changes.

2. Upload a Professional Photo. Make the first impression count, in about 6 seconds someone has crafted opinion of you through your photo and your profile. You want your potential customers/connections to answer the following questions about you.

a. Are you trustworthy?

b. Are you someone I want to do business with?

c. Can I recommend you to my friends and clients/customers?

3. Create a standout Headline. Your headline is the valuable real estate that appears next to your name in search results. The wording of a headline may determine whether a new potential client is searching through LinkedIn contacts

you. Done well, your LinkedIn headline can be used to promote your brand statement, marketing message, most enticing expertise, and more.

a. It should not be your job title/description.

b. Why should people stop and take a closer look at you?

c. What impressions are you leaving behind?

d. What do you do?

e. Use keywords or core words. Make your headline fit with SEO, Search Engine Optimization.

f. Demonstrate real value to your potential clients, customers, etc.

4. Claim your LinkedIn Username: Personalize your LinkedIn URL, own your brand. You are the brand we are talking about, claim your URL, so that when someone searches for your name, they will find your public LinkedIn page/profile. Visit your profile and select the edit public profile URL option.

5. Add Skills: When updating your skills section, make sure you use relevant, updated keywords. For example, potential buyers/customers probably won't be searching for "cold calling", try to mirror your buyer's skills/needs.

a. Use SEO keywords.

b. Add up to 50 skills to your profile.

c. The skills with the most endorsements from your connections will be listed first.

6. Endorsements: Skill endorsements are an excellent way to recognise your 1st-degree connections' skills and expertise with one click. They also let your relationships validate the strengths found on your profile. Skill endorsements are a simple and effective way of building your professional brand and engaging your network.

7. Write a summary: Why should you fill it in? For starters, it gives the reader a quick overview of who you are, what you do, what you are looking for and most importantly, what you can do for them. Think like your buyer, what's in it for me?

a. Demonstrate your expertise; make sure you include keywords.

b. Show them that you are a valuable resource.

c. Add a video; a minute video equals 1,000 words!

d. Include Call to Action Statements; this could consist of companies/clients you've helped, include your signature with contact information, keywords that are important to buyers.

e. Demonstrate the value you offer, be their solution.

8. Experience: This is the time you can treat LinkedIn as your resume. Add your previous and current jobs, making sure to include key industry words so that you will be found in searches. When you add who you worked for and you find their name in the drop-down list, your experience will then have their logo beside your name because they created a company business page.

9. Add Connections: On LinkedIn, the people who are part of your network are called your "connections". Connect with people with whom you have worked or done business with, or people with similar interests or work in your industry.

You can ask someone to join your professional network by sending them an invitation to connect. LinkedIn encourages networking by showing you exactly how your connections are related.

10. Engage with your links: Status updates are short messages that are typical of many social networking platforms. While posting updates on LinkedIn is like Facebook and Twitter, it's also different. From your LinkedIn home page or your Edit My Profile page, you can change your status update as frequently as you like.

Note: There will be more on LinkedIn later in this guide.

STAY AHEAD IN DIGITAL MARKETING

Digital marketing is in various forms, and you can keep learning about networking and its apps continuously.

The marketing is all about sites and apps. The digitised traditional media versions allow you to stay ahead in the business, but for that, you have to get going with new inventions online and stay updated.

If you ever wish to find a suitable job making a career in digital marketing, you need to have a lot of connections, an entire slate of skills and plenty of exciting ideas to offer that will appeal your future employer.

— Join a LinkedIn Group

LinkedIn is the best place for any aspiring candidate to make connections. Here you get to know the real stuff required for a position. Here you can find the profiles of more than a quarter of fortune seekers and accomplishers that you joining this group in LinkedIn is sure to offer a quick pick and you can also follow the role models and virtual mentors of this industry.

— Attend Marketing Conference

A digital conference is available to meet every skill and forte, so pick that meets your goals and creativity. Check out and acquire more exposure to cutting-edge technology, social media marketing, new internet marketing strategies and more. On attending the digital conference, you will find online marketing experts in many numbers, and you can talk to them and learn who covers topics such as traffic, design and conversion. Getting to know about marketing gurus helps a lot as you get to make connections, stay linked and to share ideas.

— Track Successes

Being something is important, but that should be apparent. For instance, you may be a pioneer digital marketer, but if you fail to prove anything, you will be no different from any of your enthusiast co-workers.

Whether you are handling an exceptional job as a challenging task or you are trying to sell your product, it is important you save the feedback, stats, other documentation and email correspondence.

It will bring a difference one beautiful day when you get an opportunity to show. You can also show this in a job interview and increase your leverage, proving you know what it means to stay connected with audiences and growing a brand to success using digital marketing strategies.

Thus, tracking successes is essential so that you know and prove you are ahead of others.

— **Brush Your Skills**

Everyone at some point or the other lags behind. Identify the skills you need to work and whet them. Digital marketing is the need of the hour to do any business or even to get hired.

Learning to integrate marketing helps develop a strategy and improve the brand's strategy overall. Embrace the business strategies that are data-driven as it is an evolutionary step in businesses.

Only with a proper understanding of the data you acquire or get that you desire helps in organising business objectives, and it revolutionises marketing. Thus, staying ahead in digital marketing demands you to work on data-driven strategy.

CHAPTER 18: DIGITAL AND CONVENTIONAL PRESENTATION OF CONTENT

Displaying content is extremely important for any marketing agency. Ultrathin tubes have long replaced the old and expensive Cathode-ray tubes. Internet connectivity, live TV streaming, videos, and images are the future of signage and modern marketing. Shopping malls, shops, and all other businesses prefer electronic display over wallpapers.

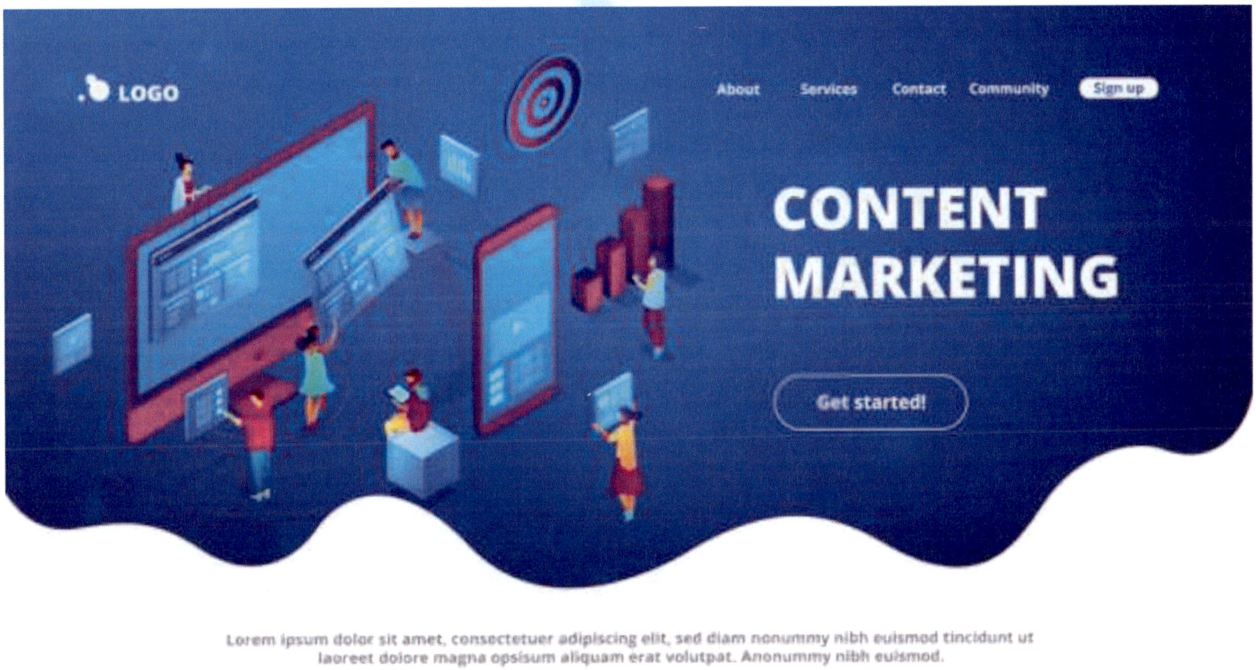

Digital signage applications include high-resolution display devices that are easy to use anywhere, indoor or outdoor. The modern way of displaying content adds versatility and innovation. For example, an electronic display can run a combination of media, including videos, images, and text that altogether deliver a specific message.

With time, the global advertising industry is growing bigger and bigger. The electronic display has become the need of every modern business. Some of the purposes digital signage serve are:

— Informational

— Commercial

— Experiential

— Behavioural

It is rightly said that there is no success without the content. Electronic signage is considered to be a new way of displaying content to an audience. It offers variety and several exciting features that allow users to be creative in content management. We often see digital signs at public places and retail stores. Therefore, it has a cultural impact on customers and viewers.

A question arises whether or not signage has emerged as a new and useful advertising source. The answer is a big yes as digital signage is gradually taking over the conventional and outdated advertising solutions. However, the significance of traditional display cannot be undermined as they are cost-effective.

Commercial places should be well equipped with information that might help customers make a purchase decision.

The internet is used widely across the globe. And the information provided on a computer allows us to check back and reach the content easily. It is easy to change and manage content on digital devices. Your success depends highly on how you are advertising your business.

Therefore, use digital signs to promote and advertise your business or cause. Digital signage is expensive as compared to those static and straightforward display means. However, the digital display has become mandatory for rapidly growing businesses.

The display industry cannot keep itself apart from technological advancements. However, some of the old-fashioned signage is still being used by many businesses in developed and developing countries.

For instance, a banner or a decal is a straightforward type of signage. The presence of highly advanced electronics signs could not outsmart traditional sign systems. However, it is recommended to use the digital and interactive form of symbols which can captivate the attention of customers.

THE NECESSITY FOR ALL INDIVIDUALS AND BUSINESSES

The world is transforming at an exponentially. To survive, individuals and businesses will have to keep up with the changing trends. Even a few years back, digital marketing was seen as an oddity. However, not anymore!

Online marketing is no more an oddity, but it has become a necessity. The Internet has assumed an indispensable part of everyday life. It is how businesses function, how humans connect and how the world goes round (quite, literally!).

Well, if you still have not embraced online marketing, here are some reasons that will compel you to. Here we go...

— Digital marketing for individuals

Online marketing is an umbrella term, and there are various tools and processes under it. Social media, in particular, helps politicians, celebrities, dieticians, doctors, dentists, lawyers, CA, youngsters and other individuals to get their message across to the mass. It assists celebrities to connect with their fans while politicians can connect with the youth and their voters to boost their campaign. Similarly, doctors, lawyers and others in professional services offer advertise their services, via social media platforms. Youngsters and the general public are also able to make use of social media sites to grow their network and get work.

In today's world, only the powerful have a voice, and that is the only voice that people listen to or look up to. But, the Internet is such a powerful tool that can help you connect with a global audience and you can make them sit up and listen to you, even if you are not a "powerful" person. Such is the power of digital advertising and marketing!

— Internet marketing for small businesses

For start-ups and small firms, traditional advertising can become very expensive. Small-scale businesses usually function on a tight budget, and therefore, investing in TV commercials, radio or print ads sometimes become a bit difficult. With the advent of the Internet, the advertising and marketing dilemma of small businesses were eliminated. These businesses finally found the solution to their marketing woes. Online marketing allows small business owners to be able to market their products or services and establish brand recognition in the marketplace, via several Internet marketing avenues.

They can reach out to their niche target audience without going overboard with their budget. It is a boon for small businesses looking to expand their operations and become a force to reckon with in their specific industry.

— Online marketing for enterprises

The benefits of digital marketing for global companies are merely endless. Businesses with means will not only be able to take advantage of free Internet resources, but they also will be able to run expensive ads across search engines and social media platforms.

It will help them in strengthening their brand name, connecting with their audience and improving their sales. If they are planning to launch any new product or service, they will be able to conduct an online survey without much hassle. From the pre-production to the completion and launch of their product or service can be done seamlessly and much quickly.

Newspaper ads and other forms of advertising can be easily missed in the crowd, but online ads are usually hard to miss. Plus, businesses staying connected with their consumers will give them an advantage over others. After all, impeccable customer service is what customers generally look for!

— The Myriad Digital Marketing Services Available to You

Thanks to the rapid growth of Internet and online marketing, there are several agencies available who offer affordable and effective digital marketing services. As mentioned earlier in this guide, the services include SEO or search engine optimisation, SMO or social media optimisation, content marketing, website design & development, web & mobile applications, link building, web hosting, paid ads, such as Facebook ad, YouTube ad, Google shopping ad and more. All of these services together are known as Internet marketing.

CHAPTER 19: RESTART YOUR SOCIAL MEDIA PLAN

The Digital era is alive and in the world, small or big enterprises are pushed by this society to be in social media networks to promote their products and generate some good feelings in your clients regarding your branding. ReThink, Remake, and it's not as tricky as a lot of people think, being in trending topics and informed about video marketing and social media. How do you stay profitable when you think to restart your media plan?

No Business is free of going on economic changes, and it is eventually necessary to renew our ideas. Making new ideas and excellent original content is going to attract more clients, they are going to enjoy what you are doing. From big and compelling brands to personal brands, the thought will need to restart. It will affect your enterprise, socially and economically.

A lot of enterprises could see problems if they don't pay attention to what a social media plan can do. Here is advice to make you know how to act in the future.

— Make original and friendly content for your media pages

First, it's good to have: Facebook, LinkedIn, Twitter, YouTube, Instagram, among others. It is good to have at least 4 social media profiles to have a backup in this matter.

After that, you should take into account that constant publishing is the first key. It will keep your clients expecting something from you. It will depend if you will be publishing weekly, daily or monthly, is good to publish at least 3 times a week, but it's better daily.

Your clients will react depending on your content, so use things as:

— Livestreaming

— 360 Videos

— 360 Pics

— HQ pics

— Short and interesting message.

Don't be left behind connecting to the Internet of Things; Video Marketing is the most effective tool in a social media plan. It will help you have formidable content. Also, you can use live streaming video, that will make your profile to be on the first page of home while you are streaming the video.

After you plan on how to publish your content in your social media profiles consistently, you will have the power of making great offers to promote products and services which will help your clients be satisfied. If you are trying to be as complete as possible, try to have a web page about your company.

You can have several social media profiles with some good job on it, but if you have a web page, your clients would be more comfortable, and you can use it to show a massive list of products or services that your company offers.

INTEGRATING TRADITIONAL AND DIGITAL MARKETING

The digital world is full of new ideas and strategies, but the value of the old, traditional marketing can never decrease. It is as vital and compelling as digital marketing. Everything depends on the target audience.

Advertisements in newspapers and magazines have the same effect as advertisements on social media sites. However, your brand and product should determine the medium you are choosing to advertise.

The strategies which are used for marketing are usually an integration of traditional and digital in most cases. Bringing both the marketing forms together creates a larger space for the customers to choose over products and brands, and this also creates a relationship of trust between the brand and the consumer.

It's essential for the brand to take along its loyal customers from the past together with them, and using traditional marketing strategies makes sure that they don't lose any of their old customers behind.

New mechanics are used to attracting more customers, but that doesn't mean that the traditional systems were ineffective. It all boils down to what product needs to be marketed and where?

Even in this digital era, common strategies like personal selling and publicity by the old customers have been successful in holding onto the old customers and bringing in new customers as well.

Advertisements through social media, giving away sample products, surprise giveaways can attract new customers, but combining both the marketing forms together would help to create a more significant customer potential and growth in the brand name and sales of the product. Inbound and outbound marketing revolves around social media marketing.

Inbound is all about attracting customers through SEO and social media marketing, and outbound is reaching the audience through various paid and natural search advertising. The limit to reach people is different for both of them. It is essential to know where to use inbound and outbound marketing.

The conventional way of advertising surely is passive while the web marketing is active and involves the target audience. Some medium work better than the other mediums; so it only makes sense to utilise both the classic and internet marketing techniques and allows the brand message to spread across different mediums.

Interactions and exposure given by the conventional way are much larger than social media marketing. It is essential to take the old and new ideas simultaneously to reach a vast audience and to be in the competition.

CHAPTER 20: DIGITAL ECOMMERCE

WHAT IS DIGITAL ECOMMERCE?

Digital commerce is the buying and selling of goods and services using the Internet, mobile networks and commerce infrastructure.

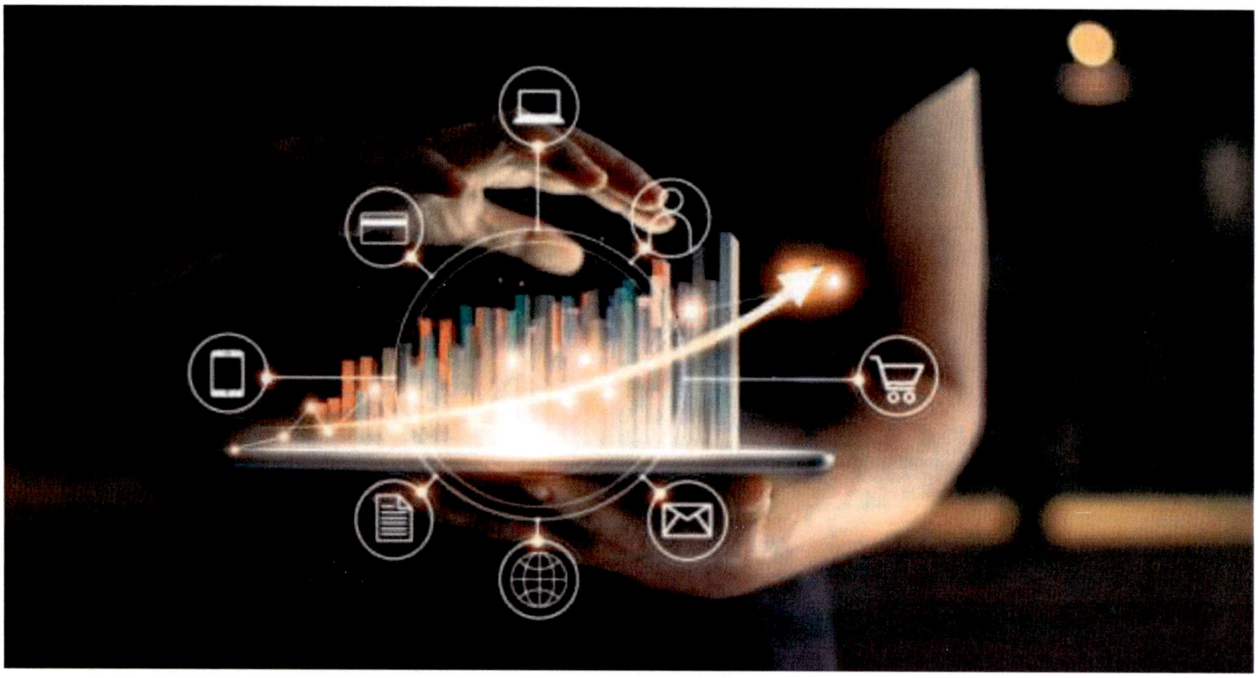

It includes the marketing activities that support these transactions, including people, processes and technologies to execute the offering of development content, analytics, promotion, pricing, customer acquisition and retention, and customer experience at all touchpoints throughout the customer buying journey.

ECOMMERCE SOLUTIONS FOR THE DIGITAL WORLD

The fast pace of the modern and digitally enabled world has put the internet at the centre of human interaction. Many transactions take place using the internet as companies and businesses have adapted to the World Wide Web for selling their products and services at the speed of light. Ecommerce simply means the buying and selling of products online. Crossing geographical boundaries and time zones, it is a continuous and constant medium for buying and selling worldwide.

So that the vast potential of the internet can be tapped and effectively utilized, ecommerce solutions such as payment gateways, shopping cart software, ecommerce websites such as Yahoo Stores now provide the much-needed impetus for online growth.

Looking into the tremendous growth of ecommerce, many ecommerce solutions have become extremely popular.

Ecommerce has demonstrated that it has a global reach, and given a B2B and B2C interaction a great impetus.

As ecommerce has developed rapidly, it has opened up the scope for businesses to develop rapidly and has narrowed down the barriers that existed previously between different countries and societies worldwide. Ecommerce solutions enable ecommerce websites to enhance the profile and corporate image of companies, while making it profitable for them to operate their business online.

Ecommerce solutions provide various tools to websites to enhance their visibility online and attract more customers to generate more conversions. At the same time, it is easier for businesses to provide seamless shopping experience to customers, right from purchasing the product to making the payment and finally obtaining the delivery.

Yet another dimension is to provide solutions to bring customers to the site and make them return for additional purchases. The ultimate aim is to help the company genuinely make profits while providing the ultimate shopping satisfaction to customers. As living standards are improving around the world, the way people buy is also changing. The internet provides a brilliant medium of channeling the buyer to the supplier and vice-versa. Ecommerce solutions provide a smooth way to facilitate such transactions and make the world of ecommerce better for the benefit of society.

CHAPTER 21: ECOMMERCE PLATFORMS TO BUILD YOUR ONLINE STORE

Today, choosing the appropriate eCommerce platform for your business is much harder than ever before because of the increasing number of options you have to choose from.

A good eCommerce platform will allow your company to make electronic exchanges on multiple devices, at anytime of the day with no hassle. Most websites are now accessible in a user-friendly format on all devices to guide the customer to checkout quickly. These newly upgraded eCommerce websites are the ones that are going to succeed because they were able to budget for a quality eCommerce platform & implementation that is the right fit for their unique business situation both now and in the future.

The eCommerce platform space has begun to mature and some of these platforms are now much more than a decade old. How are you supposed to know which eCommerce platform is right for you? I think the first place to look is the trajectory and the data behind what businesses are currently using these eCommerce platforms.

Are large companies using the platform? Are smaller companies using the platform successfully? Are the top websites using the platform? This data from Builtwith will help you decide whether the eCommerce platform is a good fit for your small, medium or enterprise size business.

— **WooCommerce**

WooCommerce is a simple, easy to use, eCommerce platform for WordPress. WooCommerce is now responsible for 30% of all online stores, which is the largest market share out of any platform. WooCommerce is an extension to WordPress and is easy to install. It allows you to sell very quickly and easily with a WordPress website, as well as ship to wherever you'd like with free shipping or flat rate shipping.

WooCommerce is a great fit if you want to get a site up quickly, as well as utilize the incredible content management capabilities of WordPress such as native blogging capabilities and more. WooCommerce has a massive plethora of extensions to improve the software. It is an ideal fit for businesses just starting out in eCommerce or that have not yet hit the million plus online revenue threshold.

Tim Griffiths

DIGITAL MARKETTING

— OpenCart

OpenCart is an easy to use lightweight eCommerce platform that is open source based on the PHP and MySQL technologies. It is more natively feature rich than WooCommerce but not nearly as impressive as the featured loaded Magento Community or Magento Enterprise platforms.

It is a good fit for a new eCommerce business that wants to get up a site quickly at a low cost. It does not have as robust CMS capabilities as WordPress for non eCommerce content so it is a better fit if you have very little non eCommerce content.

— Magento Community

Magento Community edition is the leading open source eCommerce platform among the top websites because it is built to provide online merchants with the most flexible cart system. Magento was developed throughout the year 2007 by the company Varien, and shortly released to the public just seven months later.

What makes Magento Community edition so impressive is that it comes with the features that most enterprise eCommerce platforms such as Demandware or Hybris would charge significant license fees for, at literally zero licensing cost. Features such as multi website, customizable order processing, complex catalog capabilities, and much more are native to Magento Community.

Magento Community edition is certainly the most powerful free open source eCommerce solution, especially with the newly enhanced 2.0 edition. However, with great power comes great responsibility. Magento Community is not to be taken lightly and can become very expensive to maintain and customize just like any other enterprise & complex software.

— **Squarespace Commerce**

Squarespace is a content management system which allows anyone to build and manage their brand online. They typically support both smaller companies and individuals such as local artists, as well as larger corporations looking to take their virtual businesses to the next level.

Empowering individuals is something that Squarespace strongly believes in, by giving smaller brands the ability to stand out online with high quality customer support.

For non-coders, this web platform is highly recommended in order to get your website up and running because of its easy to use website builder tools. Squarespace is not open source, and is a hosted platform, therefore customization of the platform is limited.

So if you are looking to make a more complex website with many features, you may want to look into other options. If you are an entrepreneur, local artist, or larger corporation with simpler website needs, Squarespace is for you.

— **Shopify**

Shopify is a Canadian based eCommerce company developed in 2004, originally as an online store for snowboarding equipment. Simply enough, Shopify allows businesses to set up their online stores to sell their products to the public all with one monthly cost and infrastructure, opposed to the other open source platforms which require more work to setup.

It is important to have multiple options and with this platform, there are more than a hundred different templates that Shopify offers when designing a website to make yours as personable and unique as possible.

There are plenty of templates that are modern and well designed free of charge. If you are a company that has a little bit of financial breathing room many high quality templates are $80-$180 that may pay off in the long run, seeing as it is just a single payment.

Shopify is great for smaller retailers but is not necessarily a great fit for more complex eCommerce sites or B2B eCommerce needs.

It does now offer a plus version for larger sites but doesn't seem to quite have the enterprise presence among larger sites that Magento, Demandware, Hybris, and other enterprise platforms have. Despite lack of enterprise market penetration, Shopify still shows healthy growth on all fronts.

— **Zen Cart**

Out of all the platforms, Zen Cart was one of the first eCommerce web design platforms that offers free, user-friendly, open source shopping cart software. The online store management system was renovated in 2003 making a change by moving away from osCommerce and moving toward the newly coded template system which is largely CSS-based.

The best thing about Zen Cart is you can download the system for free! They did this purposely because they wanted to stand out as a company that offers a technology that can be used by non-IT people.

Zen Cart was once much more popular and has since lost market share to platforms like WooCommerce, Magento, Shopify and more.

It has had a decreasing trajectory in usage for quite some time now.

— **OsCommerce**

OsCommerce is an "Open Source" e-commerce solution that is available for free under the GNU General Public License. Having an open source model similar to Opencart, Magento, and Zencart allows users to access all the code and customize in order to change the aspects of the software to fit the needs of a business.

OsCommerce was once very popular but has since lost marketshare to platforms that have become much modern in recent times such as Shopify and Magento. OsCommerce was started in 2000 as one of the first open source eCommerce platforms.

— **BigCommerce**

BigCommerce is an eCommerce software solution that helps businesses design their websites. They offer free premium templates depending on what you are trying to achieve. You don't need to have any technical skills in order to build your website with BigCommerce which is helpful to many start-ups that are looking to dive into the eCommerce industry.

There is a ton of flexibility when it comes to BigCommerce so whether you are selling 5 products or 5,000 products, you are still able to create the website that you desire, and because many start-ups begin at the lower end of the spectrum, this is a great ability to have.

— **Drupal Ubercart**

The Drupal extension Ubercart gives your Drupal website the ability to sell online. Drupal, which is a leading open source content management system, allows users to access thousands of modules and themes in order to give as many personalized options as possible.

As an open source eCommerce solution, Ubercart is a great platform to use if you are looking for great shopping cart functionality in tandem with the power of the Drupal CMS platform. An internal development team is able to alter the Ubercart features to accommodate many eCommerce needs because of Drupal's flexible open source architecture. Having flexibility is more important than most people realize when it comes to being successful with eCommerce.

When you are choosing which eCommerce platform you are most comfortable with, customer service, flexibility, and support are always improving at Ubercart. However, also keep in mind that the Ubercart platform marketshare seems to be shrinking despite the strong Drupal community.

— Volusion

Volusion offers hundreds of free templates that are easy to implement to get your website up and running quickly. Volusion is a California based shopping cart solution, that integrates shopping cart software with product merchandising, site design, SEO, marketing and order processing. Also Volusion provides an affiliate marketing and rewards program called MyReward.

This is a great feature for many small businesses because when customers are visiting and buying from your website, they can build loyalty points. These point eventually get transferred into a store credit, which is great for building long term relationships with consumers.

Volusion was once a very popular platform but has since lost a lot of its momentum and market share to platforms like Shopify, BigCommerce, and Magento.

— Big Cartel

This is a pretty basic online platform which is why this is one of the better platforms for companies selling a smaller range of products. Big Cartel has a range of options that are offered, one of them being free.

The trick is with the free option you are only allow to showcase five of your products that you want to sell online.

Now if you are a start up clothing company that has only five t-shirt designs so far, than Big Cartel could be exactly what you are looking for. Now if you are looking for a greater number than just five, you are more than welcome to choose from their budgeted options depending on the number of products you're looking to display.

— **nopCommerce**

nopCommerce is a free, downloadable software. This very simple shopping cart solution could be great for new online businesses. You will notice that this platform allows your website to meet all of the search-engine standards such as search friendly URLs to well-structured content.

It also has great themes for your products. nopCommerce is well known for its modular / layered structure which gives users the ability to create additional functionality and makes it as easy as possible to manage your websites.

These layers are easily accessible and user friendly on a mobile device as well as on other alternative tablets.

— **Yahoo! Store**

Yahoo! Stores is an eCommerce platform that allows you to choose from hundreds of free or paid templates for the development of an online site. It is known for being implemented for smaller companies because of its simplicity and low monthly cost similar to Shopify. The lowest rate can also be affordable by a almost any start-up as well.

Yahoo! Stores plans are reflected by it's retailers expected monthly sales unlike say Shopify whose platform is based off the number of products being sold or the amount of storage a company needs for space to satisfy their website capabilities. Yahoo was once a very popular eCommerce platform but has since lost traction to companies like Shopify and BigCommerce.

— **Fotomoto**

This Print-on-demand eCommerce system allows you to sell your artwork in multiple forms.

Once you make an account and link it to wherever you had been selling them virtually in the past, it is very easy to get your site up and running without hassle. Behind the scenes of this platform are a handful of sales representatives, professional print labs, packaging and shipping services, and software specialist.

The great thing about Fotomoto is all the work the staff behind the curtains are doing on behalf of you and your business to make sure things run as smoothly as possible.

One of those main selling points as a platform thats more directed at the website host (you) is the aftermath of the customers purchase. If you feel as though the easiest thing to do is too DIY, then by all means go ahead! But Fotomoto offers a printing network that prints, packages, and ships your order right to the customers for you! You don't have to lift a finger besides the one that you're using to complete the actual order. Fotomoto could be a great fit for smaller businesses looking to leverage a great print network like Fotomoto.

— 3D Cart

3D Cart is a software as a service eCommerce solution similar to Yahoo Stores, Bigcommerce, Shopify and more. This platform is great for any individuals that are looking to get their name and brand out into the virtual world of eCommerce. 3D Cart is known for its shopping cart solution which they claim powers over 17,000 stores, although that data is not backed up by Builtwith. You are able to choose from hundreds of themes and templates that 3D Cart has to offer.

Selling products on Facebook, as well as promoting your products videos on Youtube is easier than ever with 3D Cart. With the Facebook app as well as having a sleek Omnichannel platform, your entire website should look the same across all devices and channels. When your website is complete, you are going to want to start promoting it! You are able to promote your store by email marketing, as well as mobile commerce tools, and social media integration with 24/7 hour assistance from the 3D Carts customer service line.

— Miva Merchant

Miva is a long standing eCommerce platform for small and medium size businesses. It is great for up and coming businesses because it is a versatile and stable platform that is able to be customized for whatever kind of look your company is going for. They have a less expensive small business version starting at less than $100 a month and a more expensive enterprise edition that goes for approximately $1500 a month. Miva provides a full range of in house services to help businesses implement their solution rather than going through a third party.

— **X-Cart**

X-cart is an eCommerce shopping cart site that allows you to choose from either a cloud-based cart or a self-hosted licensed software option. Within these two options your company is able to pick from a handful of attributes such as web design, migration, installation, hosting, online monitoring, and fraud services. It has a much smaller eCommerce community than many of the other small business platforms but still has thousands of sites using the platform.

— **E-Junkie**

E-Junkie is a shopping cart service that is set up for business owners and operators who are looking to enter into the Commerce world. This software prides its self on the security of their transactions. All transactions through e-Junkie are done within their system which can be embedded into your website. Customers who purchase virtual goods from a client's E-Junkie store will then receive a secure downloadable link that expires after a certain number of downloads or a certain time.

E-Junkie is an interesting solution because it essentially allows you to add their shopping cart into your website via code snippets. They support many payment gateways like Paypal as well as have integrations with platforms like Google Analytics.

— **Drupal Commerce**

Drupal is used by larger companies and organizations. This platform is increasing in usage but at a much slower rate relative to WordPress & WooCommerce because it is significantly more expensive to implement and maintain. If you have very complex content related website needs but also need eCommerce, Drupal Commerce could be a good solution for your website.

— **Magento Enterprise**

Magento Enterprise edition comes straight from the Magento Community edition and has the same base core files as Magento Community. Magento Enterprise has many features such as rewards points, customer segmentation and more that Magento Community does not. Magento Enteprise is a very successful platform because it is less expensive than some of the major enterprise platforms like Hybris and Oracle Commerce but has the capabilities to compete with such platforms.

The other advantage is that there is a large pool of developers and agencies that support it because of its massive community edition usage.

— **Demandware**

Demandware is an enterprise cloud-based eCommerce platform technology for retailers.

This software allows them to make and manage a custom online website as well as give them full access to the mobility feature. Demandware is a public company that has become very successful by doing a revenue share model with customers. It is in the enterprise class tier as one of the more expensive eCommerce solutions on the market.

— Hybris

Hybris is an omni-channel eCommerce platform that integrates all digital and physical customer touch points into a single platform. It is now owned by SAP, a global leader in information technology solutions.

This worldwide managed company is a leader in both B2B and B2C eCommerce industries by keeping up with the everyday changes in the Internet world. It is a best in class eCommerce solution that is on the more expensive enterprise side to implement for larger companies.

— Oracle Commerce

Oracle Commerce was an add on to the companies successful CX portfolio. Oracle Commerce was originally ATG Commerce which was acquired by Oracle a few years ago. Now, Oracle Commerce continues to power some of the largest sites in the world. Similar to IBM, Demandware, and Hybris, it is on the more expensive side of eCommerce platforms.

— IBM WebSphere Commerce

This single, unified software platform framework is built for enterprise eCommerce websites. IBM WebSphere Commerce provides an omni-channel shopping experience that helps engage your customers with experiences through great content, marketing, and promotions.

IBM Websphere powers some of the largest eCommerce sites in the world and is typically a fit for larger complex sites that require extensive customization. If you do not have a large implementation budget, IBM Websphere is probably not for you.

— **NetSuite eCommerce**

SuiteCommerce enables businesses to seamlessly connect every step of a multichannel, multi-location business — from ecommerce, POS and order management to merchandising, marketing, inventory, financials and customer service.

This platform allows you to create unique, personalized and compelling mobile, web and in-store experiences that differentiate your brand and exceed customer expectations. One of the biggest advantages of Netsuite is the ability to have an all in one backend ERP, CRM, seamlessly connected with your eCommerce platform all together.

— **Digital River**

Digital River offers eCommerce, payments and top online marketing services to global companies of all sizes. Known as an Commerce-as-a-Service solution, being able to support the shopper experience at its best is something that Digital River prides its self on. Local shopping experiences in global markets and more payment options than any other company makes Digital River a leading global provider.

What differentiates DR is their full solution: reseller business model; robust, flexible cloud-based SaaS platform; and comprehensive business operation support which manages, supports, and powers users sites. They typically provide eCommerce services for larger websites not small businesses.

— **GSI Commerce (eBay Enterprise)**

Formally known as GSI Commerce, eBay Enterprises provides a globally well developed eCommerce solution and service that allows you to be ultra connected to your consumers at all times. This company specializes in running online shopping sites for larger brick and mortar brands and retailers. There are not many GSI Commerce sites in existence today as the platform is not as popular as it once was.

CHAPTER 22: LIVING THE DIGITAL DREAM

WHAT IS THE LAPTOP LIFESTYLE?

The laptop lifestyle is a new lifestyle where people choose to forego working for traditional business and instead choose to work digitally. Working digitally can mean many things from digital marketing to social media sales or even copywriting for online businesses, forums and magazines.

The Laptop Lifestyle is not a new thing, but it is something that has been coming more and more to the fore in the last few years. Many people have had success in this burgeoning industry. Of course, because there are so many opportunities available, there is always room for more people to become involved. This new business model is though not without its issues. All types of business have both pros and cons to them, and digital marketing and the laptop lifestyle are no exception.

So let's look at the pros first then we can look at the cons of this lifestyle choice;

PROS

1. Freedom to work where you want and within reason when you want.

2. Choice of direction. You no longer work for someone else, so you have a choice about what you want to do.

3. Exciting and challenging the new industry. There are little in the way of limits although ethical concerns should be uppermost in your mind if you don't trust it don't sell it.

4. Get paid for the work you put in. The more effort you put in, the more you get out.

CONS

1. Less job security. When you are working for yourself, you have far less of a safety net if something goes wrong.

2. Bewildering choice. Many people find that if they have an unlimited scope in their choice of industry and market, it is simply overwhelming.

3. Challenging new sector. Unless you are doing something, you probably shouldn't be, you won't be an instant millionaire. The laptop lifestyle requires a lot of work and learning, to begin with.

4. No salary. There is no guarantee about the amount of money you can make a living the laptop lifestyle and no guarantee; in fact, you will make any money doing so.

5. Scams. As I am sure, everyone is aware there are far more scams on the Internet than honest people. Like everywhere there is the good, the bad and the ugly, because of this, it is essential to ensure you do your research properly before making a decision about what you want to do and how you want to do it.

With all of this said, and after having done quite a bit of research myself, I would wholeheartedly encourage people from all walks of life to at least look into this new industry. After all, it seems very much like traditional industries, especially in western countries, are beginning to flounder and it is high time we all began to use the great technological tool that we have all been playing with for the last 20 years.

'WHAT & WHY' OF DIGITAL MEDIA AS A CAREER OPTION

This time of the year, most of you must be grappling with the dilemma called "What Next?" No wonder, with the host of career options thrown open in front of you, combined by the pressures from peer and family, it has made you more confused and indecisive.

Have you ever wondered, who posts the brand messages on Facebook or Twitter every day?

Ever wondered who forms and manages Websites like Sunsilk Gang of Girls or Lipton Challenge - World's Largest Puzzle. Ever felt curious to know who puts the sponsored links whenever you search for something on Google.

They are all Digital marketing/media professionals who work together to bring the brand in contact with the digital clan (i.e. you) in various forms.

OK, so now you must be wondering "Why Digital Media, what is it all about, etc.?"

The 'What & Why' of Digital Media as a Career Option:

WHAT IS DIGITAL MEDIA ALL ABOUT?

Digital Media refers to electronic media. For us, we need to keep 2 things in mind: Internet & Mobile.

Digital Marketing is the business of promoting products or services using digital distribution channels to reach consumers in a timely, relevant, personal and cost-effective manner.

So why should you choose it as a career option?

Even when the world is slowing down, Digital Media is running at a much faster pace each day. In fact, with more and more organizations opting for digital media campaigns, the media is growing by leaps and bounds. With this, is developing the number of agencies that are offering 360U services under the digital domain. And this, in turn, is opening up multiple job avenues.

However, with each day it is becoming more sophisticated and hence a thorough understanding of what, why, when, where and how of it shall empower the digital media professionals to come up with innovative ideas, thereby, breaking through the clutter.

Digital media is an apt career option for the young and enthusiastic tech-savvy generation (you again). It is this young generation that accesses the digital media the most and spends the majority of its time understanding the digital parlance, finding out newer and fresher ways to communicate and connect.

Hence, as this media is still evolving, it provides immense opportunities for you to prove your mettle. All your entrepreneurial skills can be tried, tested and nurtured here. However, the media being complicated, a course in digital marketing/media as a specialized domain shall help aspirants to hone the requisite skills to deliver path-breaking solutions.

So, what exactly does a digital media professional do?

Various Things.

To begin with, a digital media professional has a wide array of functions to choose from depending upon his / her area of interest.

— **Strategy**

A strategy is the knowledge warehouse of the organization. It encompasses thorough research about the brand, competitors, category & consumers, which after that is used to generate insights that lead to formulating campaigns that not just last long but last forever. So if you are inquisitive, observant and enjoy analyzing, then this is the right option for you.

— **Client Servicing & Business Development**

Love talking to people, meeting them, and networking? Then, this is the department to be in. You need to be a good listener and a good speaker. Not to forget, you need to know how to balance between being calm or aggressive. Getting work done aptly summarizes the role of a professional in this department.

— **Technology**

Seek logic & explanation into everything? Enjoy creating something on your own? The tech team has people just like you. Creating websites, widgets, applications and other such stuff is what these guys primarily do. You need to be enjoying working on programming languages (Asp.Net, PHP, and JAVA, to name a few) to be here.

— **Creative**

If things like imagination, designs, colours, beautiful statements rule your world, then you got to join the bunch of creative guys. Art to think through forms, situations or categories is what you need to develop.

Thinking, thinking different and creating something unique is an obvious expectation out of a creative fellow.

— **Search / Social Media Marketing**

Social networks, search, videos, blogs take significant time of your day? So much so that your family and friends feel the need to have a social network profile to get in touch with you?

Two things would summarize what people do here:

*Enjoy conversations, reading them, initiating them, managing them and placing brands into the conversational game.

*Understand why and what does one search for and how to link a brand to the relevant search.

Media Planning

Numeromaniac. Is that you?

Numbers define the media planning world. Love for numbers is a must; else, you may not survive.

Following trends, consumers, and new developments are the second primary function of a media planner. Follow anything and everything; know who is doing what and why.

CHAPTER 23: THE POWER OF THE DIGITAL WORLD IN ADVERTISING

We live in a digital world. Everything around us from electronic gadgets to communication devices uses digital technologies to function. With more and more technology advances being made in the digital world, advertising and marketing solutions have come a long way.

Digital display systems have now become by far the most preferred way to advertising for small medium and large corporations across the world.

DIGITAL DISPLAY

The uses of digital displays not only provide outstanding advertising opportunity but an interactive display board adds a punch to the whole campaign.

Digital displays board are now used for effective advertising and communication with the customers that help not only in promotional activity but also play a significant role in brand building exercise that is far more effective than any other advertising medium or displays.

Just like other advertising and display banners, digital displays are also available in different shape and sizes. You can fit your screen in any corner as per your need. So it uses the most noticeable promotional strategy for nowadays.

— Digital Signage

The trend of Digital signage advertising has picked up like no other marketing trend in recent history.

Directly speaking digital signage is a platform for electronic displays. It has just changed the state of mind and view of thinking of all marketers about marketing and advertising.

The advantages of a capable digital display are that it brings to the table the power of broadcasting dynamic content likes messages, brand punch lines and videos.

Signage is the most commercial way for advertising dynamic content compared to broadcasting ads on television or the Internet.

You will also have the comfort of updating the signage day by day yourself as it is so easy to upload a file in computer software or program.

— **Digital signage advertising**

There are several options while choosing the best digital signage advertising options for a particular brand or company.

Depending on the individual goal of advertising or brand promotion, various advertising options like billboards, LED displays, video walls and interactive Systems broadcast digital graphics in an active form to the public at large.

It also a lot depends on your product or service. No matters what you are offering but some products can be quickly promoted and more importantly get noticed via LED Displays or where else some other services can do well on video walls.

The main target of all this stuff is a brand promotion, and there is no doubt in it that none other displays can do better than digital signage advertising products. More on this later.

— **Digital Signs**

Digital signs are widely used these days in most stores, office buildings, hospitals, airports and other public and private venues. Not only can Digital signs be updated by a remote control system, but digital signs also do not use any paper or paint and hence are more environmentally friendly than traditional symbols.

Hence it can be the most effective display system in shopping malls and other public places. It is now available in different size, shape and patterns. It can display things brighter in less energy, so it is one of the most commercial as well eco-friendly display because there is no use of paper or paint in it.

NETWORKING IN A DIGITAL WORLD

A dedicated support system is crucial for personal and professional success. Networking has and will play a vital part in your business. Face-to-face networking and handshaking is still a fantastic way to do business, but with the Internet at our fingertips and available everywhere, there's a new way to connect and communicate with people.

Networking is the process of searching for contacts. Not just to be a collector of people, but to get involved, get connected and to help build each other up. It may still be about handshaking, passing out business cards, giving your elevator speech, and wearing name tags, but we should view networking as establishing and maintaining authentic relationships.

So, why do we network?

- — Engage with people who will have a positive impact on us and our business.
- — Swap ideas and stories with others.
- — Find clients and partners.

— Find a job or recruit potential employees.

— Gain feedback and insights.

— Get inspired!

— Present yourself as an SME (Subject Matter Expert)

— Generate and build leads.

— Establish meaningful relationships, personally and professionally.

LinkedIn is a global social networking site for people in professional occupations. In a sense, it is a bit like Facebook - you create your profile for others to see, but it is used for professional purposes. Members build a profile of their job history, interests and experience - an online Resume if you will - and 'connect' with former colleagues and people in their line of work.

Like most social media websites, your journey on LinkedIn begins with creating a personal profile. Many LinkedIn profiles are abbreviated resumes due to LinkedIn's professional tone, but with the new concept of Social Selling, we need to think of your profile as a brand. Employers look for inside information on candidates such as professional interests.

WAYS TO BUILD YOU AND YOUR BRAND ON LINKEDIN

1. Update your profile is the first step in marketing you and your business.

a. From the top toolbar, click Me.

b. Click View Profile.

c. From here, you can take the time to edit your profile by adding education, experience, volunteer experience, and so much more. Click the pencil next to a section to edit, or click the more button (three dots) to access more features.

d. Make sure to save all changes.

2. Upload a Professional Photo. Make the first impression count, in about 6 seconds someone has crafted opinion of you through your photo and your profile. You want your potential customers/connections to answer the following questions about you.

a. Are you trustworthy?

b. Are you someone I want to do business with?

c. Can I recommend you to my friends and clients/customers?

3. Create a standout Headline. Your headline is the valuable real estate that appears next to your name in search results.

The wording of a headline may determine whether a new potential client was searching through LinkedIn contacts you. Done well, your LinkedIn headline can be used to promote your brand statement, marketing message, most enticing expertise, and more.

a. This should not be your job title/description.

b. Why should people stop and take a closer look at you?

c. What impressions are you leaving behind?

d. What do you do?

e. Use keywords or core words. Make your headline fit with SEO, Search Engine Optimization.

f. Demonstrate real value to your potential clients, customers, etc.

4. Claim your LinkedIn Username: Personalize your LinkedIn URL, own your brand. You are the brand we are talking about, claim your URL, so that when someone searches for your name, they will find your public LinkedIn page/profile. Visit your profile and select the edit public profile URL option.

5. Add Skills: When updating your skills section, make sure you use relevant, updated keywords. For example, potential buyers/customers probably won't be searching for "cold calling", try to mirror your buyer's skills/needs.

a. Use SEO keywords.

b. Add up to 50 skills to your profile.

c. The skills with the most endorsements from your connections will be listed first.

6. Endorsements: Skill endorsements are an excellent way to recognize your 1st-degree connections' skills and expertise with one click. They also let your contacts validate the strengths found on your profile. Skill endorsements are a simple and effective way of building your professional brand and engaging your network.

7. Write a summary: Why should you fill it in? For starters, it gives the reader a quick overview of who you are, what you do, what you are looking for and most importantly, what you can do for them. Think like your buyer, what's in it for me?

a. Demonstrate your expertise; make sure you include keywords.

b. Show them that you are a valuable resource.

c. Add a video, and a minute video equals 1,000 words!

d. Include Call to Action Statements; this could include companies/clients you've helped, include your signature with contact information, keywords that are important to buyers.

e. Demonstrate the value you offer, be their solution.

8. Experience: This is the time you can treat LinkedIn as your resume. Add your previous and current jobs, making sure to include key industry words so that you will be found in searches. When you add who you worked for and you see their name in the drop-down list, your experience will then have their logo beside your name because they created a company business page.

9. Add Connections: On LinkedIn, the people who are part of your network are called your "connections". Connect with people with whom you have worked or done business with, or people with similar interests or work in your industry. You can ask someone to join your professional network by sending them an invitation to connect. LinkedIn encourages networking by showing you exactly how your connections are related.

10. Engage with your connections: Status updates are short messages that are typical of many social networking platforms. While posting updates on LinkedIn is like Facebook and Twitter, it's also different. From your LinkedIn home page or your Edit My Profile page, you can change your status update as frequently as you like.

WHY INFOGRAPHICS SHOULD BE A PART OF YOUR CONTENT MARKETING STRATEGY

As defined by Wikipedia, "Infographics are graphic visual representations of information, data or knowledge intended to present complex information quickly and clearly." In other words, infographics combine design, text and images to simplify and present complex information into easy to understand visuals.

In the past two years, the Google search for infographics has been widely increased by 800%. Known as the latest trend in digital marketing, many internet marketing services providers have joined the bandwagon and made infographics an intrinsic part of their content marketing strategy. Here are some of the main benefits of using infographics:

1) 90% of the information processed by the brain is visual. We tend to remember more of what we see than what we read. Besides, the attention span of audiences has highly decreased. People prefer to scan and get the message rather than reading the entire text. As a result, the information given by infographics is more easily consumed and understood that the long and heavy written piece of writing.

2) Audiences today are overloaded with information, with the Internet being the primary resource. The key is no longer to provide informative content but to get interested in the information you provide.

Infographics work as the best attention-grabbing tool that compels the audience to read and share information. Infographics appeal to the visual senses of audiences while making them read only the essential and necessary information.

3) A well-designed infographic embedded with your company logo enhances your brand. If the content, as well as the graphic of your infographic, is interesting, there are high chances of it being shared virally on social media and favourite blogs. As the infographic has your logo embedded in it, it exposes your brand to a broader audience.

4) Infographic is an excellent link building tactic and thus helps to drive traffic to your website. The code provided to publish the infographic on a website or a blog is an embed code. This code creates an automatic link from the site sharing your infographic to your site. As a result, you get a lot of quality backlinks and therefore, will rank higher in the search results.

5) Creating a compelling infographic with accurate statistics, figures and crisp text requires extensive research. It also requires considerable expertise and proficiency to convey the message needed in easy to understand and limited words. Thus, an excellent infographic also showcases the brand's knowledge on the subject.

Integrating infographics as part of your content marketing strategy will not only enable you to stay ahead of your competitors but will also increase your traffic, visibility and leads.

CHAPTER 24: STEPS TO MASTERING THE DIGITAL WORLD

Ever since the internet began to flourish, companies have been utilizing it to their advantage. Virtual products are being sold for real-world cash, and online-only stores are booming.

While there is a massive market for these kinds of businesses, owning one doesn't automatically guarantee you the success you're hoping for. To fully exploit this digital world, there are steps you can take to help your business take advantage of internet marketing sales funnel.

— Step One: Lead Generation

To succeed in any business, you need a product that is fresh and marketable. Without an in-demand product, you have nothing to attract customers. Finding the right niche for your business is the first place you should start when developing an internet marketing system.

— Step Two: Up-sell

To fully profit from the customers that you bring in to your business, you will want to sell as much as possible to each customer.

There are many different ways to up-sell products, ranging from charging an extra fee for items in a colour that's in higher demand to offering upgrades on preexisting products.

Because one of the most challenging parts of any business is finding customers for your product, up-selling to customers that already have a demand for what you're selling is an easy way to bring in more money.

— Step Three: Set-up Your Business To Utilize The Funnel

For the sales funnel to function appropriately, you will need to have an action plan that helps customers remember your company. While single time customers are better than nothing, repeat customers are what you're aiming for.

To remain memorable, there are many things you can do: set-up a list of customers' emails and send a monthly email blast, create a blog that posts weekly updates with informative, popular topics, have a list of your customers' phone numbers and call them quarterly to see if they are in need of your services

— **Step Four: Promote Your Brand Online**

Find innovative ways for potential customers to find your website. Promote your webpage on as many social media sites as possible. The more you get your name out there, the more your business will prosper.

— **Throw the Undesired Out of the Image**

Images are clicked every day with some purpose. The purpose of being professional or personal does not matter much. The point that matters is whether the object you clicked the image for is being displayed to perfection or not? The situations that you capture sometimes do not repeat. Some unwanted things get in between and spoil the entire photograph.

Consider you want to use some photographs for your project. You find them to be excellent except a few undesirable entities here and there. You upload the image on Photoshop and try your hand at removing those entities. The result sometimes is a complete mess up and lots of time wasted. The background also gets messed up, and you are back to square one.

— Customize your Image with the Professionals

If you want to save time and money in getting the desired image devoid of all the unwanted pixels, do not consider yourself an image rectifier and act like one. The modern digital world has professionals who use advanced tools that can easily remove things from your photographs without affecting its natural look.

Consider a photoshoot going on. You clicked several images of the model posing with all your focusing and lighting equipment around.

Somehow with the best poses given, parts of equipment came into the photographs blocking the model.

Now trying with Photoshop necessary tools that everybody uses, you can end up chopping the head of the model while removing the equipment part due to proximity.

Sometimes restoring it again is more complicated than removing was. If you think of cutting the unwanted part, the perfection cannot be achieved, and the natural aspect of the picture is lost.

What professional companies for image correction will do is that they will use modern stamping tools to perfection.

However, be the proximity of the image you want to remove and image you want to retain, the professionals will do it without tampering with the originality of the picture. The background will also be recreated and amended to get back the natural features affected because of the chopping.

— **The Final Touch**

All advertisements, presentation and video creating companies can highly benefit from this as pictures and photographs form an integral part of the media world. These processes are quite time-consuming and require high precision. There are professional companies that specialize in removing unwanted objects and can modify any complex picture without affecting the originality.

LET YOUR BUSINESS GROW IN THE DIGITAL WORLD

The Internet has provided a comprehensive forum of opportunity for its users. It includes information about most of the answers that people seek. It has helped businesses grow by enabling businessmen and women to promote their businesses online. What are some of the products that you can sell over the internet?

— **Electronics**

Electronics is a word that covers so many things. In includes computers its hardware and software, electric wires, air conditioners and other electronic appliances. You can always place an order, and someone can deliver the item to you.

— **Tickets**

Whenever there is a big concert going on, most tickets are sold online. It helps to reach out too many people who may not be so close to where the other tickets are being sold. Tickets to go watch movies are also sold online. Some transport services also sell their tickets online making them easily accessible to many.

— **Office and stationery supplies**

These include papers, chairs, tables and other office equipment. Books are also sold online and can be bought both by an office of school institutions. Other office supplies like photocopy machines, fax machines and even paper shredders can also be sold.

— **Beauty products**

Online makeup shopping is something that has evolved over the years and is generating so much income. All types of beauty products that one may need are all over the internet. Some stores have made this as their sole method of selling their products because of the many sales it makes.

— **Gym equipment**

If you are interested in selling or buying gym equipment, the internet provides you with the chance to do just that. If you are a buyer, you do not need to step out of the house, all you need is to identify what you need and place an order the rest will be brought to you.

— **Hotels and other services**

If you are planning to travel for a vacation or a business meeting, you can reserve a hotel room over the internet. This is convenient because you will be sure to have a place to sleep no matter how late you arrive or how populated the situation is.

— **Art**

All forms of artwork can be sold online. It will include your drawings, the photos you have taken and graphics you have incorporated. Is also helpful because you retain your original work.

— **Culinary skills**

If you are a chef or you love being in the kitchen, you can sell some cooking recipes online. You can sell them to people as well as hotel and restaurant owners.

CHAPTER 25: THE DAWN OF THE DIGITAL ERA

In 1851, Nathaniel Hawthorne wrote: Through electricity, the world of matter has become a great nerve, vibrating thousands of miles in a breathless point of time. The round globe is vast- brain, instinct with intelligence.

Since then, humanity has not stopped to realize Hawthorne's vision of a world where human intelligence is networked. Into the 21st century, global society lives in the frontiers of the digital age. Mass production is taken over by mass-customisation. The consumer of today applies their specific knowledge, tastes, expectations and demands on producers who have to able to meet these to succeed. We are in the era of the knowledge-based economy.

The internet has existed since 1969. British scientist Tim Berners-Lee invented the World Wide Web in 1989 and fully implemented by 1991, thus the beginning of a global network. It is today's ultimate platform for disseminating information globally, and its growth is beyond exponential. Is the print media as we know today to be a thing of yesteryears, pushed to obsolescence?

The I-WAY has created an information society. It has a significant impact on the economic, political, social, cultural, scientific, medical, educational and technological field.

Networked technology introduced the world to digitalisation. It opens up the creation, distribution, integration, diffusion, use and manipulation of information in many creative and productive ways.

Knowledge economy creates wealth through the exploitation of knowledge and understanding. Beniger states that people who have the means to partake in this form of society are referred to as digital citizens- one of the many labels that ushers in a new phase of the community into the 21st century.

THE GROWTH OF INFORMATION IN SOCIETY

There is no definite or universally accepted meaning of what exactly is information society. Theories bounce around as to this transformation in society that started back in the 1970s. Internet is not the only information technology that is widely used. There are specific media and modes of production that influences the changing ways of society.

The growth of technologically mediated information has been quantified in different ways, including society's technological capacity to store information, to communicate information, and to compute information.

Touraine wrote in 1988 referring to the programmed society- " this phrase captures its capacity to create models of management, production, organization, distribution and consumption, such a society appears at all functional levels, as the product of an action exercised by society itself, not the outcome of natural laws or cultural specificities."

In the dawn of networked technology, information of all sorts becomes digital, reduced to bits stored in computers, races at the speed of light across the global networks. It is a new world of possibilities. The digital whirlwind is sweeping society.

This digital growth is quantified in different ways. It handles how society stores information, communicate and compute the data. The technical capacity to store information grew from (optimally compressed) 2.6 exabytes in 1986 to 295 exabytes in 2017. This shows a 60% growth per year over the past two decades.

Wisegeek explains:

One thousand twenty-four gigabytes is one terabyte, and 1,024 terabytes are one petabyte. To put this in perspective, a petabyte is about one million gigabytes (1,048,576).

In the late 1980s, a large hard disk was considered 80 megabytes. Today, that amount of space doesn't even hold a current Windows operating system without butting up against storage limits.

Robust programs, music files, digital versatile discs (DVDs), streaming video and high-resolution graphics have all become memory-hungry beasts devouring real estate bit by byte. It would have been unthinkable in the 1980s that the home computer would one day require tens and even hundreds of gigabytes to store data. Though the petabyte still lies beyond the territory of the terabyte, who can say where the home computer will be in another two decades?

With the influx of computers, CD-ROMS, hard drives, USB flash drives, and other discs, the byte cannot hold larger values. With the larger volumes of information, more bytes are needed:

— Kilobyte -KB- is 1,024 bytes, but most relate it to 1000 bytes.

— Megabyte-MB- is 1,024 kilobytes

— Gigabyte -GB- is 1,024 megabytes

— Terabyte -TB- is 1,024 gigabytes

— Petabyte- PB- is 1,024 terabytes

— Exabyte-EB- is 1,024 petabytes

— Zettabyte-ZB- 1,024 exabytes

— Yottabyte-YB- is 1,024 zettabytes

Note: many hardware and hard drive manufacturers think of a kilobyte as 1,000 bytes. The automobile changed the world in many ways, economically, physically and socially. Mechanized agriculture is the only way to farm. The discovery of the printing press was a real big deal- facilitated the printing of books, as against the laborious handwritten texts.

The interactive multimedia, once again is very rapidly changing the face of the world. At first, the internet's most popular use was for e-mails and chat rooms. Then comes social networks, telecommuting, blogging and vlogging and more. Already, there is a dark side to the digital world. There is fear that technology will bring unemployment, numbing of minds and invasion of privacy.

In his book- Digital Economy, Don Tapscott writes:" the digital world, while it offers exciting promise, there is also a dark side. Social stratification, massive social dislocation and conflict are perils that man faces with this digitalisation. Violence and suffering can be seen worldwide instantly, not just in developing countries. There are new social, ethical and governance issues that will surface as time goes on."

WHAT LIES AHEAD

Critical scholars say that major critiques of concepts like information society, knowledge society, network society, postmodern society, postindustrial society and other labels tend to create the impression that we are entering into a new type of community.

According to Wikipedia, Frank Webster argues that this kind of approach stress discontinuity, that contemporary society has nothing in common with culture as it was 100 or 150 years ago. He explains that these assumptions mean, nothing can be done. Ideologically there is nothing society can do and have to adapt to the existing reality.

Webster insists on the continuities that characterize change. He stresses the different epoch of capitalism, that is, the laizzez-faire of the 19th century, corporate capitalism in the 20th century and informational capitalism for the 21st century.

CHAPTER 26: DATA SECURITY

As it goes, most 21st century businesses rely on digital communication to be able to function daily; from emails and the internet to Voice over Internet Protocol (VoIP) technology and video conferencing. Therefore, it is probably fair to say that many offices have long since relegated traditional paper-based communications and are up-to-date with all the latest technological advancements from the digital world.

Indeed, one of the most significant advantages of digital communication is the ability to store masses of information in a relatively small space which, ultimately, can save businesses a great deal of money on storage space.

But while there can be little doubt as to the convenience and cost-effectiveness of digital storage, great care must be taken to ensure that the data is safe from being lost or stolen, much in the same way as traditional paper-based information; however, there are some key differences.

And because most offices are 'networked', they are potentially at risk from hackers across the world, which means confidential information could fall into the wrong hands if adequate security isn't in place.

Furthermore, if digital data is stored on a small office-based server, it is possible that all information could be lost or damaged in an instant should there be any hardware malfunctions, or if the system is infected by a virus and other forms of malware.

So, despite the benefits of being able to store all communications in a digital format, it is essential to address all the potential pitfalls in advance, before the security of the data is compromised in any way.

However, ensuring the security of digital data can be both time-consuming and costly, requiring specialist knowledge and expensive equipment and technology. And for any company looking to dedicate all its resources towards revenue-generating activities, it can be easy to ignore this aspect of operations.

But business continuity is crucial within most organisations and companies rely on their information systems to be able to function on a day to day basis. If these systems are disrupted, then it can hinder operations in a significant way; which is why it's crucial not to cut corners when handling digital data that is central to a company's ability to function correctly.

WHAT NOT TO DO WHEN IMPLEMENTING DIGITAL STRATEGIES

The new digital world has created unlimited new opportunities for businesses to market to its customers. The amount of choice can, however, overwhelm many people causing a lack of action as they don't know where to start. While creating a workable strategy is the first step, the most crucial step is in the implementation, which usually proves the most challenging. Below are some of the basic mistakes to avoid that will save you valuable time and resources.

—

— **Thinking Every Social Media Platform is right for you**

Due to the proliferation of social networks, you may be excused to believe that optimising your prospecting campaigns means publishing on all of them. While initially, this may seem a good idea, the first step is to find out what social channels your target customers are using as they will most relevant to you. You cannot effectively manage 4-5 social media platforms if you are an SME and even most larger companies (with more resources) don't do this effectively either. Choose the most relevant 2 and do them well.

— **Not Setting Priorities and Deadlines**

Irrespective of the many marketing tasks you have, not setting priorities and deadlines is a sure path to failure. It's a great start to create a strategy, but without any timelines, in place, you will likely keep putting off key deliverables to next week. Always next week when I have time. Unfortunately, that time never seems to come so set priorities, break them into weekly tasks then diarise these to keep you on track. The key to any tactic being successful is in taking action to implement it. That is where the actual value lies.

— **Copying what everyone else is doing and not making your own rules**

Like two people cannot have the same fingerprints, copying another business is not necessarily going to reap your rewards. Being a 'me too' player will not make successful since you are not offering anything unique. Copying other people's strategies will put your business in unfamiliar territory because the strategies adopted may not suit your business goals or target market. They will also lack authenticity.

— **Not Leveraging Between Digital and Traditional Marketing Channels**

Despite the rise in popularity of digital marketing, a significant portion of your prospects could still be using traditional marketing channels. By not leveraging across both platforms, you are not getting the best return on your content messages, and you are missing out on vital touchpoints. Think cross channel or tradigital for best results.

— **Forgetting To Write a Workable Strategy and Action Plan**

A common mantra goes "if you do not know where you are headed, any route can take you there." In the digital world, a strategy is the road map that gives you the direction for your business. It will help you make the right decisions, create the right messaging at the right time and show you how and when to do it. Action is key! Creating a strategy without an ongoing action plan is a waste of time and resources.

DIGITAL SOLUTIONS THAT CAN HELP YOUR BUSINESS

In this day and age, many enterprises need to embrace digital technology to stay in touch with their competition and provide an up-to-date, aggressive service to their clients and customers. We are bombarded by the expanding digital world daily and are sometimes unaware of what is on the market, along with the added benefits that may be offered to organisations of all sizes.

Listed here are facets of digital technology that companies in this day and age should know about:

— **IPTV**

IPTV (Internet Protocol Television) is undoubtedly an excellent tv system which is delivered using an Internet Protocol network.

You will discover literally numerous remarkably useful instances of this technology which include; settling your hotel bill by way of the hotel room Tv Set, the BBC's iPlayer, the way in which education uses IPTV to send video and audio to Personal Computer terminals within a college or university and the way that hospitals provide TV solutions to their patients.

IPTV is all over the place and could benefit your company in some way. The price tag on IPTV products and services have lowered significantly in the last three years or so, so now is a wonderful time for you to hop on-board.

— **Commercial Satellites**

As a primary part of their provision of television solutions, countless companies will need a specialist, commercial satellite installation. A professional system is more than just planting a big dish on the roof of a building.

A top-grade satellite installation company would offer many excellent options, for example, a 'landlord managed system', which gives landlords total control over the dishes and a way to bring in profit from them. A 'hidden dish farm' is an additional example which offers the full array of satellite television channels without a dish in site!

— **Audio Visual Systems**

Whenever you and your employees are utilising audiovisual equipment, the chances are that this will take place when in front of an audience. As a result, good quality, reliable Audio-video devices are essential for many companies as there is nothing worse than a system that fails mid-presentation.

Some many situations and industries require an excellent AV system, for example, conference facilities, meeting rooms and even City trading floors.

— **Video Conferencing**

As verbal hints determine 55 % of communication, video conferencing is second only to being there. Consequently, this is one type of digital business solution that is being accepted by large numbers of people daily. The quality of the video, having no time delay and the ease of use have helped to make this a severe business device for a lot of organisations, especially since the charges involved have come down considerably.

CHAPTER 27: DIGITAL COUPON MARKETING FOR BUSINESS

It is said that "marketing is the life and soul of any business", put another way - without marketing then it becomes difficult for any organisation to continue to get its message out to its intended target market segments.

Marketing, of course, can be executed using different forms and methods such as...

— **Direct Mail**

— **Work Of Mouth**

— **Print Advertising**

— **Newspaper Ads**

— **Social Media**

— **BillBoard of Marketing**

... and the list could, of course, go on and on! The point is that the actual marketing strategy that any company chooses to undertake will depend on many factors such as the suite of products and services that the company produces along with the length of the sales cycle.

In terms of print media marketing, coupons have been seen to be very successful as customers like to collect the tickets to get those exclusive deals and offers. The type of cards that have been seen to work well is many and varied, such as Loyalty Coupons where customers will say get a cup of coffee free once they have purchased five cups. Another type of coupon that has been seen to work well is the Discount Coupon where the customer will present the ticket at the point of sale to claim a specific discount which will be applied to a product and service.

Now, when in the digital world, we can expand on the use of this form of marketing for which any business can make use of this channel to necessarily bring in more business. Digital marketing provides us with the ability to use coupons in the form of...

— **Scratch Card Coupons**

— **Loyalty Bonus Coupons**

— **Prize Draw Coupons**

— **Location Dependent Coupons**

— **Social Networking Sharing Coupons**

... and more which is made possible based on the use of technology. In essence, it is the use of technology which allows us to present scratch card coupons, which can be revealed on any smartphone.

It can save any company a great deal of money when it comes to printing costs; it also provides flexibility and the ability to run campaigns for shorter periods of times [as often there are minimum print quantities to take into consideration].

Printed coupons can still be used in conjunction with the technology; however; it is essential to note that one of the main differences is that clients are taken online to redeem the coupons. This gives the business a valuable lead generation system which they can use for follow-up within future promotions.

The use of digital coupon marketing is a fantastic way for businesses to engage with clients who are used to using technology in the form of their smartphones. Business owners are, in turn, able to build a database of leads while getting their offers and promotions out to a broader audience.

CREATING A LASTING IMPRESSION

The World Wide Web holds an estimated 4.82 billion indexed pages, approximately the equivalent of 136.2 billion pieces of papers.

With all this content out there battling for users' interaction, how can we stand out and create a lasting impression in such an already saturated digital world?

As a business or brand, you need to create a lasting impression on your target audiences to achieve your objectives, whether this is selling a service/product or merely promoting brand awareness and loyalty. To tackle these objectives, it is good practice to lay out a content marketing plan.

Creating and sharing content regularly is so important when attracting new customers and promoting brand awareness. However, to make an instant impression on the user, the content needs to be carefully considered and directed toward the correct target market, here are four things to bear in mind.

STRIVE FOR EMOTIONAL ATTACHMENT

Exploring the human element to a piece can help to generate a lasting impression. However, these can be extremely difficult to create. They don't tend to be directly promoting your company's product or service though it does have the brand at the forefront of the creation. Take the John Lewis Christmas ads, for example, Monty the Penguin and the Man on the Moon.

It's not slowly product-based and does not over reference the brand, but it pulls the viewer in by showing them something different, 'it's an advert with a heart'. It portrays this beautiful story that the viewer can relate to; they feel at ease with what they are viewing and enjoy the storytelling without feeling pressured into a sale.

They can develop an emotional attachment to the piece and referencing that heart-warming feeling with the brand, eventually creating loyalty and trust to the store itself.

CONSIDER YOUR AUDIENCE

Millennials, those born between 1982 and 2004, are an important demographic to consider. Researchers Howe and Strauss referred to them as "the next great generation". They are starting to become the spenders of this age and the target audience for many brands. They are also quite different from the other generations having been brought up with technology and the internet always at their fingertips.

50% would be more willing to purchase from a company if their purchase supports a cause. 46% have 200+ Facebook friends as compared to only 19% of non-millennials. This generation is used to quickly pass marketing with short bite-size content piece continually appearing in their day to day activities. 80% of the millennials want brands to entertain them, and 40% want to participate in the co-creation of brands and products.

HOW DOES THE ENVIRONMENT AFFECT YOUR CONTENT?

Where to place your content is essential in an online environment, many sites are flooded with ads that distract users from the content causing them to lose interest and move on quickly. The environment your content is going in should be studied before content creation. A thought piece might not get thoroughly read on a site like Yahoo where site sponsored ads are continually pulling the user onto the next section of content.

A better alternative would be to place it on a site like LinkedIn, where it can be studied in a less distracting context. You also need to consider where your audience is and what they have been brought to that website. Example of this is when seeding out a game: people are less likely to play it on a news site than a dedicated gaming site, as the gaming site targets passionate gamers who want to expand their knowledge and discover the next big thing.

SIMPLICITY IS KEY

You will only have a few seconds to create an impression that lasts so it should be possible to interact with your content and understand it immediately. You must keep it concrete and tangible. Aim to directly target unanswered question your audiences might have, to help break it down step by step. Keep it engaging, useful and bite-size. Often by stating the obvious and not trying to be too bright, people can relate to the message and understand it instantly and are therefore more likely to remember it.

Remember, we all work in a world of technology and are striving for people's attention. We need to create content that shows the viewer something different. Don't expose your restrictions, reveal the person behind the brand and don't feel limited by the unknown; confront your weakness.

This fresh, untouched content will look to create an emotional attachment with the piece, and the reader will relate to the honesty that is exposed.

CHAPTER 28: THE SALES CYCLE IN A DIGITAL WORLD

In the pre-digital world, the sales and marketing departments of companies often had well-defined routes from potential prospect to an actual customer. The direction a chance took from initial contact to making a purchase was known as the Sales Funnel.

And a lot of time and thought was given to understanding this customer journey, and how to fine-tune a company's sales funnel.

For instance, a potential customer may have begun their journey by filling in and posting a coupon they found in a magazine. As a result of this enquiry, they received a product brochure. And regularly, they received a sales newsletter with the latest offers from the company. On average, looking over the statistics of this process, the customers that did buy something did so in between their third and fifth mailing. And if they didn't buy anything by the eighth mailing, they never did.

DIGITAL MARKETING

If we now come forward to the digital age of marketing, we can only dream of something so simple. Nowadays, a potential customer can come into contact with a company through many different channels, technology and media.

There are still going to be off-line points of contact, such as a retail outlet or an industry conference. When we consider the online world, then there can be web browser searches, social media posts and interactions, specialist online stores (such as Amazon), videos posted on YouTube, company blog posts and articles, and so on. These all offer a company a new opportunity for greater engagement with potential customers. They also provide people with a powerful way to find the product or service they want, with a company that they want to deal with.

HOW TO MANAGE DIGITAL SALES FUNNEL?

Given the multiple ways that someone can come into contact with your business, how do you manage your sales funnel? And this is not only more complex because of the number of channels, but it is also more complicated because the same person may come into contact with your company in multiple ways before they make their buying decision.

The answer usually lies in a combination of metrics, designed to measure channel activity and sales results across the broad spectrum of your sales funnel.

ATTRIBUTION METRICS

Directly measuring activity in given channels is not enough. For example, just because your blog post was read twenty-five times last week, doesn't mean that it created any sales. Similarly, measuring just closed sales in a given month doesn't help either in determining how the customer got there.

So, the idea behind Attribution Metrics is that they combine both marketing and sales data, to give a clearer picture of what your sales funnel looks like, and how it is performing. Typically, these metrics will include:

- Traffic data from marketing channels
- Tracking your website and mobile app visitor behaviour
- Integrating with your CRM system, to connect on-site practice to sales data

Collecting these metrics is quite a challenge, given that most of this data exists on different technical platforms and in various data formats. If you have a small operation, then manually gathering this data may be feasible if you have the expertise. But for many larger companies, specialist software is needed to do this task efficiently and accurately.

INTERPRETING THE ATTRIBUTION METRICS

Having gathered the data, now the task of analysing it begins. Here are some examples of the sales and marketing insights you can gain.

1. How many interactions on average does it take with a potential customer before they buy?

2. Is there a principle channel for new potential customers (first contact)? Or do they come from many sources?

3. Over what time frame does a potential customer interact with your company before buying?

4. How many potential customers never make it to becoming actual customers?

5. What contribution do personal interactions with your company make to the final sale?

CHAPTER 29: THE SCOPE OF TODAY'S DIGITAL SPACE

Digital marketing today is a growing field. Why are so many big brands and companies opting for social media or digital marketing? The reason here is simple. Social media marketing can 'target' many of their customers in a much better way than other forms of marketing. The primary criterion for this decision is the fact that it can be personalized.

The more the brand interacts with them on a one- to- one level, i.e. as an individual, the more their consumers will be loyal to them. It adds an emotional quotient to the entire sales process. And as rightly said, a loyal customer means guaranteed sales. These are the main reasons that social media marketing is booming throughout the globe.

Since this field is still in its nascent stage, the 1st question that comes to our minds is What is digital marketing or what happens in this form of marketing? Online marketing companies or agencies handle the A-Z activity of a brand that happens online.

It includes a website or webpage designing, managing the site, regularly updating it, its presence on social networks etc. Not only these, but it also takes care of bringing in traffic to your website, increasing your ranking on organic search results and also placing you appropriately on paid ads.

In search marketing, the agency helps rank the brand's website higher than the competitive brands in the market by way of on-page and off-page optimization (SEO). It helps to get the companies webpage on the top naturally when searched through any online search engine like Google, Yahoo, and Bing.

The concept of paid search is also exciting. It is when the brand pays search engines to get their website in the top paid listing for any specific keyword. They are charged based on a single click known as pay per click (PPC). Another way is to pay per thousand impressions. It is when the search engine will project your website to 1000 users.

This scheme works in such a way that the brand has to pay the search engine whether the user has clicked the link or not, but the ad will be visible to 1000 people. It is typically used to build brand awareness. Last but not least comes the social media part.

This branch handles the brands on platforms like Facebook, Twitter, LinkedIn, Pinterest, Google+ and other accounts of social networking sites. They regularly post on these pages creating engagement, discussions, debates and notes for the brand's target audience. They even make applications, run campaigns, manage them and strive to make the content as attractive and creative as possible.

Thus, since so many people are well acquainted with the digital world, marketing companies cannot have a better option other than targeting consumers on the internet to enhance brand recognition, brand equity and of course sales.

FIND CUSTOMERS AND GIVE THEM WHAT THEY WANT SO THEY COME BACK

In today's digital business landscape, the reality is that customers talk about brands, and brands listen in on many different digital platforms. One of your goals as a digital strategist is to create a brand environment that invites customer and brand interactions, and through these interactions, collect demographic and preference information. With this customer information, you can better understand who they are and what they are looking for.

A practical approach for collecting your customer information is by setting up a demand generating (rich media) digital environment, such as a webcast, video, or podcast; another good digital option is a website resource centre. While there is a lot of attention placed on the tremendous big three social platforms, such as Facebook, LinkedIn and Twitter, productive media strategies can provide you with more engagement control and customer information (data), for sales leads, digital and email campaign strategies.

A company resource centre allows your customers to research your product or service, and as necessary, provides you with an opportunity to capture user information. This information can be converted into sales leads (where customers are in the buying cycle). Your resource centre should include not only white papers but more importantly embedded rich media and events.

In the digital world, customer demographic and preference information typically comes from email correspondences, social media, web site interactions, and transactions. This data can be collected by using forms, which provide the customer with a digital space to put their personal (preference) and business (demographic) information.

Now, this is where excellent data management skills come into play, why, because the data you upload to your marketing automation system or CRM should be error-free; the ease in which data can be pulled out from its database system, will also affect your campaign strategies effectiveness. As a digital strategist, you should have an understanding about how to use electronic forms (sometimes called short forms) as part of your plan, and also have a data plan.

A data-plan requires information to be standardized, which ensures that customer information is entered correctly; this process is called normalizing your data. Your automated data forms, where customers input their demographic and preference information, will also encourage customers to provide valuable intelligence information and enter it correctly.

Data entry forms can be useful in capturing anywhere from 16 to 20 fields of information from a customer. Generally speaking, a barometer for how much information customer will provide, depends on how many questions they initially complete. If they answer 7 or 8 items (demographic and preference), there is a good chance they will answer a total of 10 to 15 additional ones.

Remember, receiving sufficient demographic and preference information is critical to the next stage of your collection process; knowing if your leads are strong or weak (warm or cold). This information will also help you achieve a higher return (sales conversion rate) on your points.

Normalizing your customer data (writing everything the same way) before it is uploaded (by CSV or API method), into your marketing or CRM system will keep dirty data that is not labelled correctly, from entering your automation system. Allowing only properly labelled data will make it much easier to pull out the right customer information when you are ready to create leads for a digital campaign or sales team.

Ultimately you will be looking for lead information that provides sufficient demographic and preference customer data about where the buyer is in the buying process. This information translates into warm or cold sales leads. Warm leads are preferable because they are an indication that a particular customer is more interested in your product or service.

For example, proper normalization can prevent the following error from happening: August 10, 2017, and 8/10/2018 is the same date to Americans, but the following can mean October 10, 2018, if it is transferred to a database in some European countries.

Or even something as obvious as one automation system collecting customer location information using an abbreviation for a state (NY instead of New York), could cause problems in identifying the customer and potential sales lead for a campaign or first request. Why, because it may cause you to perform two or more database runs, and additional analysis to examine content with various state spelling types.

To fix this problem, you would want to normalize your data, although before you do that you would have to determine if the added person-hours it takes to correct it is within your campaign budget. On the other hand, not being able to use your customer data could cause you to lose some potentially valuable contacts for a campaign or sales lead strategy.

That being said, when data collection is automated, computer output is usually normalized. For data that is compiled and entered by humans, you should speak with your data input team regarding proper data entry rules so that you can maintain excellent normalization standards.

Once you have your customer data uploaded into your marketing or CRM automation system, you will want to decide which customers are more relevant for your campaign or sales team to contact. There is an effective and efficient way to ensure that some leads are more valuable than others, and that can be accomplished by rating and ranking your points, known as lead scoring.

This is the point when the analysis of your data takes on real value because lead scoring can improve sales conversion success rates. While It does take a systematic approach to work with your customer information, in the end, research shows that in enterprise business environments, lead scoring can increase a company's annual revenues by approximately 45 per cent, lead generation by 25 per cent, and reduce cost per lead by roughly 20 per cent.

An excellent way to begin your lead scoring analysis is to choose a scoring model that best reflects your current campaign strategy. Your sales and customer service teams should always provide input about what constitutes a good lead. Scoring of a customer's information (data) can begin at 1 and go as high as 100. Standard lead scoring models emphasize the following areas: demographics, which provide broad general customer information, and preference, which can be more granular and focus on behavioural influences.

With well-executed lead scoring, you can do a better job at managing your leads, find users, and bring them to your website or resource centre, which will then generate additional information through an auto-response back from your digital content.

An example of some widely used lead scoring models are high demand ones that emphasize user preferences (80 per cent behavioural and 20 per cent demographics), balanced (50 per cent demographics and 50 per cent preferences), and low activity demographics (80 per cent demographics and 20 per cent preferences), the last model is typically used by companies that are looking to reach as many new customers as possible quickly (generally unique companies), and may not be overly concerned about selectivity that preference information provides.

Worth noting is that personal preference information is more effective for sales purposes than demographics alone. Why, because demographics can change, while preferences tend not to. Research has shown that self-reporting conversions rates are 10 times greater, 1.0 per cent from self-reporting versus 0.1 per cent for demographics.

The lead scoring process should also be a collaborative process, with business units such as sales, customer service and marketing involved. Your scoring objectives are to evaluate data, map traits or habits of online users, understand conversion and threshold points, and determine the best-case elements of a sales-ready lead. Once you are accustomed to using this process, you will find that your customer data through scoring will lead to increased profits, better points, and added productivity.

Finally, over the past several years, a lot of attention has been placed on social media, engagement, and listening, with less on data management. Commitment through digital properties can be an exciting and motivating process, while data management is thought of like a less attractive technical task, left to a database administrator (DBA) and analytics specialist.

It is a misconception because normalization techniques and lead scoring are deeply rooted in a digital strategist's ability to be successful; to launch an effective lead generation or digital campaign that does more than engage and look great. As we move forward in the digital strategy process, we will increase our use of internet-based social technologies for business and communication purposes, and conversion rates and ROI expectations will rise.

That is why becoming more responsible and knowledgeable about the entire digital process (the funnel), through right digital strategies and practices, including using data strategically, is essential. A company's success depends on its sales team's ability to make a large number of deals in less time.

While I am not suggesting that you take on the DBA's and analytics responsibilities, but that you have a good understanding of why data management and analysis is essential and how to implement its practices.

It will also provide you with an additional opportunity to engage with your customers, create a feedback loop based on demographics and preferences. You will also be more successful as a strategist moving products or services. Having more knowledge about your customer can also extend the life of your customer relationship.

By adding a systematic approach to managing your digital data, such as using sufficient media demand generating strategies, data collection, normalization, and lead scoring, you will experience higher success rates with your digital strategy and digital properties. Why, because you will know where to find your customers, how to engage with them, and how to give them what they want, so they come back. These processes should be part of the digital strategists planning process because they are rooted in the digital engagement process.

CHAPTER 30: BRAND MARKETING - THE DIGITAL WAY

Brand marketing online has become the need of the hour. With the increasing number of net surfers who regularly visit search engines like Google, Yahoo, MSN etc. for their smallest needs and also to gain knowledge on various subjects it has become a necessity for every business to keep its presence in the web world.

Similarly, every individual and companies want their identity to be recognized through various social media sites and want all the public who are related to their business to visit their respective websites.

Thus, comes into picture the trend of digital brand marketing

As marketing is already a competitive field and its mode through the digital world makes it even more challenging. One of such processes is known as Search Engine Optimization (SEO). For the same, the brand manager has to initially do some research which involves a few steps, i.e.:

1. Understand the kind of work the business is handling.

2. Look into the competitors of the company and their websites.

3. Build a strategy for digital brand marketing.

4. Find the most searched keywords which can be used on the website so that the results of searching by net surfers will be the business website/link.

5. Build upon the content of the website following the keywords analyzed.

6. Post links on various websites.

7. Submit blogs, articles on most visited websites.

8. Do social bookmarking and press releases.

9. Gather the feedback and improvise on the process followed.

10. Upgrade the website with the input gathered and also form strategies for doing digital brand marketing following the changing trends in the web world. Through the steps followed by Search engine optimizer (the person who runs this process), the website of the business/individual is ranked ahead of its competitors so that there is business generated through this brand promotions online.

Therefore, it is vital for the search engine optimizer to have in-depth knowledge about website designing and the various modules that are included to develop a website, i.e. Photoshop, Flash, HTML, XML, CSS. As this demand for digital brand marketing is increasing, there is an increase for the employment of Search Engine optimizers and Website developers wherein web designing jobs and graphic designing courses need to be done.

A GROWING DIGITAL VENUE

The digital world is ever-expanding, and so is its marketplace. Consider this statistic from the U.S. Department of Commerce estimates consumers spent $513.61 billion online in 2018, up 14.2% from 2017.

Total retail sales increased 4.1% to $3.63 trillion, according to its figures. ... Through the first three quarters of the year, online sales grew a healthy 15.5%, which was higher than the previous three years.

The digital marketplace shows no signs of slowing down, either. Forecasts continue to show growth expectations.

In fact, a recent report in Internet Retailer shows that books and magazines sales grew by 12%, followed by computer software (excluding PC games) 7%; sports and fitness 6%; jewelry and watches 4%; video games, consoles and accessories 3%; consumer electronics 3%; and computers, peripherals and PDAs 1%.

What does this mean for the average online marketer? It means your piece of the pie could grow.

The internet is still growing in leaps and bounds, but you have to pick your primary market carefully. Niche markets showed steady improvement in sales and are an excellent place to start an online marketing business.

- **Niche markets with Growth Potential**

In addition to the exchanges listed above, including, but not limited to books, computer software, and sports and fitness, one of the largest growing niche markets is in health care. Again, statistics point to an opportunity waiting to be taken. Only 60% of companies offer health insurance plans for their workforce. Fact is internet marketers have turned to sell health care products in astounding numbers, some backed by legends in the financial world, but few offer health insurance through MLM campaigns or online marketing venues.

- **Go Green**

This niche market is in its infancy. Green products include roofing, linens, diamonds, building materials, power, plants, and just about anything you can think of that is made and designed to lessen negative impacts on the ecology. Pick a niche product with Green Seal Approval and key to it.

Online marketers should also consider affiliate programs with solid backgrounds in sales and support. Beware of the scam artists though, as some of these niche market promoters make promises, develop fictitious people to drive sales through deceit and deception, and are only in the game to take your hard-earned cash.

If you come across such a program, most states have an agency designed to handle such internet fraud. Do everyone in internet marketing a favour and report fraudulent applications immediately.

You can make a name, and a profit, for yourself with the most significant selling market merchants as an affiliate. The prominent marketers, or merchants, offer affiliate programs where you agree to put their products into the network. You draw customers to buy the products through your website. The merchants' affiliate programs offer cash or gifts to you for your services in return for the orders. Some pay as little as 15% on a sale, while others pay up to 75% of the sales for customers who purchase through your website.

But like any market, the digital venue as a marketplace is in constant change. Be ready to jump on the latest fads, market changes, and whims of consumers, and you'll be able to prosper in the digital venue.

CHAPTER 31: THE FUTURE OF MARKETING - THE CLOUD OR THE REAL WORLD

Digital marketing is the new avenue for companies to market their products efficiently to their target market. It's fast, reliable, cheap, and most of all, accurate.

The biggest concern in the field as of now is that the consumer is gaining control. Online ads are controllable as compared to their predecessors on TVs. They can be fast-forwarded, skipped, blocked if are pop-ups and if none of these, wholly ignored. The period to captivate the consumer has shrunk, and the demands have increased. Even the word 'FREE' in an advertisement doesn't quite do the job because it is evident to the consumer that there is a catch to it.

Even though it might sound like a threat, there is a bright side to it. It seems product placement is the new formula for a successful marketing campaign, especially an online one. An example is Sony that has used YouTube as a host most efficiently where movies and viewing pleasure is the primary goal, and Sony shares the same vision.

According to Forrester's, there is a definite increase in the expenditure of interactive and digital marketing in the US and also the ratio out of the total marketing budget. The most significant share goes to search marketing, i.e. marketing on different search engines and targeting every consumer according to his/her activity on the internet.

This method is quite efficient as it markets according to the query you give to the engine. It is the most effective and cheap. Display advertising is an online version of billboards, posters, etc., and the second-highest expenditure. The rest, Email, Social and Mobile marketing are equally as important as the first two.

Mobile marketing, although a young phenomenon has taken the world by a storm. Especially since the arrival of the phone like the iPhone, Smartphones, Blackberry and others, mobile marketing has opened up into a completely new avenue. Advertisements through applications from affiliations have combined all the aspects of online and old-fashioned marketing in a small and compact handheld device.

Social media is one of the quite obvious ones. The more people there are in a network, online or otherwise, the more potential of marketing therein exists. Networks like Facebook, LinkedIn, MySpace and many others generate their potential revenue from advertising sales.

Email Marketing, though it may not seem useful, is quite a massive expenditure for companies. Email cold calling works in quite a few valuable ways. If approached in the right manner, a sale can be considered definite.

The interesting fact, according to Forrester's, is that the overall advertising budgets will decline. It is quite the paradox as there will be an average of 17% increase in the total interactive marketing expenditure.

It leads us to the conclusion that online marketing is really quite cheap and will be the next milestone in the marketing world as companies will be gunning for top and be the most renowned brand in the digital world. But the right combination of these different techniques is the key.

PROTECTING YOUR BUSINESS'S DIGITAL DATA

If you have a business, it's likely that you now have some digital data or content that you are trying to protect for the long run such as digital receipts or online bills needed for tax time. This data is critical to you since it's something that you need to continue to have on hand to run your business effectively in a digital world. Learn some techniques that you can use that will help you protect this data in the long run.

The first thing that you need to do is make sure you do frequent backups from off your computer. It's a good habit to get into backing up at least once a week if not more, depending on how often you are adding digital documents that you don't want to lose.

There are online backup services that will automatically backup as often as you schedule it that will store the information offsite on a secure server. Make sure all your business information is backed up on a schedule automatically so that you don't forget.

Get spyware off your machine. You need a high-quality spyware protection tool. The problem with these programs is that they will get information on your computer habits, login information, and compromise a variety of things that you want to keep secure, especially banking information or personal accounting info.

Be sure to change your passwords from time to time. It's a good practice not always to have the same password for everything application that requires you to log in as well. There is software available that will safeguard your passwords by encrypting them as well as generating a random log on passwords with different numbers and symbols, so it is harder to crack.

Your email and contacts are critical. Be sure that you try to back up these as often as possible. Protect these in hard copy as well so that you know for sure that you always have these. Using an online backup storage solution also is a great as you can have two backups of these critical files.

Try to have open formats in your business. What these means are the formats that your files are saved in. Some forms are free meaning that they will be around forever. Other sizes are closed and owned by individual companies that could block your data in the future.

Try to move away from applications that are too restricted and have too many license issues. Open applications are something to consider for longevity. Even better is having control of your software.

CHAPTER 32: THE NEXT STEP IN THE WORLD OF MARKETING

There used to be a time when people were seen with magazines and newspapers in their hands, reading for long. It was the time when print media was flooded with advertisements of brands, both big and small. Today, the pace of life has left no time for such leisurely activities. Most of an individual's time is spent online, either for business or for fun. It is why online spaces have become the new billboards for advertising.

The trend of online activities is on the rise, and the only place an advertiser gets enough of a consumer's attention in the digital space. It makes digital advertising an exceedingly lucrative proposition.

Digital marketing has, over the years, established itself well in the eyes of the brands as well as consumers. Affording brands, a chance to develop themselves whereas giving the users the freedom to browse through advertisements at their convenience is what has brought about this change.

Digital marketing is a complex field that requires the knowledge of not only marketing but also sound know-how of how the digital world operates. Companies dealing in digital marketing have to keep track of consumer preferences, high traffic websites, trending topics and blogs, social media communication and a whole lot of statistics to device a successful campaign and execute it.

There are many ways in which a brand can use the advantages of digital marketing like emails, social and professional media websites like Facebook and LinkedIn, high traffic web pages like search engines, blogging sites like Twitter and other successfully running blogs and other channels that do not require access to the internet like digital TV etc. A strategically placed advertisement on any or all of these domains can result in handsome rewards if handled aptly.

Media planners are increasingly using rising proportions of digital marketing in their media plans devised for a particular brand or product. Owing to the changing trends in the browsing habits of consumers, the internet as a branding and advertising tool is gaining strength by the day. Marketers understand the opportunity extended by this shift in consumer preferences and are using it to the brands' advantage.

Apart from this, many new and upcoming brands are focusing just on digital marketing campaigns to boost their brand image and loyalty. Keeping a healthy appearance in the digital arena has turned out to be one of the most popular ways of staying in touch with customers, both existing and prospective. Rising global consumption of digital media offers a bright future for the field of digital marketing.

STRATEGIC MARKETING USING DIGITAL CHANNELS THE RIGHT WAY

If you are looking to implement marketing from a strategic perspective in your company or business endeavour by making use of digital channels, then it may well serve you to seek out some advice first. That's some of what we set out to do here as we look to highlight some of the ins and outs of executing marketing in the digital age.

There is more to digital marketing that ordinarily meets the eye as found in our consulting, devising and executing search engine and social media marketing campaigns.

When a company is looking to (via its marketing personnel or use of third-party agencies) market, its products and services use the available digital marketing channels such as...

— Video Marketing

— Email Marketing

— Search Engine Marketing

— Podcasting

— Blogging

— Social Media Marketing

— Micro Blogging

... all of the activities will need to be carried out via specific digital marketing channels to get engagement from chosen target market sector clients.

As an example of the statement made above; the decision could be made to use social media marketing and to connect with clients using an associated advertising platform through which to serve up ads.

Going through the process of crafting and executing specific ads necessitates that one understands who the target audience is that the business is concerned with so that time is not wasted running ads that will be ultimately shown up to people that are not interested in the related products or services that the company has to offer.

Going through the targeting process will determine where one's audience 'hangs out' so that when the message is seen, it is relatively easier to consume (or be interacted with).

When running ads within the social media marketing channel alongside that of publishing engaging and compelling content, connect, following and republishing others content.

It is essential to make sure that the ads are related to target clients likes, interests and aspirations as this will affect click-through rate, engagement and other factors that lead to the actual cost of running the ad itself.

The content aspect of digital marketing is indeed a critical and foundational one as one piece of content can effectively be repurposed for use in various formats and on differing platforms and digital marketing channels. E.g. a well-written article can be used as a blog post, then used as the basis for a podcast, this same piece of content can be developed into a video and then used to create multiple micro blogging content pieces.

Each piece of content should be used within planned digital marketing channels to deliver the marketing message through to the intended market segments.

With the world in which we live in becoming increasingly technology enabled; this is continuing to open up opportunities for marketers and business owners to present their message to clients found the world over.

However, it is essential to execute correctly and to start with the right messages, next the most appropriate digital marketing channel (some of which are listed above) are used to put the marketing message in front of the right audience. In other words, a targeted approach should use as opposed to a shotgun spray and hope approach.

At the end of the day, digital marketing is still a subset of marketing, and it has its own set of sub digital marketing channels. The strategic digital marketing approach is strongly recommended as when adhered to and the results start coming in, one will understand why it's essential to continue to adopt this approach to business promotion.

CHAPTER 33: CUSTOMER SERVICE STRATEGIES IN A DIGITAL WORLD

How to get your social media presence set up right so you can deal with customer complaints like a Pro

With social media being so prevalent, users often take to their favourite channel with their claims.

— 75% of users surveyed said they include social media when evaluating a purchase.

— 32% want a response within 30 minutes, and 42% expect a response in under an hour!

— When you set up, your social media, keep that in mind.

How to use social media for customer service

Using social media to manage customer complaints may seem like a burden, but the payoff is repeat business and happy customers.

Users often take to majors like Twitter and Facebook. Don't shy away from either even if you've received some nasty feedback in the past.

When you initially set up your accounts, you entered an email to register, and you've probably noticed unless you changed the settings you get an email every time someone is active on your page/profile.

If you find this bothersome try creating an email like customer service @example.com that forwards to your account or the account of an employee whose job it is to monitor your online presence.

If it's directed to your email, create a folder or label specifically for customer service or PR that these emails automatically go to. Don't let it get lost in your emails though or you'll miss alerts.

Depending on your email setup this will vary in execution

These alerts will let you know when you have a new comment or message on your profile.

When you get one have a response protocol ready? You don't want to jump on a complaint and then have to wait 2 days for a decision-maker to draft their response.

One single meeting with your team on customer service/PR protocol on social platforms can save you a lot of headaches.

Have canned responses ready

Canned responses refer to an automatically generated answer that is prompted by the user contacting you. You may have seen these in the past and wondered how they get set up; now you get to set them up for yourself:

TWITTER

Twitter rolled out some great tools last year for users who operate their business online:

That link allows you to upgrade your account with messages that will automatically send to anyone who messages you directly and will show users that you provide this option. Your account will show your support hours, and users will see that you take their feedback seriously.

It is an excellent signal to Google too - that you're serious about your business and helping customers.

If you want more help using Twitter, try our section dedicated to using Twitter for business.

FACEBOOK

Facebook also allows you to set up your account to help communicate with customers via instant messaging. To turn on instant replies to any instant message to your business's page, follow these instructions:

To turn on Instant Replies for your Page:

1. Click Settings at the top of your Page

2. Click Messaging in the left column

3. Below Response Assistant, click to select Yes next to Send Instant Replies to anyone who messages your Page

4. To change your instant reply message, click Change, update the message and click Save

To turn off, Instant Replies:

1. Click Settings at the top of your Page

2. Click Messaging in the left column

3. Below Response Assistant, click to select No next to Send Instant Replies to anyone who messages your Page

You can direct users in both instances towards a contact email or let them know you'll review their message within the next 24 hours and respond.

Once you have these setup, how you use them is entirely up to you. Each was only available within the last 2 years, so not all businesses have adapted yet, but those that have done it have set user's expectations.

MONITOR YOUR REVIEWS

Whether it's Yelp (who's results are now actually trending in SERPs) Google reviews or Facebook reviews (if you have them turned on) it's essential to stay on top of your studies. There could be even more players in your niche, so be on the lookout for sites dedicated to reviewing your products or services. If you get a bad one, you don't want to remove it. That would defeat the purposes of the reviews.

Instead, use the platform's response option to address the reviewer's concerns.

By demonstrating to users, you take their feedback and complaints seriously, you show them they can trust they'll be treated with the same respect should things go wrong between you and them. The point of PR and customer feedback should not be to defend yourself outright.

While some users may be serial complainers or even thieves always assume the best in the customer.

Use their complaint or question as an opportunity to possibly address something within your business you should have paid attention to a long time ago.

Often, you'll find the customer has either made an error, or there's a genuine issue you need to address with your business.

Whatever the case, keep in mind what you post will be what users see when reading up on your company. Not only that but Google looks for signals of a bad business in online engagement and reviews as well.

Position yourself as a responsible business owner who will address their concerns, so whenever someone reads about your business, they get the right impression.

Just because a lot of customer service has moved online doesn't change the fact that your business needs to give an excellent impression to potential users/customers.

Put a smile on people's faces as much as possible, and your social media can help you grow.

Tim Griffiths

DIGITAL MARKETTING

CHAPTER 34: SETTING CLIENT BOUNDARIES

Do you ever feel with today's technology, one of the hardest things for a small business owner, entrepreneur, or solopreneur can be establishing boundaries with your clients? You certainly want your clients to feel that you are accessible; however, it is just as crucial for you to have a personal life apart from the business.

Making yourself accessible to your clients is simple. You can provide them with various means to contact you:

— Email address

— Website

— Phone number - office, fax, and cellphone

— Social media account - Facebook, Twitter, LinkedIn, etc.

Even though this is a good marketing strategy, clients may start to get the idea that you are "on-call" 24/7. If this is a benefit of doing business with you... that is fine, but if it's not, you may find yourself torn between responding to a client and spending time with family and friends.

— **Where To Start**

If your clients send you late evening or weekend messages on Facebook or text regarding a new idea, they would like to run by you, and this is where you can start setting the boundaries. Responding immediately will give your stamp of approval that this is OK. Instead, you would want to wait and react in the next business day (if there is no emergency) and mention your business hours for future reference. Setting time and access boundaries can be done professionally and politely. You are the only one who with the power to take your personal life back.

— **Autoresponder**

It is a feature most email platforms offer, and people have used for years. It is most commonly referred to as an "Out of office" message. The autoresponder allows you to automatically respond to every email with a pre-crafted response that can be changed daily to reflect your schedule. You can use this feature if you are going to be in a meeting all day and want to let the sender know their email was received and you will respond personally when you return. There are also apps for smartphones that can be used similarly.

By acknowledging the client's communication with an automated message, they feel comfortable that you will get back to them with an answer. Otherwise, they may call, text, or email several times, not knowing you are unavailable.

— **Separate Business/Personal Numbers**

It used to be that you had to carry a personal cell phone and a business cell if you wanted to have 2 different phone numbers. There are now companies who offer a service where you can receive calls from 2 different number on one cell phone. The app allows you to assign distinguishable rings plus many more features which will prevent your time from being interrupted by business calls.

These are only a few ways you can begin to set boundaries, so your business does not consume your personal life.

The next step is establishing and communicating these boundaries to your clients. Remember, if you don't treat your particular time and space as a priority, they won't either.

REASONS WHY YOU NEED TO GO DIGITAL WITH YOUR BUSINESS

When the internet and digital era dawned on planet earth, it was for a select few.

The necessary equipment like computers or the software needed to be connected online was very costly, and only the top companies were able to fund the luxury of being online.

In just a few years, the scenario has flipped over as we now come to terms with the fact that the digital lifestyle is the new way of life. With online connection progressing from stationary desktops to all kinds of mobile devices and the cost of having an internet connection that is fast and reliable continuously becoming more competitive, there can be no denying that the new world is that of artificial intelligence.

It is said that the industry of social games has the highest potential with a registered growth rate of over 180% in just the last 5 years.

What about business management meetings? Well, they aren't happening in a brick and mortar room anymore. That old method of working is slowly phasing out as we see more and more companies creating virtual teams from all around the world thus increasing the potential growth for virtual data rooms which according to records comes in at a second place.

The third-place, according to IBISWorld, is handed over to Online Shoe sales (my favorite) and rightly so. The online business of shoewear is growing each year tremendously, with an average estimate of 16%. Suffice it to say, the shoe industry folks have got a handle on this digital lifestyle thing.

With just that little example, the facts scream enough that online visibility equals business visibility, which, as we know, translates to a healthy business.

Everyone is online... Are You?

Regardless of what you sell, the services you offer or the profession you might be in - it is about time for you to embrace change and ditch that old lifestyle for a new digital one. Here are 6 Reasons Why:

1. Freedom To Work With More Flexibility

Let's face it, and no other opportunity can offer you the flexibility of working from anywhere in the world at different times of the year than the online platform. From a home office, the beach, a cafe or your company board room - the internet gives you options so you can enjoy more liberty in your life.

2. Greater Fulfilment Bigger Impact

As more and more people awaken to the more significant and more accurate meaning of life, work is becoming more heart-centered and in service to fellow human beings. People are more determined to discover their talents and gifts to bless and help others. If you are reading this, I bet you are too; the digital world makes it easier to reach the right people across the world who need you the most without getting on a plane. Can it get any better than that?

3. Profit Momentum

Do you usually do some quick online research nowadays before buying what you want? If so, you're not alone. More and more people are doing online research before making a purchase causing the return on investment for online marketing to be on an all-time high.

According to a report by the Altagamma-Mckinsey Online Observatory, 20% of all online and in-store sales were driven by online marketing. It also found that total sales from solely digital marketing brought in a sweet $12.5 billion optimal profit. What's even better is that these numbers are expected to reach about $27.8 billion in just the next 5 years. If you haven't started working out your profit momentum, now would be a great time.

4. Diversity, Interaction, and Reinvention

Choosing to go digital with your business or company gives your customers a unique experience with options for their preference. Digital content can contain links, videos, audio, and other multimedia. Your audience can engage with the platform that best suits them, and it also gives you a chance ever to renew yourself.

Reinventing a business always carries a substantial cost but not on the online space because you get the chance to produce the same message in an infinite number of ways at a minimum cost thus ensuring you remain fresh and trending in your space.

5. Measuring Success

The easiest way to track the progress of a business is when it's online. There are so many simple tools, software analytics, and so on that are very often provided by the hosting company or readily available as an app. These little things go a long way in helping you scale what you are doing right and what needs to be handled before any significant issues hit.

6. Less Messy

Going digital is a must for anyone who loves being environmentally conscious and as well for anyone tired of the messy paperwork. Filing and archiving things the old way is time-consuming and highly ineffective.

How many cabinets does a business need to keep all critical documents? Are they safe? The responsible organization is the way to further progress for humanity, and there are lots of software and applications available to ensure you cost-effectively do just that.

CHAPTER 35: DIGITAL APPROACH - WAY AHEAD

We have been talking about the digital journey. Old uncertain approaches won't deliver; you need absolute clarity about digital's demands, customer's digital vision, strong leadership, and unparalleled agility. If there is one theme, I hear consistently it's that consumers expect the brands they engage with to provide a flawless digital experience in their interactions. That applies to all type of industry, be it retail, information technology, or some other and all have their way of defining a digital experience.

Project Managers in many organizations lack clarity on what "digital" means for approach. They underestimate the degree to which digital is disrupting their businesses, accounts, and projects.

They also overlook the speed with which digital ecosystems are blurring industry boundaries and shifting the competitive balance. What's more, responding to digital by building new businesses and moving resources away from old ones can be threatening to individual project managers and executives, who may, therefore, be slow to embrace the needed change.

The only way for leaders to cut through inactivity is to take bold steps to understand below areas-

You should fight the resistance to change. You should appreciate the customer's vision on a digital journey through programmatic efforts. You should envisage an active digital approach by inspecting outcome as you go. And you should fight impossibility of knowing- a constant challenge given the simultaneous need to digitize your core and innovate with new business processes.

1. Resistance to change

Many project managers and senior executives aren't fully fluent in what digital is, much less up to speed on the ways it can change how their businesses operate or the competitive context.

That's challenging. Project managers who aren't acquainted with digital are much more likely to fall prey to the "shiny object" syndrome: investing in cool digital technologies without a clear understanding of how they will generate value in their accounts/projects. They also are more likely to make fragmented, overlapping, or sub-scale digital investments; to pursue initiatives in the wrong order, or to skip foundational moves that would enable more advanced ones to pan out.

Finally, this lack of grounding slows down the rate at which a business deploys new digital technologies. In an era of compelling first-mover advantages, winners routinely lead the pack in leveraging cutting-edge digital technologies at scale to pull further ahead. Having only a remedial understanding of trends and techniques has become dangerous.

— **Improve your technology skills**

For inspiration on how to raise your accounts collective technology skills, consider the experience of a global IT firm that knew it had to digitize but didn't think its leadership team had the expertise to drive the needed changes.

The company created a digital training portal to help educate its leadership about relevant digital trends and technologies. Training leaders also brought in external experts on a few topics the company lacked sufficient internal expertise to address.

Supplementing the training effort was an organization-wide assessment of digital capabilities and an evaluation of the company's culture. It provided a fact base, which everyone could understand, about what the organization needed to build throughout the digital transformation. It may help project managers and executives to get ready on new technology skills.

2. Understand customer's vision on a digital journey

Getting left behind by digital-first movers can be dangerous to your projects/accounts future. But many of account heads or executives may perceive responding to digital-making the big bets, building new businesses, shifting resources away from old ones-as hazardous to their future.

If you want to make big digital moves, you must understand the customer's vision on a digital journey and fight the fear that your top team and managers will inevitably experience.

Projects that succeed in creating a digital customer value proposition don't get there by accident. They develop a clear vision of how they will meet their customers' digital needs, set objectives against that vision, and execute - often over multiple years. Often, projects that are not succeeding only haven't painted a clear picture of what they want - or need - to be when they digitally "grow up."

— **Design a programmatic effort**

You need to design a programmatic effort with the same rigor you would insist on to redesign key processes across your accounts or projects. It typically involves making a clear case that executives can't hide from the change's digital is bringing and that encouraging and accelerating change - rather than chasing it - can create more value.

Then you need to give executives the tools and support network they must have to succeed as leaders of that journey. Two critical points where the entire focus should go -

First, be on top of technology trends, which includes keeping apprised of relevant emerging technology and shifts in consumer behaviour as it pertains to technology.

Second, establish processes designed to generate portfolios of potential ideas for the future state of the customer journey. These processes should allow your account to create business hypotheses and vet and test them via customer research.

In turn, new ideas can be aligned to the vision for how the customer of the future should interact with the brand or business processes, iterating along the way as more learnings come in

3. Strong digital approach

Pursuing an aggressive digital strategy involves leaps into the unknown: simultaneously, you are likely to be moving into new areas and fixing existing businesses with new technologies. What's more, in many digital projects, the premium of being a first-mover makes it necessary not only to shift direction but also to do so faster than your peers. The combination of ambiguity and the need for speed sometimes gives rise to guesswork and moves that are hasty or poorly thought out-and to anxiety about whether a step isn't going to work or needs more time hence healthy digital approach with multistage to vet outcomes

— **Inspect outcomes as you go**

One way to battle guesswork is to anchor your approach decisions to a thesis about the business outcomes that different digital investments will produce. It is more about thinking that draws fast, ground-level lessons from the data to determine whether your business logic is correct.

Put another way, and it means figuring out if there is sufficient value to make it worthwhile to invest something-as part of a process of learning even more. This approach increases the odds of successful implementation: a well-articulated view of the outcomes means that you can track how well the plan is working.

4. Fighting - Impossibility of knowing

Most companies including mine, we know are trying, and struggling, to do two things at once: to reinvent the core by digitising and automating some of its key elements, for example, and to create innovative new digital businesses.

The challenge is acute because of the dizzying pace of digital change and the uncertainty surrounding the adoption of new technology. Even if the technology for autonomous vehicles pans out, for instance, when will the majority of people begin to use them? Given the impossibility of knowing, it's easy to wind up with an unfocused hodgepodge of digital initiatives.

- Experimentation re-thinking

Real success in digital is rarely about providing the same products and services, just through a digital pipe. Netflix shifted from DVDs to streaming. Uber created the world's largest car service without buying any vehicles or hiring any drivers.

Companies that successfully "cross the chasm" to digital effectiveness often discover they need to provide for free what they used to charge for, sell as a subscription what used to be "a la carte," and re-think how they derive revenue from the value that they create.

Those that do so flexibly can often find that the adoption of a digital strategy or approach offers more scale, revenue and profit than the legacy approach, but it takes experimentation, an assumption of risk, and - to be blunt - some failure along the way.

Today's leaders need to step up by persuading their organizations, accounts and projects that digital approach may be more stringent than other methods but are potentially more rewarding and well worth the bolder bets and cultural reforms required, first, to survive and, ultimately, to thrive. Your best digital opponents - the ones you need to worry about aren't taking small steps. Neither can you.

It doesn't mean that a digital approach must be designed or put to work with any less confidence than methods were in the past, though. The procedure has always required closing gaps in knowledge about complex markets, inspiring leadership team to go beyond their fears and reluctance to act.

CHAPTER 36: DIGITAL OR BUSINESS TRANSFORMATION

Digital transformation refers to the changes associated with the application of digital technology in all aspects of human society. Digital transformation may be thought as the third stage of embracing digital technologies: digital competence, → digital literacy, → digital transformation.

The latter stage means that digital usages inherently enable new types of innovation and creativity in a particular domain, rather than enhance and support the traditional methods.

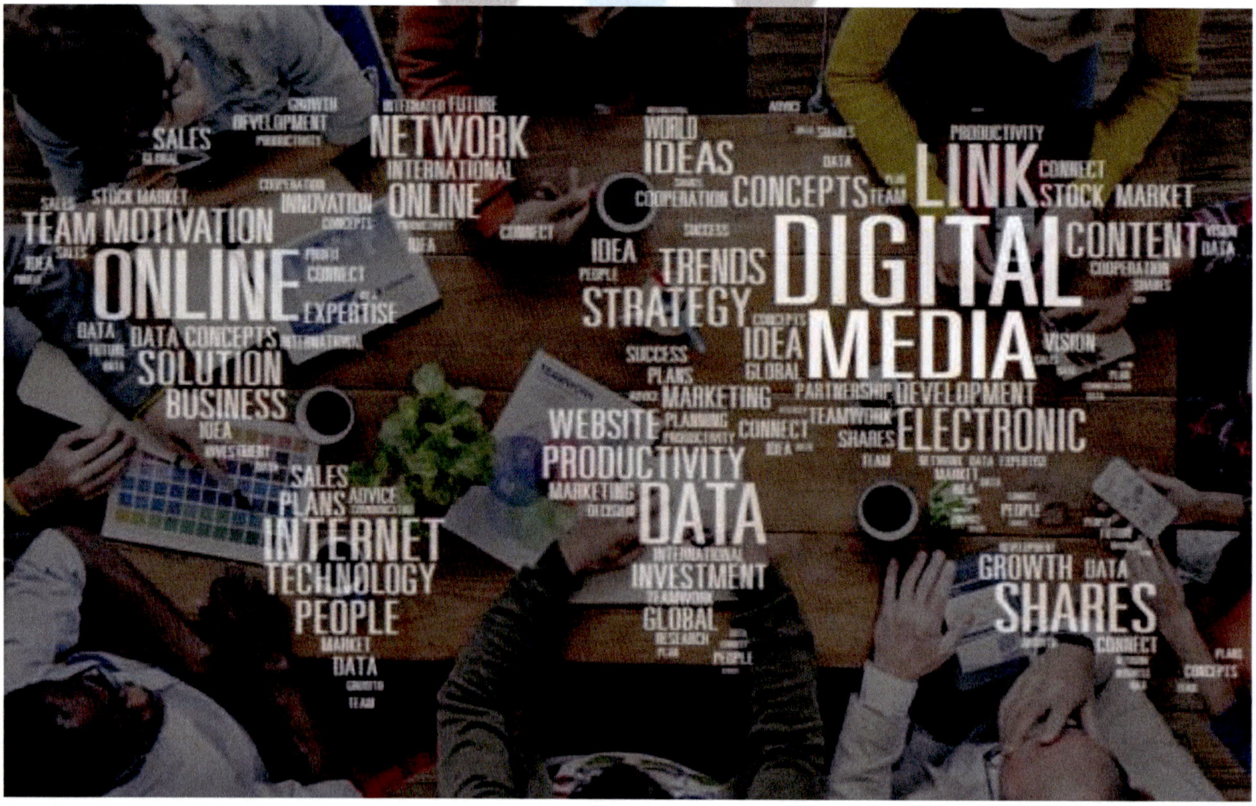

— Wikipedia

It has been more than 30 years since computers had been introduced into the business world. With the help of, powerful mobile devices and high connectivity, now we are living in a momentary world that is evolving so fast towards digital that now the digital transformation is inevitable.

Most of the C-Levels in corporations started to pay more and more attention to Digital Transformation.

They believe, without this transformation, even a long-established company may extinct. It is the Kodak example they are afraid of. The risk is there, however, is 'Digital Transformation' just enough?

Marketing, sales, manufacturing, finance processes should all be digitised to fulfil the transformation. It includes working anywhere anytime, broader and faster communication, enterprise integration that would enable performance & efficiency improvements.

That is all well planned and should be executed step by step. Can you imagine any change to be internalised without a holistic approach? Without embarking every team member, adjusting/improving their competencies, engaging them all around the same evolving mindset...

That's why we believe this topic should be handled with a broader scope, and it is the reason behind we like to call it a "Business Transformation' rather than a digital transformation.

In other words, Business Transformation shall handle the topic more broadly, including mindset and organisations, leadership and entrepreneurial mindset, education and pragmatic planning.

YOUR BUSINESS TRANSFORMATION JOURNEY IS UNIqUE

Every company has its inner dynamics, and every category has its realities; hence, your trip should be tailor-made to your business. When there is so much at stake, it is not an easy task to move the rocks around, without rigour planning, sufficient on-boarding, kicking off the new mindset with an adjusted organisational structure.

MINDSET & ORGANISATION

Any change in a company first impacts its resources, starting from a human. Top-down transformation approaches tend to stay at the top level with Digital Transformation Teams, causing manager level (or further) to think it is not their business. The only way to beat the resistance to change is to embark the resistors ASAP.

Corporate and entrepreneurial mindsets are two far ends, thus moving from one to other is not given.

However, with the power of a corporate company, an entrepreneur mindset can achieve higher goals sooner. That's why we should keep on increasing skills of the individuals in our organisation, empowering them to move forward within the team.

THE IMPACT ON CONSUMER EXPERIENCE

Digital transformation for the consumer end includes an architecture of your digital ecosystem to be able to do better listening, segmentation and tracking, enabling you to increase your digital media investments efficiency, letting you fish where the fishes are.

All these changes will have a positive impact on your consumer engagement and thanks to the new tools, and we will be able to measure the ROI of your campaigns/activities.

STEP BY STEP APPROACH

As said, digital transformation is a crucial stage throughout this journey. All your existing processes should be analysed with expert analysts according to the dynamics of your company and industry. Only after then, a solution can be determined and tailored to your needs. The gains here are not necessarily immediate; therefore, long-term investments should be planned with an entrepreneur mindset.

All in all, Digital Transformation is inevitable in this era; we need to think about it as broad as it requires to land it well in your organisation.

— What Does Digital Transformation Mean For Your Business?

Accepting and moving toward digital transformation doesn't merely mean jumping on every technological bandwagon that comes along. Doing that is like putting a bunch of cut-up vegetables in a pot and calling it soup.

Unless you put the right ingredients in the pot and turn on the stove, you'll never make soup-at least not a bowl of soup that anyone wants to eat. Instead, each company has to spend some time thinking about what digital transformation means for them.

Companies need to think about transitioning core business processes and digitalizing the client/business process first. They have to think about which applications, platforms, and solutions fit into their culture, daily operations, and budget.

There is, unfortunately, no cookie cutter solution that businesses can opt into. It's a process that requires personalization and a knack for following trends.

DIGITAL DISRUPTION AND FOCUSING ON THE CONSUMER

Digital disruption is another crucial term that describes what digital transformation can do in society at large. Smartphones created a disruption, Uber created a disturbance, and wearable technology continues to create disruptions.

With each critical technological advancement, the daily lives of consumers change a little more. The norm is shaken up, and the advancement adds value to consumers. Businesses that take advantage of the new changes, and who understand how these changes affect daily life, can modify their practices to meet the needs of the consumer.

Consumer-centrism is one way to ensure that you're meeting the demands of the digital age.

Knowing where your customers are interacting online and how you can reach them on their turf will enhance your ability to make their lives easier and to make sales.

Every business has to think about digital transformation and the power of disruptions now. There is no longer time to take baby steps and get your feet wet. It's a sink or swims environment for many businesses.

PLANNING AHEAD FOR DIGITAL TRANSFORMATION

Digital transformation is both a result and an ongoing process. You have to make the initial move, and then you must continue to evolve or be forced out. There is no quick fix for digital transformation. When you sit down with your team to discuss your company's digital future, think about the near future, but also the long-term goals of your company. To maintain relevancy, you will need to implement digital solutions that keep your company moving forward into the digital era and not standing still or moving backward.

At every step, think about the business experience. What can you implement to streamline in-house operations? What can you implement to facilitate customer interactions? These aspects that will drive your digital transformation. For some companies that may mean adopting an integrated payment solution so that customers can log in to an online portal and pay their bills. For others, it may mean getting on social media and posting relevant content on a regular basis. Any move to the digital space is part of the digital transformation.

Over the long term, the digital experience will shift. How can you make changing a more natural part of the business process? Transparency, a group mission toward digital relevance, and constant listening to customer behaviors may all be necessary for shifting your company's focus away from legacy business practices and to a more digital oriented future.

If your business is seeking to get into the race of digital transformation, it is important to act right now. Late adopters can have severe disadvantages since the competition is already in the domain. If you are looking to adopt a business model that utilizes a digital core, we can help. Embrace the digital transformation with the best developers to get to the forefront of change.

WHY IT'S IMPORTANT TO TRANSFORM YOUR BUSINESS DIGITALLY

"Digital Transformation" isn't just a buzzword. It's a core concept of the business model. And by the time you're done reading this, you'll know why it should be a core concept of your own business.

Digital Transformation many times can bring your sales and marketing from the physical world of phone calls, fliers, and mailings to the Internet. These older "analog" techniques are still valid, but they are becoming much less effective over time.

Why is that? E-commerce technologies have reached a point that they're blowing physical advertising out of the water.

People are still buying things more than ever though, but where are they doing it? They're buying on the web instead of walking into a store. Have you heard of "showrooming"? It is a term that retailers use for people who go to a store to get experience with a physical product then search for the best price online.

Best Buy, in particular, had this happen so much that they've made this part of their business model, hoping to push people to buy the product in the store through the Best Buy website. (Smart thinking Best Buy, way to digitally transform instead of continuing to fight it!)

What if you have a service business instead of a retail business? You're still in trouble. Customers aren't letting their fingers do the walking through the Yellow Pages anymore.

Instead, they're turning to Yelp and Angie's List. Yelp and sites like it have a significant advantage over older methods of service advertising. They not only can display more information, but they provide social proof of customer reviews.

Customer reviews are the dominant force in demonstrating reputation in the online world.

We used to call this word-of-mouth advertising, but now sites like Yelp allow a single person's voice to reach your entire market (at least the ones who check Yelp, 132 million monthly visitors in Q1 2014 according to the site) and color other people's perception of you for good or for ill. We like to call this "digital-mouth" advertising.

BASIC ONLINE PRESENCE IS NOT ENOUGH

Perhaps you think you're ahead of the curve. You have a website and some social media presence. Isn't that enough? Sadly to say it isn't. Many business websites don't have much more information than a standard Yelp page.

Social media is treated more like a billboard than a customer interaction platform. Worst of all, if a visitor wants to convert, they have to go back to things like the telephone or primary email to get in touch with you. They violate one of my four pillars of digital transformation, the digital hook.

The mobile web has made it so easy to convert visitors that websites shouldn't be called websites anymore. Instead, you can call them "customer acquisition engines." The fundamental shift is that your online presence needs to move from a pure marketing standpoint toward both sales and marketing. Not only that, but customer data should be tracked over time to generate an ongoing relationship with an individual visitor, urging them to convert again and again until they become loyal customers.

Impossible you say? With today's technology, it is entirely possible. You may have seen some of the tactics yourself. If you use Facebook and don't have an ad blocker on, try visiting a few business sites or talk about a topic a few times. Notice what ads you get on the sidebar. Most of the time, you're going to start seeing ads that relate to what you saw or talked about.

In fact, by merely visiting a site, companies can now start to get marketing data on you immediately.

Technologies like tracking pixels can trace an individual visitor as they come and go from a site. It allows you to push ads about your business to them on other sites. When they come back, that information can be read and let the visitor pick up where they left off in the sales cycle.

CHAPTER 37: CHALLENGES OF SELLING DIGITAL PRODUCTS

While there are many advantages to a digital business with digital products, it doesn't come without its fair share of challenges. In addition to all the regular tasks of running a business, a digital marketing also has to deal with unique issues.

First of all, because there is usually a minimal cost associated with creating and distributing digital products, the market can tend to be oversaturated. Anyone with an Internet connection and a video camera can create a training video, just like anyone with Microsoft Word can create an e-book. So not only does your digital product have to be distinguishable from everything else that's already out there, it has to be so much better than everyone else that you can sell yours and make money from it.

That's only partly true.

While you do need to be able to make money off your digital products, you don't have to make money off all of your products. Because there is no cost to store or copy these products, many businesses decide to give some of their products away for free.

In principle, this will help build exposure to their company and their brand, generating return customers, which can then lead to increased sales.

It can also help make up for when your digital product gets copied and redistributed without your knowledge or consent, which will happen. (This is another challenge; some people don't want to pay for digital products.) While you can do what you can to help combat piracy, using that detail and encouraging people to share it for free may help advertise your business.

Speaking of advertising, this can be an additional challenge for this type of product. Online marketing is an entirely different world than traditional marketing strategies and brings with its fierce competition. The world of online marketing can be challenging to master but is certainly not impossible.

With this business model, you also have to be sure your website is welcoming and easy to navigate, that people can quickly and successfully order/download/access whatever they need to (at all times; you can't just put up a "closed" or "out for lunch" sign), and that you're website is secure. Customer service can't suffer just because your product or service is digital.

However, none of these challenges is insurmountable. With the proper education and drive, you can overcome these and other problems and reap all the benefits digital products have to offer.

SAVING TIME, MONEY AND THE PLANET

For over 150 years, businesses have relied on printed media to get their marketing message out and reach their marketing goals. Even after the advent of electronic media, including computers, the dependence on and usage of print media marketing material stayed tremendous. However, the emergence and growth of digital media have changed the landscape.

Next, to business cards and advertising fliers, some of the most used printed marketing pieces are brochures and catalogues. It is especially true for businesses that sell physical products, both retail and wholesale. Brochures and catalogues are distributed usually in three different ways: at point of sale, via off-site salespeople and indirectly via mail and third-party publication inserts.

Most of the time, these pieces need to be of high quality (especially catalogues) to be effective. The production and distribution costs for this have skyrocketed, so much so that many companies either started to charge a fee for their catalogue or discontinued them altogether.

Many companies turned to publish digital brochures and digital catalogues to reduce their marketing costs, at least initially. The ability to do this was made possible by the considerable presence and usage of the World Wide Web.

Now it was possible to not only digitally produce the brochures and catalogues, but also to digitally distribute them via the web. Of course, having a "hard copy" of these pieces was still necessary. It yet could be done digitally, via putting the part on a computer CD/DVD and recently, miniature flash drives.

However, businesses soon discovered that there are many other significant advantages besides saving on costs. Today's internet world has created an enormous demand and even dependence on multimedia to get information. It also applies to actual and potential customers. People want and expect to see videos, hear audio and play with interactive graphics. It can only be accomplished via electronic brochures and digital catalogues, whether via the web or on a stored memory device.

People today also expect things to be current and very fresh, not static. They are always looking for something new or different. While it is unfeasible to satisfy the readers demand this via print media, electronic media accomplishes this very well. Digital brochures and catalogues can be revised and updated on a widespread basis. It allows companies to make a note of periodic sales and special events, take advantage of a marketing opportunity or even respond to a marketing threat.

Some of the most significant advantages are available by using online brochures and catalogues. With modern web applications, companies can now track who and where their potential and actual customers are. It is possible to ascertain which exact items in a catalogue are being looked at and which aren't.

It allows companies to identify and take advantage of trends and adjust inventories and even pricing. A huge benefit is an ability for the reader to get live online assistance and to make purchases by merely pointing and clicking.

While the continued use of printed brochures and catalogues will be necessary for individual companies, today's digital information age requires all companies to utilize digital marketing pieces.

CHAPTER 38: USE OF DIGITAL MARKETING IN THE TRAVEL INDUSTRY

Digital marketing applies to all fields of business, be it textiles, electronics or even travel. Recently, marketing is done via the internet due to the vast consumer market using the internet frequently.

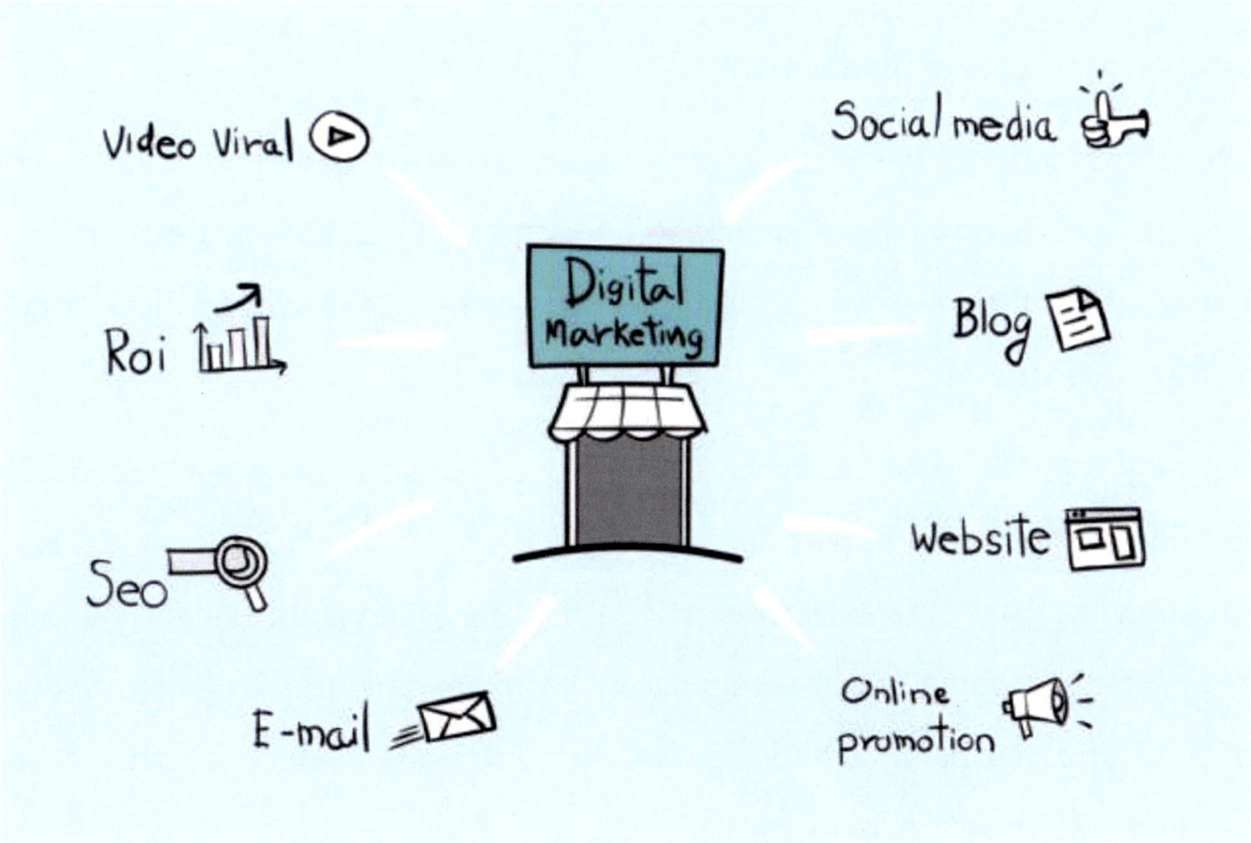

Before extensive use of the internet, it used to be focused on the radio, television and mobiles. As more and more people use the internet, from prominent businesspeople to the common public, it has also changed its focus from the above means to the internet. Now you will see numerous ads and posts on various web sites and web pages.

Why do companies all over the world use these techniques? Well, the answer is quite simple. It focuses on a large number of people at the same time. You might like to argue with the fact that so does print media, but digital media is fast and delivers information in a matter of seconds. Customers prefer knowledge in real-time, and they also prefer companies which advertise online.

Due to the significant prospects of success in the marketing field, many companies and agencies have been established due to the very fact of the worldwide success of digital marketing.

These agencies and consultancies provide services in the field of marketing such as giving advice on which digital marketing strategy would be the best for your company and they also guide you step by step on how to plan out your strategy and execute it.

Recently, it has become a significant trend for advertisers to use search engines for advertising their products. This is quite a successful tactic and is a win-win situation, as both the advertisers and the search engines benefit by this arrangement. Google, which is a significant search engine used by many nations of the world, has been advertising many products online. Recently, they have even entered the travel industry.

Google bought the ITA software for $700 million, making it the sixth-largest transaction Google has ever made.

What was the reason behind this large sum of money? Well for starters, Google wanted to expand into every industry, and the travel industry seems to hold a lot of potentials. Also, this deal would give Google an edge over its competitors, making it even more formidable as a competitor.

What is ITA? Well, it is software which provides behind-the-scenes data on flight times along with available seats and price levels. It helps not only travel agencies but also regular consumers who want information.

The deal has caused quite a lot of turmoil amongst travel agencies and Google's competitors. Travel agencies are afraid that their job would be taken over if Google could simple provide flight information on search results and Google's other competitors are worried of the fact that Google would now have complete control of the internet.

WEB DESIGN FOR THE TRAVEL INDUSTRY

— Seasonal travel

Christmas is usually a bumper time of year for every organization selling a service or product, but it can be especially profitable for the travel industry that has been struck in recent, years, months, weeks and even days.

Times are tough, and even the oldest and most mighty companies in the travel industry need a travel industry solution to see their way through the current financial storms.

Marketing online is a crucial element for all businesses, and it is a route to market that the travel industry has pioneered aggressively. Now, every travel company is jostling for position, in a frenzied dog eat dog fight that will see a few winners and many losers.

Despite the gloom, there is hope on the horizon as there are plenty of people with money to spend on travel and holidays; however, the key to attracting that cash is to update your online store so that the process of purchasing flights, taxis, hotels, car rentals and insurance is a swift, simple and enjoyable experience.

Travel web design is technically complicated because of the requirement for prices to be bang up to date and for internal links and links to affiliate websites to work efficiently and profitably.

Although the average website designer is not usually up to the task of creating an online travel agency that looks good and works well on every level, there are a few highly skilled digital design agencies that do have the know-how to undertake web design that will take off and capture much of the current online travel business.

It can be daunting modernizing or creating a new ecommerce website, but it may well be essential to compete effectively. Design styles and developing digital technology are matching each other in an online race that is engendering fear in many industries. Competition can be healthy for consumers, but too much competition will create casualties in an era where lending to business has all but dried up.

To ensure that your organization has the tools to succeed, it may be an idea to ask a digital agency that you trust to undertake an audit of your current web platforms.

Time is always of the essence, but travel web design has to work faster than most by offering fast page loading, logical navigation, up to date prices and internal and external links that work; the website also has to be found easily by coming on the first page of the generic search results. To achieve that requires expert online marketing and superb search engine optimization techniques.

TRAVEL INDUSTRY SOLUTION

For a travel web design to be effective, it has to offer more than pretty pictures and price lists; it has to create the kind of trust that specific organizations engender so well.

Building trust within a travel website/organization is usually more important than posting the lowest prices and is achieved through excellent design and good copy, rather than focusing being purely on price.

HOW THE TRAVEL INDUSTRY SHOULD BE MARKETING ONLINE

The backpacker might not know their next destination while at home, but they have some holidays coming up and need a target! Their friends are less nomadic, so what is the solution for travel inspiration when its cold dark outside?

What makes you want to travel somewhere? Is it a recommendation from a friend who went there last year? Or was it a photo that you saw somewhere. A film perhaps.

It could be a particular sport that you do that is better performed in a more suitable location; for example, Scuba Diving in the Caribbean is better than in your home area. Or you might like to ride horses up the side of the mountain in Chiapas in Mexico.

What do you look for in a destination? Perhaps like me, when you got your hands on a lonely planet from the library, you first check the night-life. You don't want to end up somewhere dull after all! So that's something that social sites can provide for people.

We want to be that coffee table chat in the youth hostel or the breakfast bar. Where nomads - backpackers collide but online in a social networking context.

Part of the fun of travel is meeting new people who like to travel. If you're in the travel industry, you will almost certainly be advertising on the internet, but if the extent of your website is a digital version of your brochure, you're doing it wrong.

Your internet presence should be partly your site, but mostly you will be hard at work marketing on other websites such as Facebook or Twitter and in the travel industry 'landed at'. Your portfolio of social networking sites becomes the online real estate you often use in addition to updating your website with news.

You should have the following tools available to you within this Social Network Site:

RSS feed enabled profiles - so you have an RSS feed of your hotels or tours or just news, right? It can be fed into your social networking portfolio so updates on your site go into the RSS content on your website and it updates automatically in the social network site.

Reviews - your customer should be able to review your services, and you should encourage them to do this.

Network with other members - Add friends and some competitors as you will see what they are doing. The best salesmen chat about their products not push them.

Videos and Photos - nothing sells a tour like energizing and captivating photos and videos. Along with reviews tagging, pictures of past customers in photos will validate the reviews they have written. If you don't have previous customers on the social site, invite them, and they will enjoy the benefits too.

Don't write too much - give enough detail to whet the appetite; the photos and videos are more important.

Share your profile pic on Facebook and Twitter - also share a link to these sites from your home page showing how networked your business is.

Being on trip advisor is not enough! Be there but don't be a part of the crowd in a sea of competitors where is the dynamic energy you will get from a great video or photos tagged with satisfied customers.

You can deep link and share as much as you like.

Facebook has a limitation of being too personal mixing with your business.

CHAPTER 39: HOW THE MARKETING FUNNEL HAS CHANGED IN THE DIGITAL WORLD

How often do you migrate from one strategy to the next when you deal with digital marketing? Innovation drives today's business, where customers shift channels of purchase to make the most of their bucks.

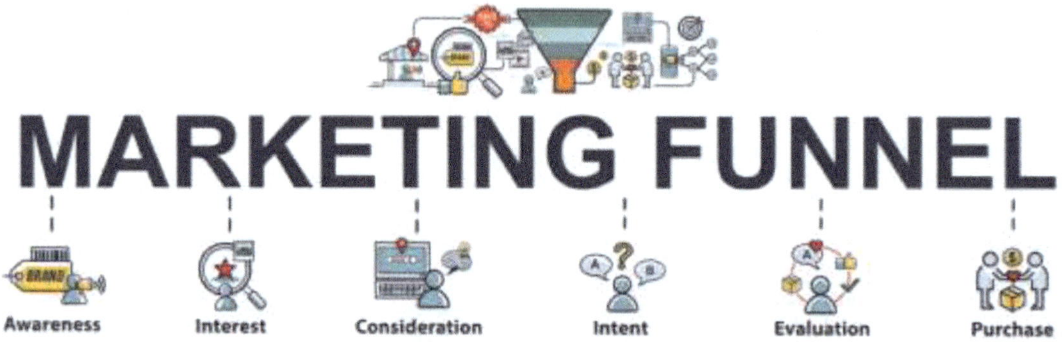

The digitized business ecosystem has flung open a multiplicity of options before the contemporary buyer to optimize the choice. While marketing has reached new zeniths of competition, especially among generic firms, customers have maintained the loyalty-price compatibility balance when it comes to purchasing a product.

With more purchase alternatives at hands, customers browse through the cyber world to economize their purchases. The parameters of successful marketing have also evolved in the digitised world. It is time to assess the evolution that the marketing funnel has undergone.

— Awareness

Marketing, at its outset, focuses on outreach. A dynamic entrepreneur counts on social media pages, e-mail marketing and online shopping portals. Data analytics technologies have enabled them to narrow down upon the choices of the customers.

A present-day customer finds the Facebook page flooding with relevant advertisements, all relevant and tailored to his choice. Awareness has been at par with the changing trends, and markers have heavily utilized new technical tricks to boost the trade.

— Familiarity

Well, how many product pages did you 'like' on Facebook last week?

Even startups have displayed shimmering growth rates when you consider familiarity of the customers with the goods. If you are passionate about electronics, be honest to state whether you feel the pulse when you find new smartphones, tablets and other electronic gadgets in the market. Social media pages, advertisements on internet pages and interactions through groups have made this process easier.

— Consideration

Companies have been engaged in virtual wars, considering the degree of advertisement and competition. Which brand comes to your mind when you think of purple? Or which tagline created the rhythmic melody in your account, which you couldn't help murmuring unconsciously? USP's may be different, but in the end, the goal of every brand is to create an extensive client base.

Customers consider the strategic edges of each of the brands, that surface in the logos, taglines and slogans of different companies through online advertisements.

— **Purchase**

It is a pivotal aspect for any business, and starting from this point, entrepreneurs focus on reputation management and customer retention. The parameters of purchase have increased in the digitized business the newcomers being availability, timeliness, return and exchange of goods, and so on.

When was the last time you purchased an unwarranted good and managed to get it exchanged, considering the quality?

— **Loyalty**

Loyalty from customers is undoubtedly an asset for any brand, irrespective of its category and size. Today's brand loyalty rests not only the call of heritage or commodifying the emotions, and but it also depends on whether the company is consistent in delivering the goods or not. Stock-offs have landed thousands of companies in obscurity. Thus, loyalty has its roots in the way the company makes its products available to the customers.

The marketing funnel has changed for the good, both from the customers' and the company's ends. While competition has gone down the wire for the companies, customers have benefitted with the best grades of goods. In a nutshell, the companies have adopted a strategy of guiding a customer to make the right decision, rather than pulling them down the funnel.

FIVE ESSENTIALS FOR BUSINESS SUCCESS IN THE DIGITAL WORLD

Digital technologies are forcing an unprecedented pace of change for the business. They are not only changing the way we communicate but are also causing us to reshape our business models. To determine whether your business is on track to becoming an active digital business, you need to ask the five following questions:

1. Do you proactively monitor the industry changes that are affecting your business?

Use web-based tools to help track the impact that converged technologies are having on all aspects of your business, such as customer behaviours, new suppliers, technology trends etc. This approach will give you a holistic perspective of your industry and enable you to identify strategic options ahead of your competition.

2. Do you encourage collaborative behaviours within your organization?

Your company must provide the tools and environment that enable the sharing of knowledge and information to tap into one of its most valuable attributes - the tacit knowledge (the accumulated skills, experience and knowhow) of your employees.

3. Do you regularly engage with communities external to your company?

It is essential to adopt a digital mindset and rethink how your business can more effectively engage (interact, listen, learn and co-create) with the rapidly growing collective knowledge base outside of your company to understand changing customer requirements, generate new ideas and gain valuable feedback.

4. Do you disrupt your business model?

Traditional business models, tools and methodologies do not adapt well to the opportunities and threats encountered in today's digital world. First, you need to understand how the individual elements of your existing model work together and then take full advantage of digital technologies to create a disruptive new business model - before your competition does it for you!

5. Do you inspire your employees to bring innovation into the workplace?

You need to encourage your employees to leverage the mobile and social technologies that they use in their everyday lives to generate innovative ideas that will enhance, simplify and accelerate the business processes within your company.

Have you answered "yes" to all the above questions? If so, yours is one of the few businesses with the foresight to understand that adopting a new mindset is essential in today's fast-paced digital environment. If you answered "no", it's not too late to follow the five steps above and begin the process of transforming your traditional organization into a truly digital one!

CHAPTER 40: CELEBRITY STATUS FOR YOUR BUSINESS IN THIS DIGITAL WORLD

You might think everyone is online nowadays. If you are an entrepreneur who has a Facebook page and a blog, then you are not among the 59% of smallbusiness owners who neither have a Facebook nor a blog. There are only 41% of small-business owners who have their websites.

If that's the case, then the number of business bloggers is not as many as people might think. It also means that a lot of smallbusiness owners have not explored the great marketing potential of blogs. And yet a lot of them want to get found.

If you are among the 41%, then now is the time for you to know the benefits of business blogging. Business blogging is the latest best way to achieve the popularity you need for your business. If you want your business to achieve celebrity status that customers and prospects will crawl over it like ants on food, then try business blogging.

SO HOW DOES THIS KIND OF E-COMMERCE WORK?

Setting up a blog is quite easy. You sign up in a free blogging site, choose a template to use, and you're good to go. Choose blogging services like Typepad or WordPress that automatically format blogs in ways that make it easier for search engines to pick up words and phrases that will help you appear quickly in online searches.

Getting a top rank in online searches is every business blogger aim. It is key to their marketing plan of getting found and achieving celebrity status for their business.

While blog set-up is relatively straightforward, it's running your blog that requires more attention and most certainly, hard work. You will need to strategize a lot on how to engage your online visitors with your blog posts and ultimately, your blog.

You have to engage your audience enough that they will keep checking your blog even after they've gone through the initial information they needed.

You can hook them more by updating your posts frequently that new information is always up in your site. This way, your audience will not tire of your blog because there is still fresh content. It is healthy to update your blog three to five times a week.

Don't put off your customers and prospects by posting irreverent details of your personal life. You can use the personal diary approach to writing your blog entries depending on the kind of connection you want to establish with your customers and prospects.

Using this kind of approach humanizes you and may endear you to some of your audience. But it may also alienate some of your audience who prefer a different type of discourse. So, it is essential to know what you are writing about and who you're writing for. If you want to sell, make sure to market your blog in a way that will encompass the needs and wants of your target audience.

Create posts that are brief but informative. The digital world is full many exciting things, and your audience may not want to devote a lot of time, or they don't even have a lot of time to devote to reading a long entry on anything. Tell them what you need to tell them in 500 or fewer words.

It is easier to pack a punch in a shorter blog. It will even leave them wanting more. And that is how and why they keep coming back to a business blog. Spark their interest in your business through blogs, and you'll be on your way to finding your business's celebrity status online.

THE ULTIMATE GOSPEL IN THESE MODERN DAYS

There is one misconception that prevails over all others, which is that of being able to earn returns from being just present on the internet. There is an immense need for adopting a particular strategy to have a fair share of views by the audience. Regular checks on the campaign will generate valuable revenue. All these duties are lined up for digital marketing specialists.

The concept of marketing is experiencing sea changes at the moment. In the past decade, companies have been hiring people who are experts at increasing business on the web. Industries and individual entrepreneurs are increasingly becoming aware that the traditional modes of marketing are passé. Digital marketing is the latest set of skills that technology geeks are gobbling up.

It is an accepted fact that in the present times the mass makes use of digital marketing more often and are more and more enlightened with each passing day. Today their whole world revolves around the digital world. Right from securing news and views to getting dollops of entertainment on their mobile phones and laptops and placing orders for commodities online, you cannot wish the digital world away anymore.

We can say that the days of a lazy approach to marketing is over. Nowadays, it is time to engage in one to one method with the customer. The companies will communicate with their customers to get an insight into the challenges and hassles faced by the clients concerning their products. Rather than being a distant organization, the company prefers to have a one to one relation with the customer, and this is possible through marketing the commodity digitally.

According to experts in the field, the term digital marketing should be the last word in this tech-savvy world. Be it in the form of response to an email, posting a blog or coming up with an online review, and digital marketing should be all-pervasive to uphold the product as the best in the market.

For the correct exposure in the digital world, a few fundamental steps have to be undertaken. The experts in digital marketing have to work along with the change in trend.

Varied categories of people have to be targeted, and unique content has to be pushed, keeping in mind the different kinds of people. A bright idea should be there about the type of interaction with the audience. Constant optimization of your web pages should be carried out regularly.

To be successful in this sphere, an individual has to understand the core concepts of campaign objectives and strategy.

There is always a three-prong approach to digital marketing. Firstly, it is that of targeting and developing the correct viewers for your commodity. Secondly, the best use of a marketing campaign with web analytics should be made. And thirdly, it is essential to produce relevant content for the commodity.

CHAPTER 41: IMPLEMENTING DIGITAL STRATEGIES

It is no secret that the world of business is evolving at what can only be called a blistering pace. What worked yesterday may not function today, and it could very well be outdated tomorrow.

There is perhaps a no better example of this modernization than in the world of evolving digital strategies. Of course, implementing a successful digital strategy to meet the core needs of any business can be easier said than done.

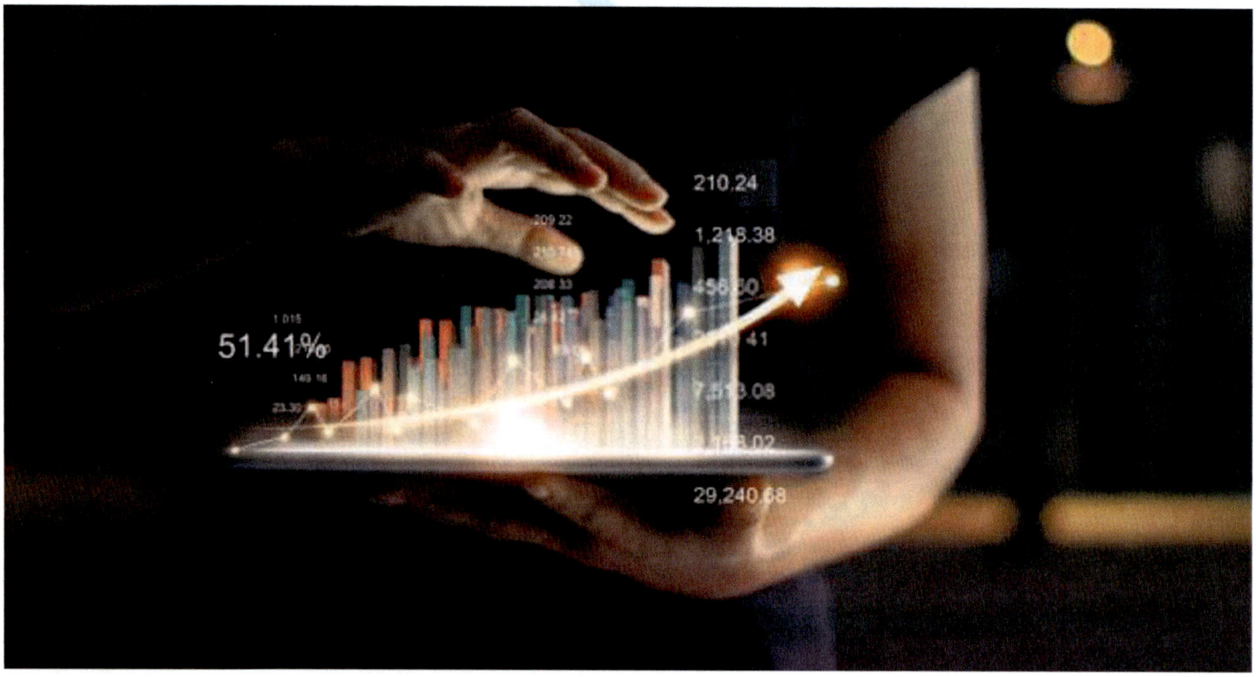

It is the primary reason why the task is generally outsourced to professionals in the industry; they appreciate the bespoke needs and infrastructure of unique companies. So, what are some of the most useful tips to follow when one needs to enter into the digital domain finally? Let's take a closer look.

— **Internal Concerns**

Just as any business is built from the ground up, we first need to consider how a digital transformation will affect the workplace. Will daily jobs be impacted by the use of digital tools?

How much information will need to be stored in the cloud? Who will have access to this data and perhaps most importantly, how much training will need to take place to complete the transition? Identifying these variables will enable management to make sound decisions at the right times.

— **Support**

In most cases, it is best to find a team of highly enthusiastic individuals that will act as "champions" in regards to your digital strategy. These players will offer firm support, which is necessary to begin the digital transition.

As we are all aware, motivation within the business tends to be quite contagious. In turn, this will enable others to take an active interest in the change. It is also a good idea to create new roles within the company (Lead Digital Coordinator could be an example here).

These roles will be attractive opportunities for those who are enthusiastic and astute; the exact type of personality that is ideal when entering the digital domain.

— Understanding Approaches

Before actively implementing any digital strategy, it is essential to appreciate which techniques are those that will be most attractive to the customers themselves. It will help to separate the business apart from the competition, which may still be lagging. Also, never forget that emerging technology is another critical factor.

What may be considered state of the art today may very well not hold that title shortly.

Once the software and the approaches are determined, these need to be communicated to all team leaders and stakeholders. Not only will this help to increase levels of inter-departmental accountability, but the strategies themselves will be much more functional as opposed to being handled piecemeal.

Finally, clear communications will help you to determine the feedback from the customers. If a strategy seems not to be working, it can be changed before it becomes what could turn into a significant issue.

— Out With the Old?

Although the core operations of the business are not likely to change, embracing the digital world will likely lead to some modifications. For example, catering to a more extensive and more international client base within the virtual world could require office hours to be modified. As mobile apps increase client engagement, a larger CRM team could be expected.

The key takeaway here is that an organization needs to become streamlined for the end customer to obtain the best possible experience. Older top-down approaches may no longer work. Flexibility needs to be embraced within all teams. Communications are likely to become faster and thus; a centralized platform must remain in place to maintain control and cross-functional accountability.

— **Using Resources**

So far, we have examined some of the primary methodologies that need to be embraced during the transition. Now, we need to look at the execution. Keeping team structures in mind (IT, sales, marketing and finance), what resources are required? For example, which demographic is likely to respond the best with this new strategy?

How long will the product be in development before it becomes available to this buyer persona?

How does a particular digital product or service resonate within this customer base? Not only will this enable the business to solidify their strategy, but all employees involved will be well aware of their discrete roles (a problem all too present within many companies that have recently undergone a digital shift).

— **Product Support**

It is expected that any new digital product will come with its fair share of questions. Not only will these need to be addressed using in-house techniques meant for employees, but outbound and proactive customer support is vital. Of course, any such support structure should be in place well before the release date.

It will also include the necessary training for the employees and any time frame should be built around the time it will take to develop a robust knowledge and support infrastructure. As there are so very many digital products within the marketplace, a business that lacks support is likely to lose valuable business while the customers will move on to a competitor.

— **Product Over Technology**

The user cares more about the functionality of the product as opposed to the technology which it employs. In other words, user experiences will be the ultimate determinant as to which digital avenues the company should explore. Otherwise, what may very well be a novel service may fall upon deaf ears. In this sense, "the customer is always right" is still the best maxim. How functional is the product, when is it needed and which platforms will provide the best user experience? Understanding these metrics will enable the business to make the right decisions at the right time.

Moving into the digital arena is all but inevitable for most companies. While this shift is indeed profound, it does not have to be daunting.

These simple tips will help any enterprise build a flexible framework that is necessary to meet and exceed the demands of their customer base. Employing these digital strategies will offer the foundation for any business to grow well into 2019 and beyond. Now is the time to plan to do that.

CHAPTER 42: IMPORTANCE OF POSTERS IN A DIGITAL WORLD

It seems as if the entire world has gone digital. Consumers do more shopping online than ever before. Businesses have been devoting more money to online advertising. However, there is still a place for advertising in the real world. Creating a memorable poster is always a great way to attract attention to your product.

— Movies Are Nothing Without Posters

Almost every movie comes out with a poster. A poster from an iconic film can be worth a lot of money. It means that they are still an effective way to promote a product.

Seeing an advertisement for an upcoming movie gets you thinking about that film months before any real promotion begins. The same thing can be done for any other product a company wants to promote.

— Small And Portable

Posters can be placed almost anywhere. Putting a sign in your store is a great way to attract attention to a featured product. A poster that is placed in a high traffic area can attract new customers who may be curious about your business. Well placed advertisements can still be a great advertising tool that can get your message out to the public.

— It's All About The Presentation

A well-made poster can attract the attention of the people who see it. Restaurants could hang a banner of a juicy steak with a fine wine to wash it down.

The colours and texture will immediately jump out if the poster is made right. A picture of a family about to sit down to Christmas dinner could remind you of your holiday memories. No digital advertisement can tug at your senses like that.

POSTERS CAN GIVE YOUR COMPANY A RETRO FEEL

Sometimes it is just right to be different. Advertising through the use of non-digital means can give you company a retro feel to it. Nostalgia can be a great way to get customers to do business with you. It is even more real if your company caters to an older clientele.

These are the folks that aren't going to be as impressed with some digitally enhanced advertisement.

Posters do have a place in the advertising scene these days. Banners are a staple in the movie industry. They must be valuable ways to advertise if Hollywood is still investing in them.

A quality poster will tend to resonate well with the customers that your company is trying to attract. Colours, textures and emotional responses are more natural to get with signs as opposed to digital advertisements. Doing these things well are what you want out of an ad no matter what medium you are using.

REASONS FOR FLYER PRINTING IN DIGITAL WORLD

Print media for promotion is so familiar yet very useful. Although people have completely transferred their attention to digital media that many people do not feel the need of paper anymore. And in such a case, you must be wondering if we still need flyer printing to influence people? The answer to that is yes. Here are a few valid reasons for that:

Now, when you do not have your laptop with you, how can a promotion reach you? I am sure you do not carry your digital media all the time with you. Most probably, the mobile would be handy.

So, when you are out the only effective way of reaching you are flyers. It is one reason you will find them getting distributed at the entrances of some public building, malls and restaurants etc.

These can reach you even when you are not at your place by mails, so when you come back, you will find them at your doorstep to catch your attention.

Now even if you have your laptop with you, you have to start it first and then look for the promotion. And what if your computer runs out of battery and you cannot charge it there. While these papers can be easily read anytime, you want.

Carrying these promotions is also very easy. Since they are very lightweight, they can easily fit your pocket or wallet. You have to fold it and make it fit inside the purse.

You can keep it as a proof or a copy, and whenever required, without any hassles, you can show it.

These flyers have a profound impact on the receiver. As people still prefer to keep a hard copy of everything digital too. There is a creation of personal touch in them, which you will never find in your digital promotion.

So, you can quickly see how they are so effective in the modern world. They have not yet reached the stage of obsolescence. But their success can happen only if they are created keeping customers' expectations. The reader always tries to find the bargain he is getting. So, it's not just appearance, and it is, the presentation of content and the content itself, which becomes the reason for the success of these business flyers.

Therefore, the need to focus on the content is most important. And the content should offer something that the prospective customer needs. And you also need to ensure that the offers should be highlighted so that there is no chance for the reader to skip them.

Flyers are still one of the most powerful means of promotion. Therefore, even in the world where 'going digital' is a need, these have always managed to occupy a prominent place.

CHAPTER 43: DEMAND FOR DIGITAL OUTDOOR ADVERTISING

The world of outdoor advertising is growing from strength to strength and shows no sign of slowing down. The ability to opt for a canvas so large and reach so many people at once has made every company sit up and take notice of this medium. It is one which is confined to the larger companies, however, given that costs are rather high. However, the returns have been s promising that most companies are looking to exploit this medium fully.

The business of outdoor advertising has come a long way. From the conventional large billboards which could make the campaign larger than life, there were soon mobile mediums like buses and trains employed, which could get to different locations and reach more significant sections of people. There is a new dimension of advertising which has opened up and is giving everyone something new to look forward to.

Outdoor digital advertising is the newest, most significant form on the block. This form replaces the conventional billboard with a digital screen. The most significant advantage of this form is that it allows for moving pictures and running images, making the whole campaign more appealing. With the size and dimension that this is available in, this is larger than life in many more ways than one.

There are several reasons why outdoor digital advertising is a great form. For one, the digital world has evolved so considerably that it has become easier to replicate advertisements into digital style rather than in the regular, still form. The quality of the publications is also much better, as is the resolution and colour.

The moving factor almost adds in a new dimension, which makes it more attractive and catchier. Digital outdoor advertising has also allowed for the incorporation of sound, which gives unique depth.

When you think of digital outdoor advertising, it becomes much easier to remove and replace the advertisement.

Usually, companies would sit with the same campaign and same look on the billboards for several months at a stretch. With the digital option, it is possible to update and modify the campaign continues, with a little cost incurred. Correction, removal or additions made to conventional billboards could cost several times the amount of money.

With the introduction of digital outdoor advertising, the dynamics of this business has undergone a significant change. In the way that it is viewed and handled, and also in its scope, it has given numerous reasons to believe it in, and also rely heavily on its benefits.

ARE YOU FACING A DIGITAL DISADVANTAGE?

The advantages of the digital revolution are clear to see. You can reach more people, more quickly, more cheaply than ever before. You would think, therefore, that most businesses would be rushing to digital. The fact is, though, most companies are not.

Recent research shows, for instance, that only just over half of small businesses have a website. Some 47% of firms in the digitally advanced USA have yet to get a website. Considering the first website went live 23 years ago, you have to wonder why are they waiting. Even big firms, like those on the Forbes 500 list, are still waiting for some aspects of digital activity with around a quarter of them yet to do anything with social media.

Even in the marketing sector, where you would expect lots of digital strategies, less than 10% of companies have employed content producers - a key role in digital. Wherever you look for data, it appears that most businesses are tentatively touching the digital world.

However, there are some companies which have understood the power of digital and what it can achieve. Research conducted five years ago showed in an analysis of the world's Top 100 Brands, those that were doing best as a result of their use of digital were mainly high-tech firms, such as Microsoft and Google, or they were retailers like Amazon.

Indeed, most other sectors at that time were losing money as a result of not having a strategy that was focused on digital.

Now, new research shows that the high tech and retail sectors are still leading the way digitally, with other areas mostly again "playing at it". Worse yet, the study found - just like the research from five years ago - that the digitally-focused firms are increasing their profits at the same time as companies who are digitally behind the times are losing benefits.

It is the second major piece of research which confirms that a strategy based around digital results in more profits. Indeed, the study found that digitally based companies increase their profits from their physical assets by 9% over those companies that are not digital.

Whichever way you slice or dice the data, it confirms - once again - that the sure strategy for a profitable business is one based digitally. Companies without a digital focus are gradually losing out. Bit by bit, the digital world is eroding their business and their profits.

It all suggests that if your business strategy is not centred upon a digital future, your business may well not be in business in that future.

CHAPTER 43: DEVELOPING A WINNING DIGITAL STRATEGY FOR YOUR BUSINESS

Central to every Greek city and town was the agora, a marketplace and meeting place. The literal meaning of the word is "gathering place". One can quickly figure that in one of the cool areas of the agora, friends and families would exchange pleasantries, people could meet and discussed community and political issues, while traders could make proposals and closed deals.

Agoras were more than markets; they were centres of life. The conversations that happened there and the ideas that erupted from there could have brought down governments, gave rise to new revolutions, and brought about unique philosophies of life.

— A paradigm shift in the marketplace

Over the centuries, some of these places in every civilisation made it to the textbooks of the universities promoting research and exploratory studies to understand their centres of life.

In the modern times, whether it is Trafalgar Square in London that is used for political demonstrations and community gatherings or Times Square - better known as "The Crossroads of the World", one of the world's busiest pedestrian intersections having people gather from different countries and continents.

— Digital Agora

Today, with the convergence of internet, mobile devices, and communication mediums, the surge in social media networking, the agora made inroads into the individual's centre of life to a click.

The conversations in social media spread like wildfire. People have an instant opinion almost about every sphere of life. Whether it is politics, sports, business, religion, or science, everybody is either listening or talking.

Google, Facebook, Twitter, YouTube and the like introduced a virtual marketplace and an online meeting place called digital agora.

The members of these movements surpass populations of several countries. For instance, Facebook has a user base of 1.2 billion people, which is close to 16% of the world population.

80% of online users search on Google and other search engines to find products and services they are looking for. What are you doing to ensure your business is seen by your target audience?

Conversation builds trust, trust builds community, and the community creates brand perception. Dialogue is the heart of the city in the social media networking platform. On average, about 350 million photos are uploaded to Facebook every day.

The sheer volume, velocity, and variety of content are changing the unit of data from gigabytes to terabytes and reaching petabytes, thanks to billions of conversations in the digital agora. The communications could be about your company, your product, your service, and it would be a new idea or a shortcoming of your current product, it is essential to listen to the community and humanely engage with them to discover the treasures in the digital marketplace.

LOGO DIGITISING FOR BRAND MANAGEMENT PURPOSES

In today's computer-operated world, embroidering intricate logo designs on any fabric is easy and fast. It is because of logo digitising service. When we say digitising, it is a process of converting your logo into a digitised embroidery pattern, which is the only format that embroidery machine can read. The process is complicated; however, guarantees excellent results.

A digitising logo is not only about enhancing the aesthetic feature of a particular item. It is also a perfect and cost-effective solution for companies who want to increase their branding. Companies can incorporate their professional logo on the promotional products they will be using through quality digitising service. To personalize the t-shirts, bags, caps, and other items used for brand management purposes, the company logo must be converted first on digitised embroidery design.

And to have the digital file, the original logo is scanned using the digitising software. This converted file will serve as a guide of the embroidery machine as to how the stitches will be sewn. The creation of the most compelling combination of textures, lines, and looks for the embroidered design still depends on the digitizer since he is the one that decides for the thread colour, where to set the digitized pattern as well as the stitch parameters.

Logo digitising can also help maintain the professional look of your employees even if they are just in their casual dress code. A custom shirt with embroidered logo on it helps your employees establish a professional and respectable image. Just make sure the embroidered company logo is something you and your employees can be proud of.

And when it comes to quality logo digitising service, there's nothing much to worry about. Lots of custom apparel shops are now offering affordable custom embroidery digitising service for all types of logo. All you need is to look for a reliable service provider to ensure you're spending the money for the right quality.

CHAPTER 44: DIGITAL MENU BOARDS

Digital menu boards are now considered as one of the best advertising platforms today because they offer a lot of benefits compared to conventional static banners. However, there are still a lot of business owners who are unaware of the things that they can get from it.

Some don't even know the different types of digital boards that they can use for their business. Today, I will be showing you the two types of digital menu boards, to help you determine which the perfect example for your business is.

Here are the two different types of digital menu boards:

— **Standalone Digital Menu Board**

As the name suggests, this is a digital board that can be operated independently. All you need is a media player connected to your board, software that will help you manage the content being shown on your board, and a digital display where you will be showing the information that you want your audience to see.

It is the most common type of digital board and is often used by small business owners who are operating the business on one location. Standalone digital boards are also the cheapest that you can have. Some companies can install and manage it for you, for as low as $300.

— **Networked Digital Menu Board**

It is a more complex system of digital boards that are being used for large businesses with several branches on different locations such as McDonald's and Starbucks. Networked digital boards are made up of several boards connected to a single media player.

The main advantage of a using a networked digital board is that it allows you to change everything on your boards simultaneously with a few pushes of a button. It will help you save a lot of time because you don't have to manage several boards one by one.

These are the two types of digital boards that you can use for your business. Always remember that the budget and the scale of advertising are two of the main factors that should be considered when choosing the one for your business. There are a lot of companies that you can approach if you want to learn more about digital menu boards. All you have to do is to use the Internet to find the one that is capable of enhancing the performance of your business with the help of digital menu boards.

— **Primary Components of a Digital Menu Board**

A digital menu board is a dynamic display for menus, promotional items, product images, and even animation used by companies to promote their product. Usually used by restaurants, particularly by quick-service restaurants, digital boards have replaced the old static painted or printed signboards used before. Advancements in LED Display technology has pushed the boundaries of digital menu boards. They are now cheaper to buy, lasts longer than before, and have more functions than the old standard board.

Three primary factors maximize the use of a digital board. These are:

— Hardware or Equipment

— Software

— Design

— Digital Menu Board Hardware

The equipment that comprises a digital board varies. Some of these boards are attached to rotating extenders and toppers to give the board some motion and more visibility. But the heart of the system of a digital board is the LCD TV screen. The LCD lets the establishment show vivid bright images and animation that will attract the customer to products and promotions that the company offers.

The control board is also essential. It is the brain of the digital board system. It controls what and how a particular image is displayed on the screen. Some advanced control boards have integrated communication functions to handle order taking, such as in drive-through windows.

— **Digital Menu Board Software**

During the old days of static boards, establishments would give the sign maker a mockup or drawing of how the sign should look like. Afterwards, the flag is produced, delivered, and mounted.

With a digital board, the image or display is uploaded to the control board where it can be programmed with various options such as animation, time of day display, and 'Happy Hour' rates. These can be done in-house by a trained employee or a commissioned to a professional digital board designer.

— **Design**

As mentioned, the look and feel of a digital menu board can be done in-house or through a professional. To maximize the full potential of a digital menu board, the establishment must study how best to implement a digital display.

Factors such as space, product, promotion, and location influence the effectiveness of a digital board. Companies are willing to offer these kinds of services. Some even offer in-house training in the use and design of the boards. With the advent of the digital displays, extra planning is required to take advantage of the opportunities this kind of equipment can offer. With the right hardware, software, and design, the digital menu board can generate additional sales than a standard painted sign would do.

— Advantages and Disadvantages of a Standalone Digital Menu Board

There are a lot of different types of digital menu board that you can use for your business, and one of these is a standalone digital menu board. Unfortunately, there are still a lot of people who are not aware of the things that an independent digital board can do for them.

Here, I will be showing you the advantages and disadvantages that you and your business can get from this digital display. Reading this article will help you find the one that is perfect for your business.

— Advantages of a Standalone Digital Menu Board

One of the most prominent benefits that you and your business can get from a standalone digital menu board is that it will allow you to reach your audience without spending more than what you have allotted. It is the purest form of digital advertising, and you can have this installed and operating for less than $300.

Another advantage that you can get from a standalone digital board is that it will allow you to be more flexible with your advertising campaign. Although it is not advisable for businesses with several branches, the standalone digital board will still help you get more from your advertising campaign.

— Disadvantages of a Standalone Digital Menu Board

Standalone boards are cheaper, but you need to spend more money if you are going to have it installed on different locations. Businesses with several branches won't find this option as the best for them.

Standalone boards are not designed to work as a network, and a business owner will have a hard time managing different boards at the same time.

Aside from this, you won't be able to manage a standalone digital board remotely. It should be installed in a place where the digital signage player is located.

Since this option is hard-wired, you won't have the ability to operate this type of digital menu board wirelessly.

These are some of the things that you need to know about the standalone digital board. Always remember that choosing the best for your business is very important because this will determine the results that you will get from it. It will be easier if you are going to look for providers who can help you find the one that is perfect for your business.

It will also save you from the trouble of learning everything about a digital menu board to find the one that is perfect for you.

Making Digital Rain

To be an effective marketer in today's digital age, you have to understand the basic concepts and strategies used by marketers online. Today's marketer has to be a digital rainmaker, assuming that making digital rain is about the generation of business results online.

Digital rain begins when marketers know how to generate customer leads and evaluate online consumer behaviour data being made digitally across multiple platforms and technologies. In essence, today's digital rainmaker needs to know where and how to meet its customers with a digital handshake.

But those who aspire to be a digital rainmaker should have a basic understanding of marketing principles before they set out to making digital rain. They should understand that digital marketing is an exchange whereby one side creates a market to satisfy a consumer need in exchange for something of value. Most often, the cost is a currency, but it can also be a barter arrangement whereby the provider receives something in return that he or she perceives to be of equal value.

Before any transaction can occur, marketers must first assess what consumer needs or wants are either not currently being met or are only partially being satisfied. Product and service concepts are developed and tested to gain feedback on consumer acceptance and production viability.

Then, the marketer has to determine what type of market there will be for the new or adapted product and calculate the cost/benefit of mass production based on forecasted sales targets and investment returns. Pricing, distribution, promotion and customer service need to be well thought out before launch.

With sound marketing knowledge as a basis, there's also much more to being a successful online rainmaker than just creating a Facebook and Twitter account and pushing out promotional messages. Today's digital rainmaker needs to know how to integrate traditional marketing principles with new platforms that target consumer behaviours, lifestyles pursuits and content consumption preferences online.

The rainmaker needs to know everything possible about its target market. When and how often are they online? What do they search for, and how do they interact with information? Who and what influences their product interests and purchasing decisions? Are they sharing or observing social content? And what technologies are helping or impeding their conversion probabilities?

These are just some of the countless questions online rainmakers are continually seeking answers to sharpen their digital marketing strategies. And like any other new platform, the key to success is understanding both the benefits and shortfalls of every marketing vehicle.

YouTube might be a perfect channel for the marketing of restaurants or food products, given the visual nature of food preparation and setting. But technology product equipment discussions might be better suited for LinkedIn groups or technology forums.

Picking the right digital marketing channels is only the first hurdle because it's just as important to understand how consumers react to your attempts to interest them in something you're offering.

Are they apt to click through a paid search engine text ad, if the copy is intriguing? Will, a rich media display ad on one of their favourite websites, put them in your new leads' category? Or is better to send them a time-based mobile incentive message to visit you when they've checked into a nearby establishment?

Once you've moved them through the online marketing funnel from awareness and information gathering to conversion, you've made it rain. But was it a light sun shower or a torrential downpour? It's time to kick in your high-powered social customer relationship management (CRM) initiative to help encourage customer loyalty.

Using site tracking tools, you can better serve their unique interests and only serve up relevant product offerings in your database marketing initiatives.

The digital rainmaker also needs to know how to make it easy for existing customers to share their favorable product experiences, encouraging online influencers to accelerate word of mouth marketing efforts.

Social media is also being used as a 24/7 customer service channel by many brands. Rainmakers can and should immediately listen to and address any less than flattering feedback on popular channels like Twitter and Facebook.

Being a successful digital rainmaker requires basic marketing knowledge and experience, a positive stance on the art of salesmanship and an insatiable thirst for information and evaluation of metrics that can improve your efficiency.

CHAPTER 45: DIGITALIZATION

HIGH TECH OR HUMAN TOUCH?

There is a fact that is entirely understood and realized among leaders in the majority of the leading industries around the world, and this is: How the digital technology is disrupting all the models we know so far.

Digitalization happens to be at the moment the primary source of tremendous transformations in different aspects of our lives. Digitalisation is the new connectivity for citizens, policymakers, societies and governments. It presents unlimited chances to the creation of more value to businesses, although if not undertaken carefully, it also represents a risk.

Much has been discussed and analyzed, very specifically the economic or societal implications of the digitalisation phenomenon, questions are rising and contest widening, while important issues are just appearing while the process of the digital transformation is taking place.

Who is the operator behind a machine? To whom are companies targeting their augmented or virtual reality gadgets? Who is behind all this digital transformation show? Is what some economists from the EU business school name: the unitary cost of production, say, the human being, say, you and me.

Some great personalities around the world from various cultures, this is about supermen who undertook time to scrutinize our inner and outer nature. Those great philosophers agree that the present humanity's evolutionary state is that of the mere intellect, nothing else nothing much. Understanding has enabled us to go beyond the unexpected in the material world.

It has enabled us to progress in many fields of thoughts from the material point of view, say, what our senses experiment as a stimulation that comes from the outside: object and subject.

However, paradoxical as it seems we are perpetuating our dependence to devices and decreases the natural abilities we have been born with, making us in many cases, mentally lazy and acting like slaves of those devices. Otherwise, can anyone explain if they know how are thoughts are formed or how can we undergo profound changes in our sincere personality and have an integrated life? Statistics show a terrible projection in this so far.

Exponential growth which defines most of the scenarios we are living can help us understand all this material phenomenon. Universal laws from a physical point of view limit our senses and way of existing. Exponential growth, therefore, releases unlimited possibilities in graphics, virtual realities, holographic realities or astral realities.

When a computer's speed continuously increases its rate the more fantastic or even science fiction like computers or devices comes up. Processor chips- "Computer's main component is called the Central Processing Unit, or CPU for short. The CPU is a tiny piece of silicon and is often referred to as the silicon chip or the processor chip.

This tiny little piece is the brain of the computer, equivalent to the engine of a car"-double in speed every eighteen months according to Moore's Law, the rule of thumb in the technology industry. Therefore, computers as we know, up to 2025 will tend to be more than 70 times faster than it was now in 2019. Photonics ("the branch of technology concerned with the properties and transmission of photons, for example in fibre optics"), says the more data are coming out of fibre-optic cables, faster connectivity, this increase at more than double rates every nine months.

Meanwhile, as an exercise analysis, changing customer expectations, cultural transformation, outdated regulation, and identifying and accessing the right skills - to name just a few.

These challenges need to be addressed by industry and government leaders to unlock the substantial benefits digital offers society and sector. Machines increase efficiency, provides lots of tools to deal with ailments, health problems among others, in the other hand also decreases our intellectual coefficient not allowing to use discernment or analytical abilities, it even disintegrates our personality making us sometimes too much ego or selfie (The Internet of Me) driven causing us to lose vision of a holistic life view.

After placing a debate above on the real meaning of the human being behind the devices, we want always to emphasize very clearly that technology is useful. Technology is beautiful. Nothing more than that: "The word technology comes from two Greek words, transliterated techne and logos. Techne means art, skill, craft, or the way, manner, or means by which a thing is gained... So, technology means words or discourse about the way things are gained."

Bearing these premises in mind, quite many recommendations can be given out, but asset information to aid incumbent industry leaders in their efforts to achieve a proper digital transformation this can apply not only in companies but in any groups such as families, students, social organisms, etc.:

Place the human factor above everything and anything. It includes a solid ground human resource philosophy in the company.

Have moments of silent, periodical moments of conscious silence (this is far different from sleeping), away from all type of technological devices. Turn them all off while you are into these precise moments of silent. If in the group, the better although is strongly advised to do it individually as individual mental peace brings forth collective peace. It all starts with each one of us! Regularity is advised, hopefully, twice a day, 30 minutes.

Start practising meditation twice a day. 30 minutes. In the morning, 30 minutes. In the afternoon.

Meditation creates new neurons, increase the brain's grey matter, widen brain connection. It makes us more intelligent. Intelligence doesn't mean just having a high IQ. Meditation increases immune function and decreases pain. Meditation reduces inflammation from the cellular aspect. Meditation decrease stress, depression and anxiety.

Training to each one of the members on how to breathe correctly (a vast majority of people don't know how to breathe even though they have noses!).

Start training on what you eat. Yes, you are what you eat. The purer the food, the more intelligent is our mind. Food goes to the blood. The blood nourishes our brain and overall system.

The creation of a new digital culture consists of involving everybody, shareholders, stakeholders, etc.

Start searching and identifying, developing and later on launching new, digital business models.

Setting up successful corporate venturing businesses inside the company is a must.

Every aspect of operations must be re-examined.

Leveraging data and the right digital traction metrics must be part of the new culture. It also includes investments in security.

— **Build a high-quotient digital workforce**

The company that wants to thrive into the digital enterprise must go beyond the mere implementation of new technologies just for the sake of it. What gives a digital enterprise that long-cherished competitive advantage is its culture, strategy and way of operating, never forgetting that in your new digital business models, always ensure these two things: The employees as unitary costs of production and customers as the centre of everything you do.

ADVENT OF DIGITISING

With the advent of computerized technology, things have changed at a rapid pace. For instance, the way we communicate and the way we perform various tasks have become a lot faster and automated. The use of computers has proved to be the most beneficial and logical step in the evolution of humanity.

While not more than half a century ago, people discovered that most of the physical work could be replaced by mechanical machines, now we are getting more and more used to having computers do the work for us. However, that does not leave us without a purpose; we are the ones that need to tell computers what to do and how to do it. Software programs have the role of acting as an intermediary between humans and machines, and one of the operations they do is called digitising.

WHAT IS DIGITISING?

The arid definition of digitising says that it is the conversion of an analogue signal into a digital signal. Each point and each sample in the analog signal converses in digital form, and what is obtained is the digital form of the same source - be it an image, a sound or a document.

Digitising is what makes the transmission of information so easy in this day and age. A copy of a text no longer needs just a copy machine, and you can transmit the digital form to a virtually infinite number of copies that do not need paper or ink. The same thing happens with images, sounds or signals.

TYPES OF DIGITISING

Digitising is very useful in many various domains. For instance, scanning images and videos are beneficial for the editing process. The same source can be used to operate all the needed modifications, using only a computer and a software program.

Audio files that are digitized are scanned, using their sampling rate as the basic unit. Image sensor devices are also used for recreating the digital representation of objects we use in real life. Digitising is used for creating electronic maps, using the images caught by satellites.

Embroidery digitising software is used for creating embroidery machine codes that are loaded into a machine to recreate the patterns on fabric. These are just a few applications of digitising, that many people use now day by day.

— How does embroidery digitising work?

Embroidery digitising consists of translating the artwork - done by a professional digitizer - into code that is stored in a stitch file. This file is then read by an embroidery machine that interprets the system as a stitch type. But is it all that simple?

There are specific steps that must be accurately followed to obtain the desired results. Editing the artwork for the embroidery digitising process. Not all artworks are designed for embroidery, which is why they often need to be simplified to be interpreted correctly by the embroidery machine.

Creating the stitch file.

Once the artwork was transformed in a digital form, a digitizer (or a puncher) must establish the path for it. This term describes the actual process through which the machine must follow the pattern from start to finish.

Determining the stitch types. Various parts of the design must be created using multiple stitch types. During this stage, the digitizer will identify the best stitch types for each part of the plan.

Avoiding shifting in the design. When working, embroidery machines create a push and pull effect, which may cause shifting.

For this reason, the digitiser must use their skills to compensate for the possible shifting.

Knowing the fabric. Last, but not least, the digitizer must know what kind of material will be used, as various effects will be obtained based on this aspect alone.

CHAPTER 46: DIGITAL SIGNAGE

WHY DIGITAL SIGNS ARE IMPORTANT

We've spoken about this earlier in this guide, often in this space, you can explore a small slice of digital signage development, such as the role of digital signage in meeting the evolving media appetites of people.

The ability of digital signs to blend the functions of traditional symbols with the interactive aspects of digital kiosks; or the potential of digital signage to command an increasingly larger slice of the media budget of marketers.

While those are important topics, let's get back to the basics of digital signage -expressly.

Why should professional communicators turn to digital signage to convey their essential messages?

There are several reasons, including:

— **To increase a company's visibility**

One of the biggest problem's retailers have when it comes to self-promotion is cutting through all of the marketing noise generated by every other business - be it on radio or TV, in newspapers and magazines or from competing for storefront signs. Digital signage can cut through those distractions by attracting and directing the attention of the most important potential buyers of all -those in a store who are ready to spend money on a purchase.

— **To help solidify relationships with customers and vendors**

Consider an auto dealership waiting room with customers seated waiting for their cars to be fixed. With well-positioned digital signage messaging -as opposed to an ordinary TV displaying a cable news channel- the dealership can promote special offers aimed at its captive digital signage audience as a reward for choosing to do business with the dealership.

Or, in a corporate setting, a digital sign in the lobby can be used to welcome scheduled vendors, guests and other visitors as they arrive -a simple move that builds goodwill.

— **To deliver critical information more efficiently**

In times of emergency, an existing digital signage network can be a lifesaver, providing critically essential messages alerting employees, customers and other patrons of exit locations, storm shelters and additional vital information.

— **To save time**

Preparing a static, printed sign is labour-intensive, expensive and time-consuming. The same message can be created and displayed far more quickly with a digital sign.

Add to that the recurring expense of printing new posters as needs change versus simply updating a digital sign with a few keystrokes and it doesn't take long to begin earning a tidy ROI from a digital sign.

— **To attract more considerable attention than is possible with static, printed signs**

The other drawback of print is that it is static. Human brains are programmed for motion. Our eyes are automatically drawn to moving objects. Digital signs displaying full of motion video are dynamic, not static. They tap into something innately human to demand attention and hold it.

— **To increase the efficiency of employees**

Imagine a small industrial plant where management wants to communicate vital information to hundreds of workers. Perhaps it's production quotas vs. actual performance; maybe it's mean time between accidental employee injuries; it's probably delivery information regarding vital components that are en-route.

In all of these instances -and others too numerous to recount here- digital signage can convey important information to a workforce that is vital to employees maintaining a safe, efficient environment.

There you have it -several reasons why digital signage is a valuable, effective communications alternative that professional communicators cannot ignore. Sometimes it's good to get back to basics.

Digital Signage...

1) Can increase your company's visibility,

2) Can help solidify your customer and vendor relationships,

3) Can deliver critical information more efficiently,

4) Saves time,

5) Attracts attention better than static signs,

6) Can increase the efficiency of your employees.

And, digital signage can be less expensive than what you are already using.

DYNAMIC VERSUS STATIC MESSAGING

How about the signs hanging in your establishment? Week after week, month after month, customers and prospects see the same printed message on those signs. Do you know the similarity between the opening paragraph of this column and those signs? Sure, your customers and prospects might have read those printed signs the first -and even the second- time they walked into your establishment. But what about now? Have they given them a second glance for months?

The tendency to not want to change printed signs is understandable. Printing is expensive, both in terms of money and time. Think about the process for a moment. You or someone in your organization must conceive the message, create the design, assemble the pieces and -depending upon the complexity of the project and the quality desired- hand off the project to a printer, which puts it in his queue of jobs, or drives to a quick-print service and waits for the job to be completed.

Once printed and displayed, the new sign has a brief life as a new communications tool. Soon, it's been seen by customers and prospects numerous times, and it fades into the background somewhere between the pictures on the wall and the paint. At that point, the cycle begins again.

Contrast the effort, time and expense of creating static printed signs with the dynamic, quickly changed messaging that's possible with a digital sign. Scrolling text, animated clips, motion graphics, video and sound are all useful components on a well-integrated digital sign messaging.

Each is easily added. Doing so is made even easier by templates that are about as difficult to use as a Microsoft PowerPoint template.

Many digital signs users report being able to playback their initial messaging within a few hours of loading digital sign software and templates onto their computers. Updating those messages also is simple, requiring as little as a few minutes to a couple of hours per week, depending on how extensive that messaging maintenance is.

The dynamic messaging offered by digital signs also exploits the human response to the motion. A printed sign is static; it does not move, nor does it change. Digital signs offer dynamic communications. Text can scroll across the bottom of the screen. Weather graphics can be automatically modified in response to changing conditions. Animated logos and graphics can fly through view, and video is filled with motion.

Incorporating some or all of these elements into a digital sign message adds movement. That taps into the natural human tendency to direct one's eyes and attention to something in motion, which is a tremendous advantage for anyone with a message to convey.

Thus, leveraging the power of digital sign versus using static print delivers two crucial advantages: the flexibility to change messages quickly and efficiently and the ability to attract the attention and interest of patrons.

ASSESSING THE EFFECTIVENESS OF DIGITAL SIGNAGE

Using digital screens for advertising and promotion is becoming a common form of advertising. Digital advertising and outdoor digital signage are springing up all over the place. With quite a high initial outlays, there is undoubtedly a considerable investment involved in embarking on the digital route, but is it worthwhile?

Assessing the value of any advertising medium, let alone something as new digital signage can be difficult at the best of times, but many potential digital advertisers are put off as they are unsure as to whether the effectiveness of the campaign will lead to a return on the initial investment.

Quantifying the success of digital screens can be tricky. Unlike other promotions digital advertising is an indirect sales medium and accounting for its success can be challenging to measure, even with better than average revenues; however, some research has gone into the subject, and there is now more evidence as to the effectiveness of digital advertising.

Research conducted by Brunel University and ROI Team (an independent retail research company) looked in-depth at the effectiveness of digital signage in the world-famous Harrods store in Knightsbridge, London.

They discovered that digital content, combining both visual imagery and informative text, has the most significant and positive effect on shoppers' consumer purchasing behaviour.

The research centred on nearly 500 face to face interviews conducted in spring this year. It concerned a digital advert for a holiday in the Maldives which was shown on three different mediums, including a digital signage campaign and a control advertisement with the viewers responding more favourably to the digital advert.

INCREASING EFFECTIVENESS

While the effectiveness of digital advertising is undoubtedly less in doubt, thanks to the latest research, there is still much that can be done to increase the efficiency of a digital advertising campaign.

Perhaps the most fundamental thing you can do to increase the effectiveness of a digital sign is to increase the audience size, and the simplest method of doing that is to take the digital display outside.

Outdoor digital signage will reach far more people than a similar indoor campaign. Although there is an added cost of protecting the screen from the rigours of an outdoor location, the extra viewership can soon recoup any additional investment.

TOP 10 PITFALLS

So, you've decided your business or institution will be well served by adding a new digital signage network. Now what?

Where to turn and what to do can be confusing, especially if you're responsible for your organization's communications or IT department, but don't know anything about a digital sign. While there are many good companies in business to help you achieve your goals, you can make the endeavour easier and far more successful if you avoid the problems many before you have encountered when rolling out and maintaining their digital signage networks.

Having worked with hundreds of customers on their digital signage needs, we've seen a lot of difficulties that could easily have been avoided -along with the associated delays and added expense- with a little knowledge upfront. As the saying goes, forewarned is forearmed. So, keep these Top 10 Pitfalls in mind as you plan your new network to make the experience smooth and rewarding.

— **No. 1: Lack of a definite purpose**

Someone in your organization has read digital signage can make marketing messaging more effective. It can reach potential customers at the point of purchase, promote the desired behaviour, target different demographic groups associated with different times of the day, and do so many beautiful things.

But what exactly does your organization need to accomplish with it? That's the fundamental question. Without clearly defining the purpose of a digital signage network, it is impossible to find success in any phase of its deployment or use.

Taking the time upfront to define the expectations for the system and write them out on paper for the approval of key management will provide direction and focus effort on attainable goals. Struggling to fulfil a nebulous purpose for the flat-panel sign network will rack up unnecessary expense and leave everyone connected with the project frustrated.

— **No. 2: Taking on digital signage as an IT project**

"Digital signage network," the very words sound IT-oriented. While there's a lot of IT technology involved with it, taking it on as an IT project is dangerous.

While highly skilled, the typical IT manager does not have the background nor the experience needed to roll out a successful digital sign network. There's a powerful temptation on the part of IT managers to look at dynamic signage playback as if it were a Microsoft PowerPoint presentation. It isn't.

PowerPoint does an excellent job at making business presentations, but how many TV stations rely on PowerPoint to create and playback the programs, commercials, news and promotions you see nightly? Exactly zero.

Concerning playing back video, graphics, text and animation, layering multiple visual elements and building and maintaining a playout schedule, a sign network is much more like a TV station than a boardroom with a projector and a PowerPoint presentation. Keep that in mind if an IT manager volunteers to take on your organization's project.

— **No. 3: Lack of content**

Congratulations. You have a digital signage network. What are you going to display? Having a system without content is like having a newspaper without print. There's just a whole lot of nothing and an overwhelming sense of emptiness.

Communicating in some form must be part of the reason behind the decision to add a sign network. However, there is no communication without content. Fortunately, many organizations have existing resources to draw upon that can be repurposed as digital signage content. Logos, commercials, promotional video, print advertising, plans and drawings can all be reused in whole or part to communicate a message on a sign network.

Additionally, RSS Internet feeds are a tremendous resource for updating a sign network with fresh "newsy" content, weather and sports scores that can give an audience a reason to take a second or third look.

Regardless of where it comes from, content is critical to the success of a sign network. Knowing where it will come from is as important as actually having the system in place.

— **No. 4: No one assigned to manage the project**

While it's not like designing the International Space Station, putting a digital signage network in place can be a complex undertaking. For that reason, it's essential that any business or organization taking on a sign network assign someone to manage the project. Having an individual identified to own the project will minimize the impact of the unforeseen problems that inevitably creep into any complex undertaking.

Just as bad as having no one assigned to manage the project is its closely related cousin: management by committee. Offering up conflicting directions from multiple individuals will leave your system integrator bewildered and your project incomplete.

— **No. 5: No one to update content**

While RSS feeds and subscriptions to news wire services are two sources of current information for a digital signage network, where will updated material conveying your company's specific messages and current offerings come from?

A dynamic sign network that attracts attention has an insatiable appetite for fresh content. Thus, it's essential that an organization taking on a sign network assign a qualified, competent person to the task of creating that content. Without someone in charge of the network's content, the text, graphics and video being displayed will soon grow tired. Stale content will have the opposite of the desired result for a digital sign. It actually will drive viewers away and impart a sense of "been there, done that" that will be difficult to reverse.

— **No. 6: Taking the cheap way out**

There's nothing wrong with being budget conscious about a digital signage installation; however, selecting products, including displays, controllers and software, and services like content creation solely on their price tag can result in a system that in the long wrong will cost an organization dearly.

Systems designed solely on the price of the component miss the point. Digital sign networks are about communicating information -perhaps a marketing message, maps and directions or instructions- to their intended audience. Spending money on an inexpensive system just because it's cheap could cost a business or organization far more than the money saved in lost opportunities.

— **No. 7: Not knowing the locations of the signs**

Knowing where your organization wants to locate the flat panel monitors in its digital signage network is essential for a few reasons. First, establishing the digital sign media players needed depends on where the sign or signs it's controlling are located.

The length of cable runs between player and sign must be taken into account. Clearly defining the location of the posters will allow you to minimize construction/renovation expense and avoid paying for "do-overs."

Second, understanding exactly where the signs will be positioned will make it easier to understand what will be needed to mount the flat panels in use. Are wall studs available where a warning will be located? Or, will a freestanding structure be required? What's the condition of the wall studs? Is electrical power available? What's the status of ambient light sources? Will a window or skylight need to be shaded to reduce glare?

Third, not knowing where the signs need to located may be a symptom of a bigger problem, namely not having a clear idea about the purpose of the digital signage installation.

— **No. 8: Installers without general contractor capability**

Installing digital signage can be messy. Drywall and plaster may need to be cut. New electrical plugs with isolated grounds may need to be installed. Beyond those distinct construction challenges, less apparent structural modifications may be required. Those can vary from relocating HVAC ducts to re-enforcing walls.

For that reason, choosing a digital signage installer without the skill and experience to serve as a general contractor for the project can be a big mistake. Depending on the specific installation, it's not unreasonable to assume carpenters, electricians, plumbers and even heating and cooling contractors might need to be involved in making necessary structural modifications. Having an installer who can serve as a general contractor to bring those diverse resources together and manage them properly can save lots of time and expense.

— No. 9: Failing to allow adequate time to learn the system

Far too often, the people responsible for new digital signage installations at businesses or organizations are so excited about their operations that they can't wait to show them off to upper management.

After all, a significant sum of money went into making the digital sign network a reality. So, showing it off as soon as possible only seems natural.

However, creating content for a system, scheduling it and making changes to playback along the way requires some skill. It takes time to be adequately trained to use a sign network.

Failing to allocate sufficient time to learn how to use the system not only could be embarrassing in front of management but disastrous to your communications efforts with the general public, if they're your first audience.

— No. 10: Failing to keep future expansion in mind at the time of initial design

Designing yourself into a box when first contemplating a digital signage network can be costly. Without casting an eye towards future needs, it's possible that portions of the system might need replacement before they've been amortized to accommodate expansion.

Without exception, experience shows that businesses and organizations that fund the addition of digital sign networks express interest in expanding their systems after they're installed.

CHAPTER 47: 5 MUST-HAVES WHILE LOOKING FOR A DIGITAL MARKETING AGENCY FOR YOUR STARTUP

Every startup or small-scale business holds the potential to grow if it has the right ingredients. The ingredients are the right idea, funding & a professional digital marketing agency to hoist the digital campaigns & plans for such business.

To expand any business's horizons, it has become vital for them to be a part of such a digital era.

Digital marketing over conventional marketing is becoming one approach that is no doubt output-oriented, steadfast resulting and most of all, cost-effective.

A brick & mortar business in today's time requires a website, social media presence & some key strategies & actionable tasks to evolve as a recognized brand in the market.

But before starting with the process, the key is to understand what your startup must look for in a digital marketing agency before partnering with their services - apart from their digital marketing startup package.

Here are the 5 must-haves to look for in a digital marketing firm of today other than digital marketing startup package:

1. Hard to miss - their website

The first thing you need to approach is their website, and their website will help you decide how well they can plan for your website's marketing. Check if their website is up to date and has all the capabilities that any site should host.

Their website will speak volumes about their agency, their achievements, competency and the efforts they may be willing to put in your startup's website to make it trending & best-selling.

2. Referrals for the credibility

It is the most crucial thing to do - to check the company's profile & market image before extending a contract with them for their service.

You can contact their ex-clients or customers to get the preview of their work pattern & check how well they have managed to publicize certain brands in the search engines. The best way could be testimonials & the portfolio embedded on the website.

3. A veteran of the current technology, software & marketing methods

Digital marketing is effortless if it doesn't house the latest technologies, software, tools & the methodologies. Look for the veterans or experts that are familiar with the most recent social media performance monitoring & analytics tools, knows the search engine's guidelines and can come up with customized strategies suitable to the brand/company profile.

4. Complies well with your startup's goals & ideas

A well-reputed online marketing agency knows how to come in terms with any startup's shared goals, nature & purpose behind it. An agency must comprehend the kind of business & must revert the strategies or plans that work in their demeanour.

5. Flexible in terms of making communication with the client

Such marketing firm should be comfortable in terms of bringing the right conversation on the tables. They should not lapse in terms of communicating the core messages like the process, progress or the suggested actions for the individual project.

NETWORKING BLUES

Networking is a skill that requires a lot of time, planning and organization for it to be effective. Being efficient also involves correctly managing your contacts. It is essential to not only attend events but nurture and grow relations. There are many tools and resources for leveraging networks and connections.

Listed below are simple tips for engaging and being responsive to your networks.

— **Digital Age**

Lean on technology to keep your networks in order and productive. There are plenty of apps that you can download to stay consistent and available for your connections.

Download and use apps that offer frequent updates and reminders about individuals in your groups. Reaching out to congratulate a counterpart on a promotion, anniversary or other achievement are excellent ways of staying in contact. Also, utilize apps that can be interconnected with other platforms that you use frequently.

— **Traditional Communication**

Although we are in the digital age, receiving a handwritten note or making a phone call are still proper methods for reaching out. It shows sincerity and genuine value for others. It can also catch the attention or be a pleasant surprise for the individual on the receiving end. Once again, setting up reminders to make this type of personal touchpoints can be extremely beneficial.

— **Outside Assistance**

If things get too overwhelming, then consider hiring outside help. Invest in a virtual assistant who can manage your contacts and even increase your connections. Along with organizing information, meetings etc. the assistant can also provide services in editing, marketing etc. Outsourcing can also be beneficial in time management and allow you to focus on other tasks.

Use these valuable tips to scale your networking process and grow your connections. Being focused, organized and intentional about your endeavours provide significant returns on your investments.

CHAPTER 48: TOP 5 INTERNET MARKETING STRATEGIES IN 2019

Internet marketing and digital advertisement have gained prominence throughout the past couple of years like wildfire. With the massive digitization of media and entertainment industry among many others, internet marketing gained fame.

It has grown to become a popular choice of advertisement strategy alongside banners, billboards, and commercials, etc. Every day, with over 3.5 billion search queries, there is no doubt that Internet Marketing Strategies is among the trending topics.

Thus, here we are going to enlist top 5 internet marketing strategies to implement in 2019. They are listed below: -

1. Chatbot Marketing

In this era of being a busybody, running a company and interacting with every customer becomes a real challenge. This is where the chatbots come into play.

You can create your chatbots, with automated replies via text or message, and the customer will not even realize whether they are interacting with a customer care provider or a bot.

The Facebook messenger connects over 2 billion people, so Facebook chatbots have become a real and accessible solution to boosting up the digital market. Since chatbots can be used to generate human dialogue, it can be used to reply to customer queries, spread important information, and to provide user-friendly assistance to the buyer/page visitor.

2. SEO

Search engine optimization is the best way to remain on the top of the search list by using and enabling specific keywords which increase the hit score according to the type of business. For long-term strategies, this is possibly the best way out, as it is cost-effective also.

The investment is not indefinite as once a site gets ranked, it will remain so; increasing the influx of traffic and in turn, increase in sales. If a company is looking for outsourcing on a digital platform, opting for SEO is no doubt a suitable choice, given it is maintained regularly.

3. Inbound Marketing

Human judgments integrate emotions. So, emphasizing on the attachment of value and sentiments to a product and not only superficial advertising also plays a significant part in successful digital marketing. Not interrupting the thought process of a customer, instead of giving choices for personalized products is the base of inbound marketing. It is also a long-time investment, with high returns if the market is consistently maintained.

4. Influencer Marketing

People nowadays not only look for the popularity of an influencer but also look for the quality of follower. Classic marketing strategies like word-of-mouth marketing and advocate marketing, are now being popularized in the digital marketing field.

An advocate influencer instructing and convincing the people who are entirely away from the world of advertising does a great job of gaining organic customers. Reaching out to the masses on social media, promoting a product, and creating a good community of netizens in bulk, influencer marketing is sure a bold and new technique.

5. Digital PR s

Everybody, nowadays, spend a lot of time on digital platforms. With a lot of spam messages and time-consuming news and contents, digital PR plays a very crucial role in creating a niche for brands and businesses. Though it is not a very new technique, and public relations date back to the beginning of marketing; still, PR cannot be ignored nonetheless.

It is just about the right exposure to the target customers in a positive light. A personal brand can also be popularized using digital PR. It takes less work than traditional PR but is more effective.

Due to global digitization Internet Marketing Strategies, like the ones listed above, have grown to become prominent contributing factors in the field of media and mass communication.

The better you have your strategies figures out, the better shot you have in reaching the boulevard of success.

CHAPTER 49: SERVICE MANAGEMENT

Whatever business organization is ventured into, the capital gain is what gets the most attention. Business procedures naturally generate a handsome amount of lucrative revenues. Service management is the term used to refer to the administering of serving producing companies.

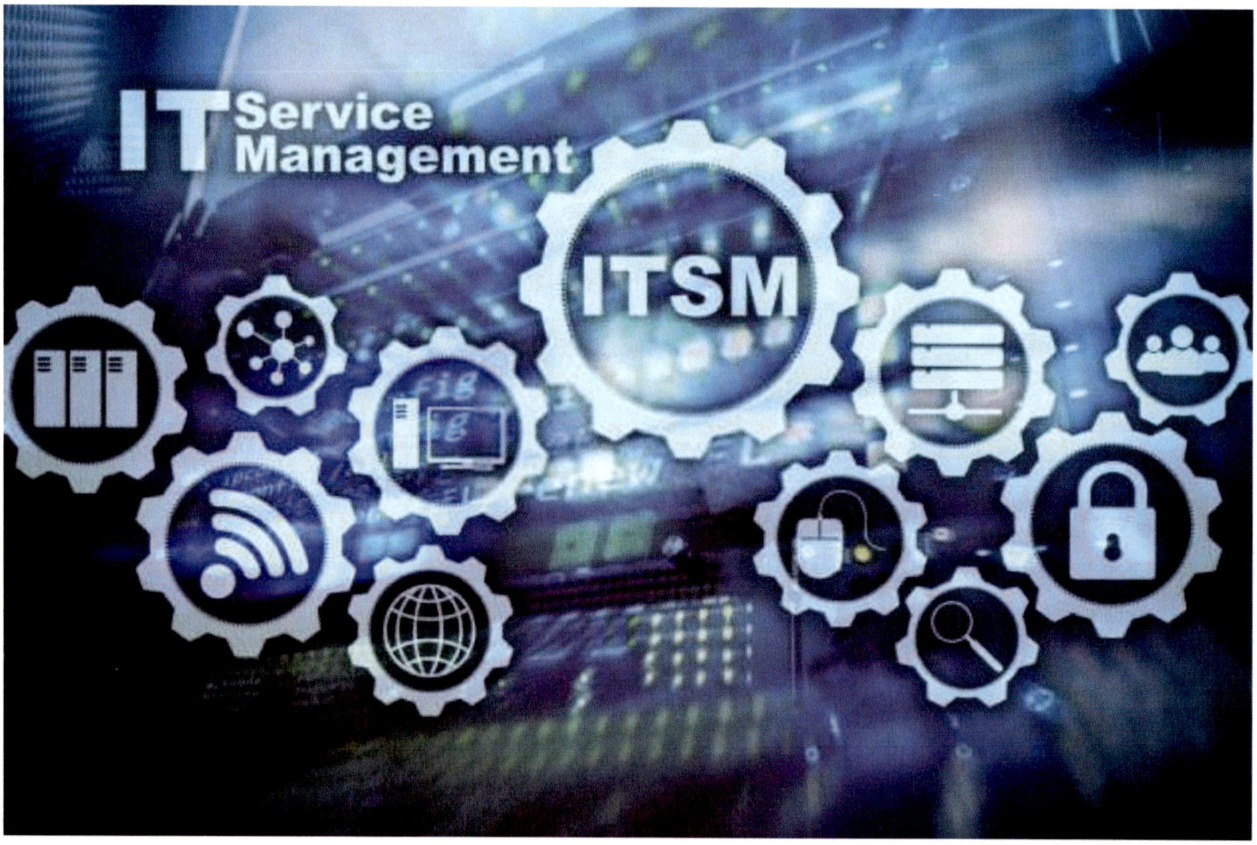

It is mostly in contrast with that of the agricultural and manufacturing companies because the term service management mostly applies to information and technology sectors and at times to auto repair and housekeeping industries.

These days procedures have become automated. Meaning, an IT technological breakthrough has paved the way for the practical materialization of the business process. Among the particular advantages surfacing are commerce methodologies such as the Internet and web technology.

Service management is synonymous to the administration of operation's support. The service management arena by and large covers the areas of order management, service delivery, inventory, and network maintenance, the firmness of the communication providers and the maneuvering of their networks. It is the service management arrangement that ensures a flawless flow of these service areas.

The constant monitoring of the IT sectors places the IT organizations under enormous pressure. The management of daily operations and securing the proper flow of the IT assets and answering the demands of the clienteles are strict responsibilities to handle.

The IT-related service management staff must ensure the availability of persons who are versatile in troubleshooting network problems and averting technical tribulations.

Doing business via the web has long become a trend. More and more individuals commit to negotiations online. A helpful service management team will save the day for all parties involved in any online business transaction.

Various service management providers house effective solutions to cope with the growing demands of their consumers. They make services available and products that are of great help to their clients. Among these products are the comprehensive lineups of service desk, support automation, service intelligence, service catalogue, and service accounting.

By capturing consumer demands and providing current optimum and affordable services to all business needs, IT service management can make the IT-related business a worthwhile experience.

EXTENDING ITSM TO NON-IT ORGANIZATIONAL UNITS

The role of technology in business is more important than ever before. There is new pressure on IT and financial resources to help other departments, such as Human Resources, Facilities, and Customer Service, automate their business processes. Besides, tech-savvy end-users are demanding self-service for everything they do.

Traditionally, companies have utilized standard forms or purchased singularly focused, point tools designed to automate specific functions driven by separate business requirements and funding streams.

Unfortunately, these Business Process Management solutions are usually disconnected from the business, require extensive customization and are too expensive to fit the budget constraints of a single organizational unit.

Not to mention the burden on IT to acquire, maintain and support multiple point solutions.

The fact of the matter is that most organizational units are interested in automating similar workflow activities.

For example, receiving a request from an end-user, assigning that request to a team member, obtaining approvals, tracking and reporting progress, and so forth. At the same time, organizations are trying to cut costs and seek inventive ways to get more out of their current systems.

RESPONDING TO THE DEMAND

How does an organization respond to the demand for business process automation solutions without breaking the bank or placing an undue burden on IT resources?

A single solution that is:

— Agile enough to meet the rapidly changing demands of today's business

— Flexible enough to meet the needs of various organizational units, their processes, and their users

— Secure sufficient to maintain confidentiality between data from varying organizational units

— Simple enough to deliver value in a short time and without customization

— Extensive enough to integrate with a variety of department-specific tools

BEYOND IT

IT Service Management solutions that are based on the ITIL (IT Infrastructure Library) framework are a perfect match for non-IT business functions. ITIL is a set of guidelines that advise on how to run IT as a business.

These are loose and generic guidelines that can easily be translated to other organizational units.

All organizational units provide some service. For example, Facilities provides cleaning, office equipment, and safety services. All service providers receive requests, and they manage approvals, they require metrics and following a process will likely help the business run smoothly.

ITIL has helped IT move from constant firefighting to more careful planning, better communication, and structured service delivery. Leveraging standardized best practices to help non-IT organizational units "run like a business" certainly cannot hurt.

NON-IT BUSINESS PROCESS USES

— Facilities Management

— Human Resources

— External Customer Support (Call Centers)

— Accounting

— Security

— Legal

— Sales Tracking

— HIPAA Patient Management

— Training

— Marketing

— Project Management

GETTING STARTED

Many organizations that have extended their ITSM solution to other departments started the journey with a Service Catalog. The catalog of services demonstrates that business services can be requested and automatically tracked. Presenting business services in a familiar and straightforward structure to users encourages them to submit requests formally.

If you are having trouble demonstrating how an ITSM solution can extend to non-IT business processes, create a sample business service catalog to start. Stock this catalog with services from various departments, such as requestable office furniture, name change requests and keyboards, and mice.

Demonstrate to the other organizational units the different functionality and intelligence that can be configured to route the requests to the proper teams based on automated workflow. For example, the process employed when there is a request for a New Hire.

The new hire requires office space, furniture, telephone, and IT equipment. The fulfillment process involves the coordination of tasks across multiple groups including HR, facilities, telecommunications, and IT.

Without automation, the onboarding process will be chaos.

Just imagine the ability to request office space for a new hire within a service-catalog, automate routine maintenance checks on fire alarms and report on trends within your external customer service department, all in a process controlled environment.

BENEFITS

Leveraging the once traditional ITSM functionality (such as ticketing, service catalogues, self-service portals, change management, approvals, knowledge management, service level agreements, and workflow) for non-IT Service Management using standardized best practices makes a lot of sense operationally and financially.

Achieve better return on IT investments - Extending a single Service Management solution across organizational units has a much lower total cost of ownership

Justify budget spend - Allow disparate business units to share the cost of a single solution

Improve service quality - Deliver faster response to end-users/customers through self-service, automation and knowledge sharing

Improve internal communication - Share knowledge and connect end-to-end processes across multiple departments such as HR and Facilities

The marked similarity between IT processes and non-IT processes, from submitting a request, accepting the invitation, verifying the entitlement, gathering approvals, fulfilling the request and verifying the successful fulfillment with full audit trails, tracking and reporting, makes extending the right IT Service Management solution to non-IT processes a no-brainer.

Better processes, fewer manual errors, and automation will lead to lower costs, employee morale improvements, and much happier customers.

CHAPTER 50: CRITICAL SUCCESS FACTORS

Digital transformation is critical not only regarding short-term growth and market share but also to ensure their long-term survival and relevance. Digital platforms and ecosystems can drive efficiencies, and through new and unexpected collaborations, create new value for businesses and customers.

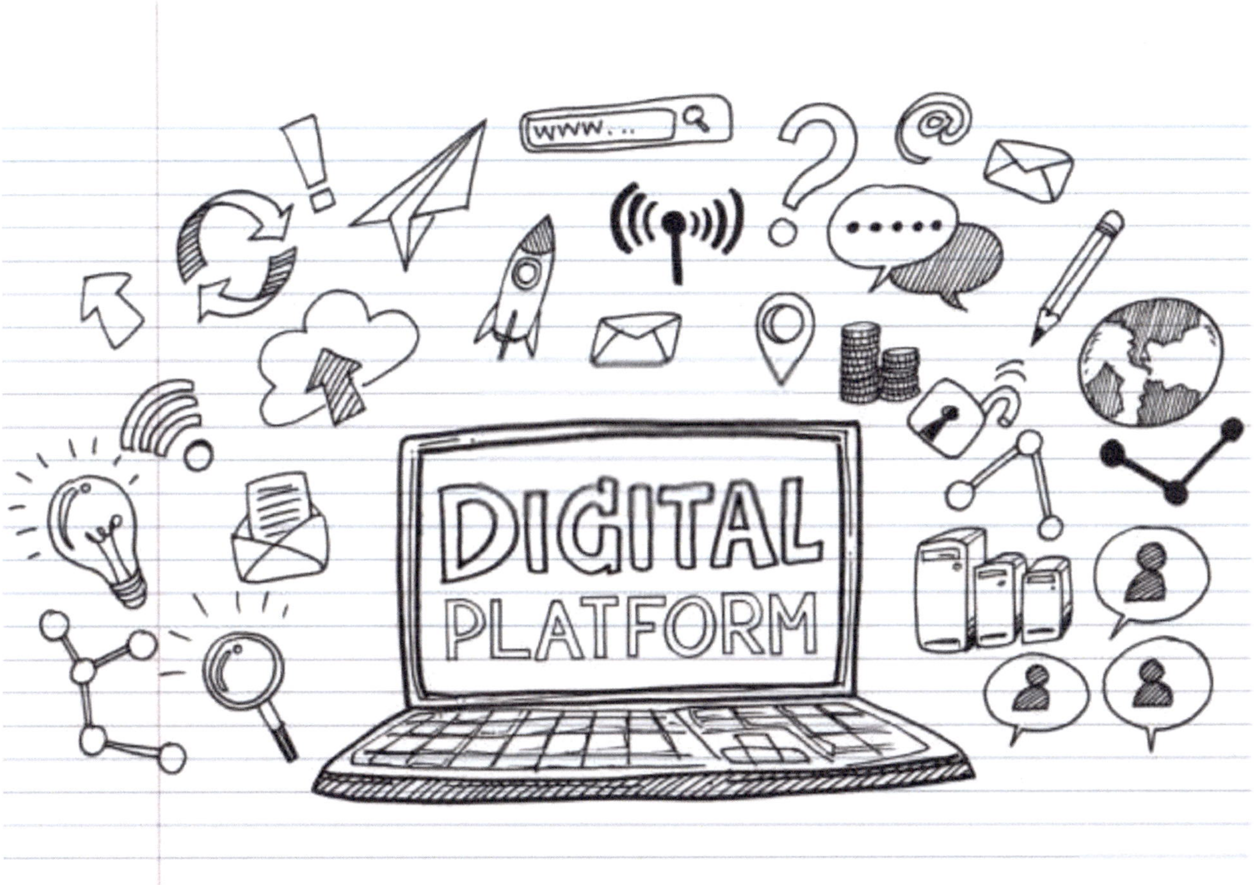

Digital maturity across industries has been classified into personas such as beginners, conservatives, fashionistas & digital masters with digital and leadership capability driving their business transformation.

The digital age has brought about a new way of thinking on process and operations. Smart devices with digital capabilities are seamlessly offering direct benefits to industries around productivity, efficiency, innovation and decision making.

Today's millennial enterprise CEO priorities are innovation, speed to market, public trust and human capital which leads to initiatives around the digital and data-driven business.

The CIO priorities are to manage both change and operations. While on the one ,hand it is to increase transformation, efficiency, security, on the other hand, it is to cut costs & time for new service, maintain, simplify IT models & infra and improve business process.

The business outcomes of a digital transformation program decide its critical success factor or value proposition. These could be around customer experience transformation or enterprise user efficiency. People, process and technology, are essential factors for the success of any transformation program.

It is imperative that a digital transformation is applied to the end to end process and not in a piecemeal manner.

A stimulating and digital customer acquisition front end with a manual/semi manual process at the back office or vice-versa will never lead to the desired business outcomes. So complete digital process automation leads to innovation, efficiency, and trust and that becomes one of the critical success factors for the transformation program.

Change management is another critical success factor for a digital transformation. People/resources directly or indirectly involved in such a transformation determine the fate of any such initiative.

Concerns around the perceived loss of control of a manual / semi-automated process, push back on any change, an adaption of any innovation should be managed by a structured change management process comprising of clear communication, management direction, creating a collaborative environment to address organizational cultural challenges.

Technology plays a vital role in the success of an adaptable digital transformation. However instead of technical know-how or features of a software or hardware, it the ease of implementation, design thinking, smooth transition and program management with a finesse that stands out and results in an acceptable digital transformation which gets applauded both externally and internally.

FACTORS INFLUENCING YOUR DIGITAL TRANSFORMATION TEST STRATEGY

Digital transformation implies connecting every system and processes of an enterprise to achieve a slew of outcomes including quicker decision making. It has come about as a result of increased internet connectivity and a proliferation of digital technologies.

Digital transformation has spawned many new age companies that are agile, lean, focused and result oriented. To compete with such newbies, enterprises saddled with legacy systems and used to the traditional ways of doing things need to transform themselves.

Although Digital transformation services aim at reorienting the systems, processes, and stakeholders in an organization, they are prone to risks as well. These risks can be manifold from having vulnerabilities in systems, methods, networks, and products to dealing with new resources.

Moreover, since digital transformation services aim at accelerating the time to market as far as the products and services are concerned, quality is often given short shrift. It often leads to the failure of products in meeting customers' expectations. When enterprise digital transformation initiatives do not yield the stated business objectives, the need for digital quality assurance becomes critical.

WHY DIGITAL QUALITY ASSURANCE?

- To identify and eliminate glitches present in the systems, processes, networks, products, and services.
- To meet the rising customer expectations for better quality products/services.
- To stay in competition by delivering quality products/services with reduced lead times.
- To accelerate the time to market with better products by using Agile and DevOps methodologies.
- To adhere to quality and security regulations.
- To prevent hackers from exploiting the systems, products or services.

— To ensure brand loyalty among customers.

— To achieve business objectives and ROI.

A robust digital testing strategy requires incorporating the shift-left approach. It is mainly to pre-empt the creation of glitches by testing the product during the development phase itself.

With Agile and DevOps paradigms becoming the benchmarks for a digital testing strategy, how can test automation stay behind? Digital QA through test automation helps businesses to future-proof their systems, products or services. It does so by increasing the test coverage area and carrying out repetitive functional and non-functional testing seamlessly.

— 7 factors influencing a digital transformation test strategy

1 Security: Security is arguably the most significant factor influencing the digital software testing of products. It involves aspects like vulnerability scanning, penetration testing, risk assessment, and security auditing among others.

Here, testers identify the weaknesses in a system or product by using automated software. Also, a simulated attack is carried out a la penetration testing to check for potential vulnerabilities, which when removed, can prevent the system or product from external or internal hacking.

2 Cost: This can have two different connotations. On the one side, the cost incurred by the business when a product fails to live up to the users' expectations is taken into account.

While on the other hand, the cost of implementing manual/test automation is considered. In the case of choosing a test automation software, the need for an open source or licensed software is decided based on the overall cost and the type of tests to be carried out.

3 Presence of legacy systems: Digital QA involves the testing of a software product across devices, networks, platforms, frameworks, browsers, and operating systems.

It requires faster systems with the latest test software. However, if an enterprise is beset with legacy systems, then the test strategy needs to be looked at again. It is done by considering the capability of such systems and the cost of replacing the same.

4 Reliability: The software s ystems that enable digital transformation should be tested to know the extent to which specific functions of these can perform on a continuous basis. It includes feature testing, load testing, and regression testing.

5 Scalability: The changing dynamics of business requires an enterprise to be flexible. The flexibility should be regarding expanding the capacity of its systems and processes to meet any future demand. The test strategy chosen should check the scalability aspect of the operations.

6 Interoperability: An enterprise will have some software programs running its digital transformation initiative. These programs should have a better interface

with each other to achieve the overall business objectives. Hence, the test strategy should check the programs' interoperability.

7 Skillset: The success of a test strategy depends on the expertise of the test team. The test strategy should consider this aspect along with the need and cost of training.

The success of digital transformation initiatives by a business enterprise is critical for its sustenance. The systems enabling this transformation should be rigorously tested based on the factors mentioned above.

DIGITAL TRANSFORMATION IS VITAL NOW

With decreasing retail sales, more people buying online, and new sales and marketing tactics smashing competition through the digital space, the old business models can't compete for much longer. Get started today and start the transformation now before you get out-transformed by your competitors!

For businesses to excel in today's increasingly competitive environment and remain agile in the midst of constant change, organizations need to automate processes wherever possible. At the same time, IT is being pulled in a multitude of directions and assisting non-IT units with business process automation is not at the top of the priority list.

Presenting a solution that consolidates all of the requirements of various organizational units, is simple to implement and extend, and makes process automation available where it did not previously exist, may cause IT leadership to move a "shared service management solution" up on that priority list.

CHAPTER 51: LINKEDIN FOR BUSINESS

HOW IT CAN HELP YOU

LinkedIn can be another platform for staying up to date with the newest information in your industry. A great example in LinkedIn Today that was launched in March this year. LinkedIn Today picks up Top Headlines and stories from multiple sectors that are shared the most by LinkedIn's network of professionals.

Members can also view top trending news strongly related to a particular industry and what is being shared those most from people within that industry.

It shows the Top 3 stories that are strongly related to you which in my case includes Social Media Marketing and Advertising, Internet and IT.

For anyone who is unhappy with the information delivered, you may change your profile, so you are offered the Top Stories for various industries or from different sources. LinkedIn Today can be accessed when you go to the Home Page.

— LinkedIn Signal

Like LinkedIn Today, LinkedIn Signal also delivers information to you from your professional network.

LinkedIn Signal, it marries the concept of LinkedIn and Twitter by taking the stream of info from Twitter and making sense of all the Tweets. Mostly it is a view of Twitter via LinkedIn's eyes - you can refer to it as the Twitter for professionals.

You can locate LinkedIn Signal in your profile panel by going to the News tab at the top of your profile and then scroll down to Signal.

Once you are in the Signal dashboard, you can sort through the Tweets by 1st-degree connections, 2nd-degree connections, company, industry, time, location and much more. It can be an excellent means of picking up interesting information from your professional network.

— LinkedIn Is a Search Engine

These recent innovations from within the LinkedIn team, indicate that LinkedIn is much more about content mainly curating content from around the web and delivering relevant information to its users.

In some ways it is fast becoming a search engine in its own right; comparable to Facebook has grown to be.

The fundamental difference between Facebook and LinkedIn when compared to Google is that information is being found by users rather than users having to search for it. Google isn't quite there yet however it is changing rapidly and trying to evolve.

WHY LINKEDIN IS ATTRACTIVE TO MARKETERS

Previously the hunting ground of recruiters and Human Resources personnel, LinkedIn is also beautiful for Marketers targeting businesses. LinkedIn's statistics tell a portion of the story:

- Globally Facebook has over 500 million members (with 300 million active users),
- Twitter has 40 million
- LinkedIn has 50 million members.

LinkedIn might lag behind Facebook when it comes to users, but it carries a very attractive demographic which advertisers and business to business (B2B) marketers find very attractive.

It is because, according to Cliff Rosenberg, LinkedIn members have an average age of 43 years and an average income of $100K, which is more than average income.

There are also millions of users around the world so using the tools inside LinkedIn can assist you to reach people that you previously found challenging to target. Just as exciting is the fact that LinkedIn keeps growing, every second new user is signing up to LinkedIn globally. Marketers like growth.

WAYS TO GET IN CONTACT WITH HARD TO REACH CONTACTS

LinkedIn has some free and paid tools making it easy to reach your target market depending on who you choose to target.

— **Paid Options**

Of the paid options, LinkedIn Ads are a great paid option to target prospects because you can target prospects by Geography, Company, Job Title, Group, Gender, and Age.

There is a lot of talks that the ads are much more expensive but bear in mind you are reaching a more attractive demographic with higher disposable incomes as well business professionals.

If you are in recruitment, then the obvious way to reach potential candidates is by upgrading your account to Business, Business Plus or Executive which allows you to send messages to potential candidates outside your professional network.

Otherwise, you can go the path of Rio Tinto and Vodafone which have an annual license to allow them to approach LinkedIn members directly.

— Free Options

An excellent method to interact with members is to join groups relevant to your profession. It is a potent tool.

By joining a group, you can take part in conversations, ask questions, and get advice or opinions. Hint: It's a pretty effective way to do informal market research and find out the essential requirements are for your potential customers.

The key is not to sell but to add value and build your authority within your industry or profession. As you become more known, you will probably find people approaching you rather than you being the one to approach them.

Another way is to look at your connections to check out who they are linked to. If they know someone you know, you could approach your contact directly and ask them to introduce you.

If they are satisfied with your service, and know like and trust you, they will be more than happy to recommend you to their contact.

The other alternative is to request that your contact recommends you in LinkedIn. If they make a recommendation about you, it will appear in the updates section of your prospects home page.

Speaking of recommendations, it is essential to also get recommendations from individuals who can influence your career.

When you ask for recommendations, send a note explaining how people can recommend you.

Some people don't know how to go about it, and LinkedIn does not have a significant button highlighting people to support you.

Be sure your profile is 100% up to date; keyword rich and that you use a professional looking photo.

— **Use Linkedin As Tool To Help You To Rank Better In Search Engines**

There are some things you can do to help you rank better in Search Engines - individually if you are a business owner or Managing Director.

1. Set up a company profile so that it will appear in search results. Use good keywords. If you aren't sure, engage a professional to help you refine keywords. Do put your website URL on your company page. Make sure you also nominate yourself and at least one other person as admin in case one of you is not available.

2. Request that your staff put themselves on LinkedIn. It might sound crazy since many people see LinkedIn as a job board, but it is a right way of getting multiple backlinks back to your website which will help you rank in search engines.

3. Participate in group discussions - groups discussions appear in search results, so it is an excellent tool to build your brand and your company in search engines.

GENERATING LEADS WITH LINKEDIN

LinkedIn is a business-related social networking platform that is mainly used by people for professional networking and forming strong business relationships. For entrepreneurs and businesses, LinkedIn is a great medium to promote their brand and make new working relationships by generating more leads.

If it is used the right way, LinkedIn can be a powerhouse for generating great leads, especially for B2B's.

Even though most of them depend on business to business, there are some tried and test ways that businesses have been using to generate as many leads as possible for high business profits.

It is not easy for B2Bs to get the same type of results like other social networking websites mainly because B2B target other businesses and professionals while social networking sites target audience. LinkedIn is one such site that caters well to the B2B market and if you use this medium the right way, getting the anticipated results become easy.

The most important tip to generate more leads with LinkedIn is to demonstrate your knowledge and show how well informed you are regarding the ins and outs of the industry.

Check out the questions related to your field and utilize your knowledge to provide answers and solutions to others. It would not only help to assert yourself as a well-informed person, but you would also assume the role of a leader whom others will seek to get solutions to their problems, and as a result, you will get more clients who need your assistance. Letting others know what you can do for them is the best way to generate more leads and become more popular on LinkedIn.

Along with demonstrating your prowess, it is equally essential to optimize your LinkedIn page. It will help to improve your search engine visibility and give others a bright idea of which category of business you belong to and how you can help them in their business.

By optimizing your page, you can also appear in top searches and promote your products and services well.

LinkedIn provides its users with the facility to share content with others. You can use this to generate more leads by posting engaging and exciting content that others would love to read.

It is a great way to promote your brand and sharing will help to keep the content fresh and rolling so that every time you have visitors, they get something new and exciting to read.

Make sure the content is not only fresh, but it also offers relevant advice and tips to readers to generate more traffic.

Another great tip that would help to generate more leads on LinkedIn is joining groups and making networks. It will result in making new friends, meeting more professionals and finding people who could help in better business.

It is essential to ensure that you join groups that have a good reputation and are related to your industry instead of joining groups that con people and shady bear status. Joining groups would help to meet people in the related sector whom you could help and who could help you.

Posting ads on LinkedIn is also a great way to get more exposure and in turn more leads. You can advertise your business and services the best possible way and create more effective leads that lead to better profits.

However, it is essential to ensure that the posted ads are good enough to get public attention. All these tips for generating leads on LinkedIn are targeted to help B2B companies to do better and reap good profits by comfortable as well as practical means.

CHAPTER 52: TOP REASONS TO USE LINKEDIN FOR B2B

Most people use LinkedIn to stay in contact with coworkers, colleagues, make a sale or form a partnership.

Over the past several years this online network has seen more than 9 million professionals become part of this community that is continuously growing.

With more than 160 different industries present within this network, LinkedIn has become one of the top networking sites for professionals worldwide.

However, in many ways, LinkedIn is still under-utilized and should be looked at as a precious resource.

Here are some ways to increase the value of LinkedIn for you and your business.

1. Publicize Yourself

It is extremely important for those individuals or businesses who are looking to generate traffic or merely increase their presence within a particular industry. By adding valuable connections, you increase the likelihood that people will not only view your profile but may be interested in doing business with you or your company. A good suggestion for businesses on LinkedIn is to place the URL of your company's website within your profile; this allows your company's site to be accessed more readily and helps increase site traffic.

2. Improve your Image

To capture the full potential of LinkedIn, it is important to understand that it is not enough to reach out to people in hopes of getting them to be a part of your network or to join your group.

When people view a profile, they are looking for information about that particular business or person, such as their previous experiences, years in an industry, or business capabilities to identify whether or not you are a relevant contact or connection.

With your profile filled out correctly, along with a picture to promote yourself, you can maximize the views of your profile and the number of relevant connections within your network.

"People with more than twenty connections are thirty-four times more likely to be approached with a job opportunity than people with less than five."

3. Promote your Blog

It is vital to know that you can also promote a blog or business website through your LinkedIn profile and do so efficiently. There are various applications out there, but the best one (in our opinion) for promoting your blog is called WordPress.

Although this is known as a Content Management System, it is also referenced as an application with LinkedIn.

This type of application allows your blog to run in real time on your LinkedIn profile. So when you post a blog, it will automatically appear on your LinkedIn profile for all your connections to view.

It would be wise to make sure that your blog content is current, exciting, and optimized for the web. It helps catch your viewers' attention and could ultimately lead to an increase in traffic and could uncover potential business opportunities as well.

4. Learn about certain industries

If you're thinking of working within a specific market or sector, LinkedIn is an excellent tool for identifying market segments whether niche or broad. The search fields within LinkedIn are elementary to use and return excellent results.

With LinkedIn, you have the opportunity to search for people or business within a specific industry or specific groups to help you make educated decisions about contacts or future business ventures. These search features allow users to efficiently obtain the results they want without having to sift through vast quantities of results.

5. Analytics

LinkedIn, if utilized appropriately can be a handy marketing tool. LinkedIn allows its users to identify who has visited their profile over a particular date range giving some great insight in determining or identifying potential business opportunities.

Although this tool is free on a limited basis, LinkedIn offers a paid service that provides you greater insight and more detailed information about the users who view your profile.

Along with being able to identify who has been viewing your profile, LinkedIn is referenced as a "referring" site within Google Analytics.

When running an SEO campaign or just using Google Analytics as an analysis tool, you can see how much traffic has been directed to your site specifically from LinkedIn which is a great help when gauging marketing efforts.

NEW LINKEDIN APPS BENEFICIAL FOR B2B STRATEGIES

Many businesses to business advertising firms and their respective clients are already on LinkedIn using site features such as LinkedIn Groups to engage with prospects and connect with other professionals in their industry.

Recently, LinkedIn added three new features to its site and opened public access to another.

The following is a breakdown of these new features that are designed to give users the capability to forge stronger connections with other professionals in the LinkedIn community.

— **InMaps**

Provides a graphical representation of all the connections in a user's LinkedIn network. User connections are divided into groups by categories such as school or employer.

The name of each connection is sized according to the number of contacts they have in that particular InMap group. It allows the user to see which connections in their network are gateways to other contacts.

— **LinkedIn Skills**

The Skills page allows users to search for other LinkedIn professionals according to a specific skill.

Search results provide users with a list of others sharing that skill within their community as well as in related companies, jobs, and individual locations.

— **LinkedIn Signal**

This feature provides a real-time feed of posts from social media sites such as Twitter.

The posts are typically organized by a user's connections. The signal can provide real-time information also on what people are saying about a particular topic by typing in keywords in the application search box.

— **LinkedIn Today**

This application is a new page consisting of stories shared by a user's connections and other professionals in the LinkedIn community. LinkedIn Today allows users to follow as many as 22 industries and an array of news outlets.

The "Today" feature can also be accessed remotely via the new LinkedIn iPhone application. Its emphasis on business already makes LinkedIn the premiere social media site for B2B agencies and their clients.

But, by actively using some of the new tools offered by LinkedIn, B2B companies can enhance their level of engagement with colleagues, customers, and prospects.

CHAPTER 53: LEVERAGING LINKEDIN FOR YOUR BUSINESS SUCCESS

Small business-to-business (B2B) businesses that focus on LinkedIn as one of their main social media channels have been and are continuing to be successful at getting more leads that eventually lead to increased business. It is a worthwhile tool.

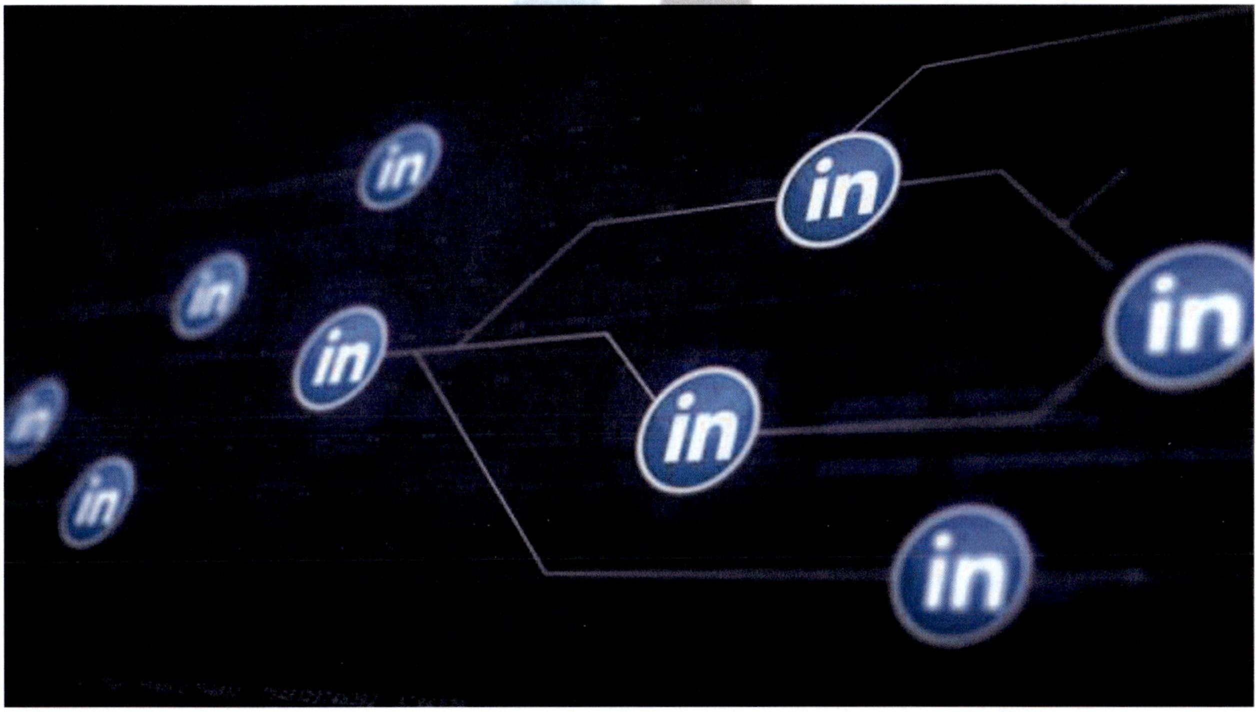

Many business people seem to be having a difficult time using social media channels for business. If you are one of those people who are not so well acquainted with LinkedIn, the following information should help you to understand why it is so essential for your business. Leveraging LinkedIn will help you to achieve positive results for your business and before long; you will not know how you managed to leave it out of your online marketing strategy.

GENERATING LEADS FOR YOUR BUSINESS

Undeniably, LinkedIn is widely used by professionals. The reason that it is so popular is that it is a beneficial social media channel that is easy to use and extremely user-friendly. When it comes to lead generation, you need to identify what works for you and your business and what doesn't work. If you find that something is working for you, use it as much as you can.

Of course, if you have tried something that doesn't seem to be working, don't waste your time and effort on that because your time will be much better spent on things that cause positive results.

To successfully generate business leads, the first thing that you must do is to complete your LinkedIn profile. Completing your profile doesn't mean just putting your name and a few details about who you are and what you represent professionally.

You need to fill in as many details as you can so that you allow other people the opportunity to get to know you. After all, you need to build relationships with people so that they will eventually buy whatever you are selling.

Building a relationship means that you are going to make trust and credibility as well as your positioning yourself as a subject matter expert. Your goal in that regard is for the other person to think of you first when they have needs that you can fulfill.

— **Realizing the fullest potential of your social network**

LinkedIn is a much more powerful tool than a lot of people understand, and it can help you to achieve your business goals in an advantageous manner. It won't cost you much money if any. The only things that you will have to invest our time and effort. Those are investments that you would make for your business no matter what tools you used to achieve success.

— **Handling customer service properly**

It is essential for you to examine precisely how your business is handling customer service and how it is tending to the needs of your clients. You can tie on LinkedIn with this as well.

The discussions through LinkedIn are critical to your success, and all sorts of exciting and stimulating pieces of information can be discovered through that particular form of communication. If you want to achieve greater success with your business, you need to pay a great deal of attention to the timing. You must always respond in a very timely manner, and your clients must still feel that they are your priority.

— **Engage with people on a very regular basis**

You should regard LinkedIn just as you would any other social media channel except for the fact that it is one of the top social media channels for business and should be respected for that. Engaging frequently can take on many different forms. You should synchronize your blog posts to LinkedIn as well as other social media channels with which you engage so that you increase your reputation and exposure.

— **Use LinkedIn to Effectively an Implement Employment Strategy**

Many businesses large and small make use of the employment resources LinkedIn provides. The job search and employment features of this network will connect talented people with talent seekers.

LinkedIn members can directly contact business seeking applicants for open positions. Human resource solutions and expertise are available through the Group feature on LinkedIn as well.

INCREASE B2B LEAD GENERATION WITH LINKEDIN

LinkedIn is arguably the best social medium for business-to-business companies. This network has an astonishing visitor to lead conversion rate of 2.74%. This is three times the conversion rate of Facebook and Twitter. The key to success here is to post information that is high value, decidedly relevant and offers unique industry insight. As this is a social website after all. The hard sell is not the way to go, no matter how tempting.

— **Increase Sales with LinkedIn**

Customized add banners that link back to your company website are free of charge with LinkedIn. Company pages that offer specific content targeted to LinkedIn member profiles are also provided. These features can drive sales through the over 1.5 million member Groups or communities that reside in the LinkedIn network.

— **Build and Strengthen Your Business Relationships**

Information sharing in the form of posts are allowed with LinkedIn. Adding meaningful industry content that is beneficial and interesting to LinkedIn promotes visibility for your business. LinkedIn analytics will monitor the effectiveness of your posts and enable you to change post updates to optimize your reach. It will vastly increase your chances of connecting with the companies that can benefit the most from business with you and vice versa.

IMPROVE YOUR B2B MARKETING TECHNIqUES

It is critical to think of new ways of creating credible customer-driven content constantly, online distribution channels, search terms, Internet links, etc. in B2B marketing. Traditional mass media has little or no relevance. That is why the B2B channel mix will look very different and may comprise:

— Search engines

— Niche websites such as LinkedIn

— Industry related online marketing

— Industry listings or online forums

— Accreditation with respected organizations

— Industry endorsements

— Case studies

— Client referrals and testimonials

— Thought leadership articles

— Awards

— Certifications

— Media relations and press mentions

— White papers and research studies

— Customized demonstrations

— Low-risk pilot tests

— Trade shows

— Trade directories

— Industry spokesmen

— Industry rankings and awards

— Industry publications

— Customer events

— Corporate videos and podcasts

— Executive bios etc.

Often, B2B communications output is best tailored to each target customer. Make sure your agency can also create significant PowerPoint decks in-house so that you can customize them for your corporate presentations.

— **There is a season for everything**

Always gear your B2B marketing towards your customers' planning cycles.

There are different financial year-ends in different countries, and it is essential to make your business pitch at least three to four months before your customer's year-end, to ensure your company has a chance of making the vendor shortlist for next year!

— **The grey line**

Unlike consumer marketing, where you can offer seasonal sales and gifts in exchange for individual purchases, such tactics are not always viewed as 'ethical' in B2B marketing.

CHAPTER 54: MAIN TYPES OF LEARNING

Machine learning is the core driver of AI. It's the concept of having computers learn from data with minimal programming. There different ways in which an ANN learns and we will discuss that in this chapter.

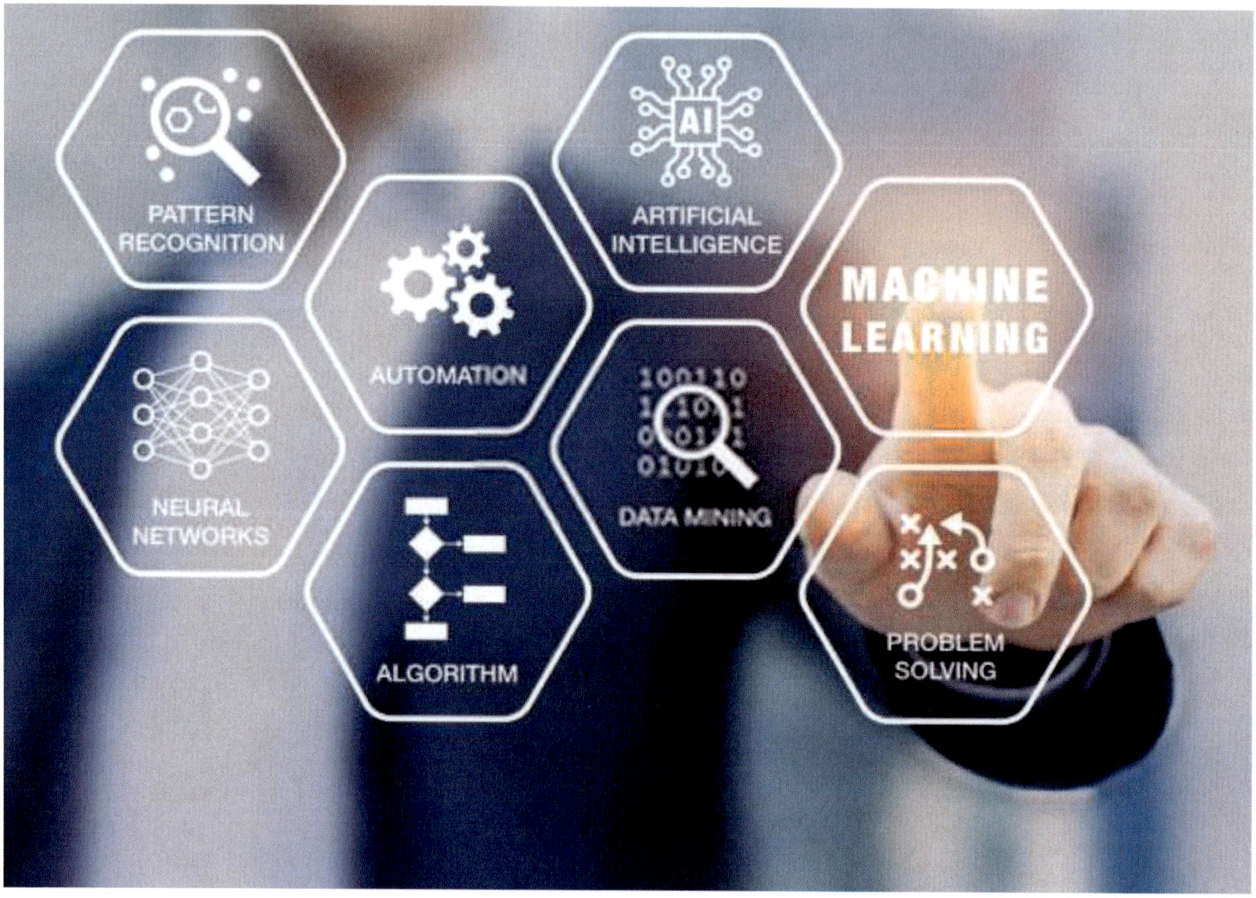

— **Supervised Learning**

In this type of learning, training data consists of input object and its corresponding desired output. The system is provided with the labelled training data. After sufficient amount of observation and learning system can categorise the input.

Supervised learning Algorithms can be used in many applications. Background data analysis, front end presentation, recommendation engine, database marketing, spam detection, pattern, speech, object and handwritten recognition.

— Unsupervised Learning

In Unsupervised Learning, the system is allowed to response for data without any training.

We have unlabelled and unclassified data. The system is allowed to produce response for unlabelled data without any prior training. It is used for creating labels, classes, customer segmentation and identification of associated patterns.

— Reinforcement Learning

This type of learning allows the system to learn from the environment feedback. There is a need of human expert in this learning scheme. It can be used in manufacturing, power systems, inventory management and finance sector. It is a semi-supervised learning.

— Types Of Neural Network Architectures

Different types of neural network architectures are:

Perceptron: This architecture has two input units and one output unit. There is no hidden layer present in this architecture.

Multilayer Perceptron: It is a deep feed forward network in which more than one hidden layer are present.

CNN: Convolutional Neural Network is a feed forward network mainly used for image classification, object detection and recommendation system.

LSTM: Long Short Term Memory Network consists of a memory network inside is hidden layer.

RNN: It is a network in which the hidden layers have self connections. Activation function is provided from lower neurons as well as previous one is used.

Radial basis function network: It is similar to feedforward network, except it uses radial basis function as an activation function in it.

Hopfield Network: It is an interconnected network where the value of neurons are fixed with a particular pattern and then weights are calculated which are not changed.

HOW NEURAL NETWORKS ARE USED IN MARKETING

Data is probably the most important raw material for the transformation of an economy to a digital economy. However, this raw data are hovering in the air untapped, unprocessed, and useless. Artificial Neural Networks can be deployed for data mining, and processing of big data in a few minutes to provide information on business insights. And this is why ANNs are used across different industries such as medicine, engineering, finance, and others.

Artificial Neural Networks are also transforming the available set of marketing technology resources, giving marketers new, more efficient and more dynamic tools for predicting consumer behavior creating and understanding more sophisticated buyer segments, marketing automation, content creation, sales forecasting, etc.

The most widely used application of artificial neural networks is in the field of predictive analytics. Predictive analytics is a confluence of two statistical methodologies, data mining and predictive modeling, which can be augmented by the machine learning capabilities of neural networks. By learning to recognize the current and past trends and behaviors, artificial neural networks can make predictions on future outcomes within a campaign.

For instance, Microsoft used the BrainMaker neural network to fine-tune its direct mailing campaign, increasing its mail response rate from 4.9% to 8.2%. Each year the company sent out about 40 million pieces of direct mail to 8.5 million registered customers. Most of these direct mailings were aimed at getting people to upgrade their software or buy related products. The first mailing usually included everyone in the database, but the second was only sent to individuals most likely to respond.

How? The network analyzed data associated with 25 variables such as the recent product purchased by a customer, the date of first product purchase and the time elapsed between the release of a new product and the purchase of the product.

By analyzing behavioral patterns associated with each of these purchases, the NN was made to score each of the users according to the likelihood of them opening a mailer. This allowed Microsoft to incisively target only those users with a higher likelihood of opening a second mailer from them, and thereby increase their mail response rate.

With a virtual sea of data to input into a neural network, it's now possible to achieve sophisticated, accurate predictions that can help CMOs make smarter decisions about what actions to take and what channels to allocate more resources to.

Likewise with market segmentation, sales forecasting and content creation and distribution, the neural networks, fed with enough data, are able to provide more precise insights and predictions, helping marketing decision makers better gauge expectations.

This technology is also allowing for a more dynamic level of automation, which isn't only evolving the marketing workflow but is creating an even more seamless experience for the consumer.

NEURAL NETWORKS IN ACTION

AI along with neural networks decipher discrete data in no time, and make sure a perfect solution is placed at the decision maker's fingertips. The data being generated is continuously being updated, which also means the machine learning models too will be updated at regular intervals. The enterprises would be able to access up-to-date information - breakthrough insights that can be useful for rapidly changing business environments.

Faster decision-making with more confidence: What if something goes wrong with the manufacturing plant at your industry, what would you fix first? I am sure most of the employees working on that plant would be clueless. In such cases, AI helps the maintenance team to decide what to fix first with confidence, as AI would automate and line up the decision-making processes for the maintenance team.

Accessing insights from Big Data: An exciting opportunity after implementing AI in your workplace is AI's ability to recognize and understand patterns in Big Data that humans cannot.

Protecting sensitive data: AI enables elimination of human error which in turn helps improve output quality and strengthen cyber security.

A noticeable difference has been seen in the roles of employees, after deployment of AI. More attention is given on managing and on implementing strategic initiatives and at the same time analytic tools automate and scale data to facilitate better decision-making.

ARTIFICIAL NEURAL NETWORK IN DIFFERENT FIELDS

Since Artificial neural Network are found in any applications in a wide range, some of them are explained below.

Nowadays these are used in medical field such as cardiology, disease prediction, recommendation, electronic signal analysis, faint detection, clinical research and many more. Basically these are different mathematical algorithms build for different tasks.

In real business these are used in betting system, stock prediction, finance, telecommunications, insurance and business management. Due to such applications it is becoming pervasive in common business operations and goals.

PROPER SORTING OF DATA

Business intelligence obviously requires the collection of all sorts of information and then analyzing this information to provide relevant data to the people in an organization, most of the time, these would be the members of the upper management. It's vital for marketing companies to collect as much data as possible, from as many sources as they can.

The reason is simple. Better insights deliver a company the ability to enhance strategies and also react faster to changing preferences and trends. However, collecting data from disparate sources can become problematic if it isn't uniform, and there's no process to standardize it.

This can lead to difficulties when attempting to produce actionable insights that aren't outdated in a few hours. For industries where marketing is around-the-clock such as online gaming, spending days on reports instead of hours can mean losing customers to competitors.

However, it doesn't have to be that difficult. For online gaming mega-site NetBet, the problem wasn't the amount of data, but the disparate formats and sources it was arriving from.

Their marketing team depends on data to target their events and promotions better, but incompatible sources meant a substantial portion of time collecting information was spent unifying these data streams into a usable format.

One of the biggest benefits of business analytics is that it is programmed to capture data from several sources and convert it into a clean stream for parsing and visualization. By cutting down on the time it takes to standardize data, companies can react to an ever-changing market.

Business intelligence requires the use of tools and several of these data tools would include data warehouses, data mining, and data modeling. These data tools make it much easier for a company to collect the data it needs and then analyze and interpret it appropriately.

These tools are to be used for organizational purposes and would also be used in conjunction with OLAP or Online Analytical Process. Another term for OLAP is Analytics and the basis for this procedure is actually the Cube Dimensional Analysis. A business intelligence (BI) strategy will help you to choose the right tools and platform for your business.

KPI, KEY PERFORMANCE INDICATORS

key performance indicators, or KPIs, are the metrics that are used to monitor business activities that are critical to the success of the company. They help to quickly cut through the massive amount of information that is a part of day-to-day business operations, retrieve key insights, and to maintain a pulse on business performance. This last point is especially critical, as it allows businesses to make adjustments in real time.

Still, there's no universal list of KPIs that every company must use. Even though there are guidelines for similar types of businesses, at the end of the day, each company has to decide for itself what it needs to measure.

This decision depends on several factors, such as specific business goals, philosophies and many others. Even companies operating in the same marketplace might have completely different approaches when it comes to choosing which KPIs to track.

However, although the specific key performance indicators that are tracked often differ, the approach for choosing them is relatively similar. It's mostly a matter of figuring out which KPIs are the most relevant to the company or each of its departments. The present state of business is assed by the use of Key Performance Indicators (KPI) in business intelligence. As more companies implement KPI, data is becoming available to business faster and more efficiently. Data used to be available for business only after one or two months. This untimely availability did not help business adjust their strategies.

More recently, banks have tried to make data available sooner and with shorter intervals. Banks do this especially for businesses that have higher credit/operational risk loading. This allows many companies to get new data weekly, and adjust their strategies faster than ever before, leading to increased customer satisfaction and retention.

While KPIs are used more often for tracking financial operations, that's not the only way to implement them. Key performance indicators can monitor product quality, the supply chain and customer satisfaction, all while providing web analytics data.

Also, it's vital for marketers to not simply ask questions but to pose the right ones. Defining success and metrics to track it are vital components of planning a strategy. They can also be easily misapplied, however, and lead to a misunderstanding of the data that can lead to inefficiencies and lost opportunities.

One of the benefits of BI is the ability to sort through massive amounts of data and generate actionable insights from it. To work optimally, it needs to ask the right questions of the data being produced. For this, the best marketing dashboards include the option to define a variety of key performance indicators and other metrics.

PREDICTIVE ANALYTICS

Predictive analytics is the idea that you can use a combination of data, statistical algorithms and machine learning techniques to put yourself in a better position to identify the probability of future outcomes based on historical information.

Essentially, you're taking the lessons that you've learned in the past and are applying them to better predict the future.

Predictive analytics are used in a variety of different ways in nearly every industry that you can think of. For example, cybersecurity experts use them to help detect fraud or cyber-attacks while they are still in their early stages, thus giving them a better chance to do something about it before the problem grows too large.

Predictive analytics are used to analyze all of the information going on across a network in real-time, aiding researchers in their effort to spot the types of suspicious activity that could lead to intrusions and other instances of fraud faster than ever.

Other companies use them to optimize their omni-channel marketing campaigns to reach their own audiences in a more effective way. Based on past customer purchases or responses to certain types of marketing collateral, predictive analytics can be a way to do everything, from creating better, more informed collateral in the future, to helping promote opportunities, to assisting in cross-selling or up-selling to existing customers.

What predictive analytics are NOT, however, is a silver bullet that is guaranteed to make an organization better, stronger or faster. As the old saying goes, "There is no fate but that which we make for ourselves.

" Predictive analytics are not a guaranteed way to confirm that something is going to happen. Instead, it's a way to give yourself access to better, more informed insights based on what has already happened to better prepare for certain things that are likely to occur down the road.

PUTTING PREDICTIVE ANALYTICS TO WORK FOR YOU

When it comes to the major nexus between predictive analytics and business intelligence, it's important to keep in mind that your goal is less about predicting the future in a literal sense and is more about putting yourself in a better position to achieve desired outcomes by leveraging past behaviors to your advantage.

Case in point: many companies use predictive analytics to gain insights into potential future trends. You see this happen in the electronics industry all the time. Based on market research data about what people are buying, what they're responding to, what they like and what they don't like, you begin to get a better idea of where an entire industry might be headed.

This puts certain savvy companies in a position to get in on the ground floor of something poised to be the "next big thing."

In other cases, discovering a potential future trend is just a question of applying what we learned from our trend as it behaves across different seasons and mixing that with the most recent behavior of the trend. Together you can create a forecast that can take into account the seasonality of your business and your most recent performance so you can better plan ahead. Applying that technique in a Business Intelligence tool such as Dundas BI may look like this:

Another example commonly used in a variety of industries has to do with how companies leverage predictive analytics to recognize inefficient business practices.

A warehouse, for example, might uncover new insights into how their resource allocation (think equipment) is affecting their ability to load or unload trucks on a regular basis. Or, predictive analytics might be used to show that when X, Y and Z conditions occur, trucks have to wait in a loading dock before they receive attention for far too long, thus severely harming the overall productivity level of the entire warehouse.

With this knowledge, you could simply correct X, Y and Z conditions to achieve the desired outcome - turning over more trucks in a faster way, thus cutting costs and increasing efficiency at the same time. One common predictive analytics algorithm to be used in this scenario is a clustering algorithm that can help identify those conditions.

Software companies are another example of this type of idea in motion. Many use predictive analytics to help improve the original value proposition that their products are offering in the first place.

This in turn provides users with advanced proof that they can do what they say they can, thus creating a unique competitive advantage (and likely decreasing that company's overall time-to-market as well).

For example, Netflix improved its services through predictive analytics by having the software determine what movies and shows would fit a customer's list based on what they've previously watched, how often they watch certain shows and movies, and how often movies are rated and recommended to others.

Regardless of how predictive analytics are leveraged in your current business intelligence solutions, the end result is almost always the same. Someone in a planning position can use the past to better predict what next week's schedule might look like, helping them mitigate risk from gaps in coverage or sudden capacity influxes.

Resources in the field can be better allocated to help get employees where they need to be at exactly the right moment. Even representatives in a call center could use past appointments to predict future ones, thus reaching out to customers who may be on the fence and offering an appointment with a high probability of success.

The end result is the same: you're left with a better, faster and more efficient organization that offers better, faster and more enjoyable service to customers. At the end of the day, that truly is the most important goal of all.

MARKETING CAMPAIGN ANALYTICS

BI software can help you easily plan, monitor and assess the success of your promotional activities to see what marketing campaigns/promotions your customer base is reacting the best too. That way, marketing budgets can be shuffled and allocated to the more successful campaigns that produce the best possible ROI.

For instance, if Promotion A generated $1000 in sales but cost the company $250, that program is not actually more cost-effective than Promotion B that generated $700 in sales but only cost $100 to run. By leveraging information from your BI system, you can maximize the revenue returned from each advertising dollar spent. By comparing actual to expected results by campaign, you can "market" smarter and better identify opportunities to increase sales and growth.

Effective use of business intelligence by the sales and marketing team can lead to improved customer retention rates, higher revenues from up-sell/cross-sell campaigns, and enhanced levels of customer satisfaction. And at the end of the day happy customers mean more revenue for your company.

Another major pain point BI can solve for marketing professionals is narrowing down demographics to find the right audiences. The most successful strategies and campaigns work because they are able to send the right message to the right people at the right time. One of the biggest benefits of business intelligence and analytics is its capability to collect information from a variety of disparate channels and provide a complete view of a company's customers across every channel.

More importantly, BI can organize this multi-channel stream and create more actionable data that considers a variety of factors. By targeting not just demographics, but also engagement, ROI, purchasing and interaction patterns, companies can build a complete view of their target customers.

The best companies who use marketing analytics to evaluate demographics can better define their audiences and thus target them more easily by looking for the right metrics.

SOCIAL ANALYTICS

Use of social media has exploded in recent years. It has quickly invaded almost every aspect of our lives – to the point that we wonder how we ever managed without it. Business use of social media is also growing rapidly, as sales, marketing and communications departments and enterprises clamber to better segment, target and interact with customers.

Social media provides a wealth of information that marketers can use to understand their target audiences' behaviours and preferences. But, it is also a tumultuous hubbub of thoughts and opinions. Therefore, to arrive at any reliable, quantifiable or generalizable conclusions requires the capture of vast amounts of data, which then need to be analyzed and visualized.

So, let's looks at how Business Intelligence software can help marketing departments harness these social platforms as new avenues to market.

Social media marketing provides perhaps one of the best sources of real-time marketing and target audience feedback, offering a great way for companies to interact with customers, understand their preferences and gain direct response. But, while social media platforms produce a large amount of data, how can marketers collect, collate, analyze and act on that information in order to derive valuable insights and drive smarter decision-making?

Business Intelligence (BI) solutions – which deliver API connectors for third-party Web applications – offer marketers the capability to analyze data captured and generated by popular social media platforms, such as Twitter, LinkedIn or

YouTube. This analysis provides a quick and cost-effective way of understanding the impact of social media marketing activities.

PROVING ROI

What's more, BI software with such capabilities can be an incredibly useful way for time-pressed marketers to demonstrate the ROI of their social media campaigns. Furthermore, integrating such data with other data sources and types, within a BI platform, can also assist marketers to understand the relative value of social media activities compared to other tactics and campaigns.

Using BI in social media marketing can also help improve resource management, increase conversion rates and predict future trends and issues. Social media is an ever-changing environment that needs a reactive and flexible marketing strategy cemented by data-based insights.

By enabling users to automatically connect to third-party Web applications and analyze the data produced, BI software is empowering marketers to gain a holistic view of multiple social media platforms. In turn, this ensures quick and reliable decisions can be made based on myriad of data sources.

CHAPTER 55: CUSTOMER DATA

Data, a word when read, seems simple, but in an organization or business, it means a lot. Data has the power to change the whole perspective of your organization; it can make or break the game. It's a realm of multiple possibilities.

Whether the data is, on-premise, edge, or on cloud, it has the capacity to bring new opportunities forward and give detailed insights for your business.

On the other hand, consumer data is the information trail customers leave behind as a result of their Internet use.

This data, which sometimes comprises personal information, comes from such sources and channels as social media networks, marketing campaigns, customer service requests, call center communications, online browsing data, mobile applications, purchasing history and preferences, and more.

Companies collect and analyze customer data to attract, engage and retain their most profitable customers as part of a broader customer relationship management strategy. Companies use this information to target relevant advertisements, offers and other products and services to consumers, as well as provide them with a personalized experience based on individual preferences.

Many companies face challenges in walking the fine line between using consumer data to enhance the customer experience while also ensuring they do not breach customer trust or mishandle their personal information, particularly as data privacy and cybersecurity concerns grow.

IMPORTANCE OF CUSTOMER DATA IN MARKETING

Your initial goal in business is that people become your customers and buy what you are selling and/or your existing customers buy what you are selling over and over again. You need to capture how they are using what they buy from you and apply it to your business growth.

While a loyal customer can be described as someone who purchases regularly from you, there are levels of loyalty which every business owner should be aware of. After analyzing your customer data, you can find that your regular customers can be further segmented. This will allow you to devise different messages to each group of customers, depending on their profitability and loyalty to the company.

FOUR CATEGORIES OF CUSTOMER

True Friends: These are customers who are loyal and profitable.

These represent the highest profit potential. By communicating consistently (but not too often) and delighting these customers, organizations can nurture a really profitable relationship. Customers in this segment will be advocates of the organization.

Butterflies: These are customers who are disloyal but profitable.

These represent high profit potential. The customer is basing the exchange on the transaction not the relationship and organizations should look to engage with (but try to not marry) the customer at every transaction.

Barnacles: These are customers who are loyal but not profitable.

These represent low profit potential. There is a limited fit between the company's offerings and the customers needs. There is potential for cross or up-selling here, however it does depend on the size of the customers wallet.

Strangers: These are customers that are not loyal or profitable.

These represent the lowest profit potential. There is little fit between the company's offerings and the buyers needs. Organizations should not put any resources into these relationships.

LEVERAGING CUSTOMER DATA FOR YOUR BUSINESS

By analyzing customer data with a fine tooth-comb, businesses can become more aware of their profit potential from existing customers. Not all customers are the same. Just as friends, we have levels of friendship and that sits well with us. The same applies to our business life. Customers are not equal. Once you identify who are loyal and profitable, you can invest more in those relationships. Similarly, you can divest your time and resources from non-profitable relationships and see them for what they are. Explained below are different ways customer data can benefit your business.

1. You can learn a lot from capturing customer data: The fact is that the data that you obtain from your customers can be extremely valuable for you and for your business. You can learn a great deal about your customers' activities (and identify patterns of activity), you can extract information about social media profiles, customer preferences, and exactly what motivates the customers to buy the way in which they buy.

In short, you can gain entrance to the customers' minds through the data. In fact, if you leverage the data properly, it will reveal all sorts of useful information, such as capturing metrics on conversion rates, identifying issues as they occur, and taking measures right away to fix whatever needs to be fixed. Here is a more detailed explanation as to how you can use the customer data.

2. Identify the most problematic issues (and problem areas): Customer data can help you to identify specific issues that may lead to the loss of customers. That is very valuable information to get your hands on. If you are able to identify an issue in one area of your business, you can manage to fix it and if you can fix it, you can prevent your number of customers from decreasing. There are several different tools available online that can help you to go through that process, including a funnel analysis, which will enable you to keep close track of your conversion rates at every milestone.

3. Capture the strongest customer areas: It is critical to your business that you are able to have a clear understanding of where you are doing the most selling. Those are important data to capture because, as a business owner, it is critical that you understand where your selling strengths lie. If you have that information, you can continue to enhance those products and/or services that are doing well and potentially discontinue what is no longer working for your business.

Some other pieces of information that are included in the data are what the customers like to buy when they like to buy those particular products and/or services, etc. Once you are armed with that information, you can really focus your offerings on satisfying your customers' needs on a deeper level.

4. Add to your list of customers: The best of all possibles is that you have a healthy list of clients who have been with you for a while and are loyal to you. Additionally, you should continually be increasing your list of customers as well. You want the combination of the existing and new clients to serve you and your business well.

In fact, the more close relationships you develop, the better your chances will be of getting people to tell other people about how wonderful your offerings are.

5. Gather data on how your ever-improving products and/or services improve the lives of your customers: It is essential that you constantly improve upon what you have to offer.

However, it is just as important for your to capture how those improvements positively affect your customers. You can do that by paying close attention to the reviews that your customers write and by the surveys that they answer.

The information could be invaluable to you. In fact, the information can give you insight into not only making improvements but also you will get a deep understanding of exactly which changes you want and need to make to make your customers happy. That is a key factor in ensuring that you keep those customers over time.

6. Come up with ways to make your offerings easier and easier over time to use: After you have been able to study all of the customer data, you can use that information to help your customers improve upon what they are doing with their businesses.

They will understand quickly that you and your business are making a positive impact on their lives and on how they run their business. Another really valuable result will be that they will respect you for doing everything possible to make your customers' lives easier.

HOW COMPANIES ARE WORKING WITH CUSTOMER DATA

Companies are trying many different ways to aggregate customer data into a single place where they can view and use it.

Here are the primary ways that companies attempt to do this.

— **Custom In-House Databases**

Building and managing custom databases and data warehouses is an enterprise-type solution that works well as a long-term data storage challenge, but doesn't support real-time marketing use cases or provide API support for ongoing integration and export of audience segments.

— **Tag Management**

Tag Managers are used to collect and route event data from websites and sometimes mobile, but do not transform various events into user profiles or segments that can be used to support marketing.

— **Marketing Suite**

These marketing applications are loosely integrated with specific tools to create limited user profiles and campaign extensibility.

They typically require ongoing custom services and manual integrations to support customer data capture and export.

— **Email Service Providers**

Email tools store a small subset of customer data and only deliver audience segments back into email, and not to other marketing tools or systems.

— **Traditional CRM**

CRM tools are limited in the types of data they can collect and store and the primary use case is to manage sales opportunities and sales accounts, not consumer relationships.

— **DMP**

DMPs are designed to support ad tech use cases for targeting by combining third-party data with a batch upload of marketer's first-party data.

It's not a true customer database since it has limited extensibility to other tools and use cases.

— **CDP**

CDPs are purpose-built to create a central repository of all your customer data and to make cross channel audiences available to all your marketing tools for coordinated targeting and personalization.

USING CUSTOMER DATA PLATFORM

Companies like Netflix, Pinterest, Amazon and LinkedIn build great consumer relationships. They grow their businesses around serving customers and fully understanding them through data.

Traditionally, companies have tried to understand and manage customer relationships in two separate types of systems:

— Channel-centric tools like email services, ads, web analytics, mobile apps, etc,.and/or

— Databases or Data Warehouses that store various data sets in-house by IT

Both methods result in storing and using customer data in different places. Siloed data is difficult to stitch together and makes a customer-centric approach much more difficult.

Marketers seek building omni-channel experiences to cater to how customers interact across multiple touchpoints when and where they want. The traditional customer data management model leads to a disjointed experience.

Not being able to act on the signals that your customers provide in real-time is a missed opportunity to create delightful experiences.

CDPS GIVE A DEFINITIVE CUSTOMER UNDERSTANDING

Many marketers continue to work with glimpses of customer understanding because they don't have the means of putting the entire picture together. Most organizations connect customer data from different business functions, like email, loyalty programs, web, and point-of-sale, to name a few.

They struggle to combine both static and real-time signals to gain a better customer understanding. Customers know what a great experience looks like from their interactions with stellar, customer-centric brands like Netflix, Amazon, and Pinterest, and they expect nothing less. Companies must organize around their customer to deliver great experiences in today's data-driven world.

— Enter: The Customer Data Platform

According to Growthverse, Customer Data Platform (CDP) can be defined as new marketing infrastructure to pull data from disparate systems, create and manage customer profiles, discover new customer segments, and make these segments available back to all your marketing tools.

A CDP delivers the next tier of customer understanding by connecting data from various channels and siloes within your organization and unearthing rich, holistic profiles built to power your customer experience.

CDP's make the data-driven customer-centric horsepower of a Netflix, Pinterest, Amazon and LinkedIn much more accessible for marketers.

— What Does a Customer Data Platform Do?

The role of CDPs is to collect lots of data about customers who do business with a company, create a detailed image of the customer, and deliver effective, personalized communication across all channels.

Why is it important to gather so much information about the user in the first place? Simply because the more you know about your "perfect" customer, the easier it will be for you to implement lookalike modeling to find similar people you can target your marketing to.

A Customer Data Platform will do the following:

- — Get your customer data together in a single, easy-to-use place
- — Coordinate marketing around next-level customer understanding and use behavioral signals to reach customers more effectively.
- — A CDP brings together all of your customer data
- — Use predictive science to find audiences that matter
- — Sync those audiences with your marketing tools
- — Gain a holistic understanding of customers across touchpoints.
- — Improve targeting and personalization using cross-channel audiences with all of your marketing tools.

BENEFITS OF A CUSTOMER DATA PLATFORM

Efficient Marketing Operations: Create a centralized, customer data asset that marketing can own and manage

Data-Driven Performance: Apply predictive science to customer segmentation to optimize ad spend.

Right Content, Right Time: Coordinate campaigns in an omnichannel manner with maximum effectiveness.

Increase Conversion: Providing contextual ads or content throughout the customer experience based on how customers will likely engage.

Increase Retention: Fully personalize and optimize loyalty and support programs with a customer-centric approach.

WHAT TO LOOK FOR IN A CDP?

Use this checklist to make sure your CDP features the following:

A Marketer-Friendly UI

— Visual custom audience builder

— Visual custom audience builder

— Pre-built integrations for many popular Martech tools

— View universal customer profiles easily

A Wide Selection of Martech-related APIs

— APIs for data collection, enrichment and export of data

— Real-time profile API for personalization

— Real-time notifications to see live changes in audiences across tools

Platform Flexibility

— Cloud-based, secure data service

— Resolve and merge multiple user identities across channels and tools

— Collect structured and unstructured real-time event data

— Dynamic, progressive user profiles - from unknown web visitor to known via any identifier

— Data Onboarding for multiple data sources and types (e.g. loyalty database, web, email service provider, point-of-sale, third party)

— Support for real-time data streaming and batch processing

— Customizable, adaptable data schema: no need for predefined fields or long implementations

— Automated data export to marketing tools for execution, or Big Data tools like Google BigQuery or Hadoop for analytics or visualization

— Data Replay to incorporate historical and new data sources

Predictive Analytics

— Predictive engagement scoring and metrics gives you next-level customer understanding

— Classify content and determine customer intent to influence your content strategy

— Classify content and determine customer intent to influence your content strategy

— Lookalike audience modeling finds current, best customers from other data sources

— Pre-built lifecycle segments so immediately predictive marketing use

— Progressive audience discovery via machine learning

CONCLUSION

Thank you once again for downloading **"DIGITAL MARKETING: A Guide to Marketing in Today's Digital World."**

Digital marketing provides small businesses with resources to perform sales and marketing that were previously available only for large companies. It ensures the survival of online businesses. Today, brands are putting more focus on digital marketing than ever before. Digital marketing skills are in serious demand and provide a unique competitive edge for one's career. It offers excellent opportunities around the world.

There is a wide range of digital marketing roles which include jobs related to social media as well. It also provides a variety of opportunities to start your career as an Entrepreneur.

There are lots of benefits that digital marketing professionals can look forward to in the upcoming years. More companies embrace digital marketing as their primary marketing strategy which creates plenty of job opportunities for freshers. The future of digital marketing seems to be very bright at the moment.

In an age where systems are everywhere, businesses need to understand how to exploit Digital Marketing as it is a means to improving the service to your customers, driving down costs and making your organization more agile.

For all brands and businesses, digital marketing is easily one of the best routes to go down and should be considered when you're looking to increase awareness, engagement and reduce cost.

To Your Success.

Tim Griffiths,

CEO TJ's Business Solutions.

Tim Griffiths

DIGITAL MARKETTING

Made in United States
Orlando, FL
04 November 2026

90200298R00252